A WORLD
HISTORY
OF RAIL

A WORLD HISTORY OF RAIL

FROM THE STEAM REGIME TO TODAY

JEREMY BLACK

AMBERLEY

Half title page: Stock of 500 francs of the Imperial Ethiopian Railway Company dated 14 December 1899; Emperor Menelik II is illustrated awaiting the first train with his court. It is signed by Alfred Ilg, Swiss engineer and adviser to the Emperor. (See page 119.)

For Jonathan Johns and Sam Wellbeloved
With thanks for good friendship.

First published 2023

Amberley Publishing
The Hill, Stroud
Gloucestershire, GL5 4EP

www.amberley-books.com

Copyright © Jeremy Black, 2023

The right of Jeremy Black to be identified as the Author of this work has been asserted in accordance with the Copyright, Designs and Patents Act 1988.

ISBN 978 1 3981 2101 0 (hardback)
ISBN 978 1 3981 2102 7 (ebook)

British Library Cataloguing in Publication Data. A catalogue record for this book is available from the British Library.

1 2 3 4 5 6 7 8 9 10

Typesetting by SJmagic DESIGN SERVICES, India.
Printed in the UK.

CONTENTS

PREFACE

A rail survivor. The Slovak Arrow was an express introduced in 1936 on the line between Bratislava and Prague. Apart from the duration of the Second World War, the service has run ever since using various locomotives, from steam to electric. This is the restored M 290.002 Slovenská strela pictured at Valšské Klobouky railway station in 2021.

There is still the thrill as they go through; the spotters and photographers eagerly recording the occasion. The scream of steam for long held generations in awe, as locomotives thundered through cuttings and tunnels and over embankments, putting the march of travel onto a new level of scale and speed. The excitement of rail, the energy of builders, the trains cutting through the landscape and the transformation they brought to economies, societies and countries, can all be readily seen. The surge of steam, the scream of the whistle. In the 1974 film *Murder on the Orient Express*, the steam train leaving Istanbul station, ostensibly in 1935, is a powerful image of drama and adventure, the lights blazing on the 1922 locomotive as the music rolls forward gathering speed. The power of the appeal was clearly present, and the shrill whistle signalled the departure from the station.

Yet, not all countries had railways, just as not all were accessible to steamships. The history of railways in Afghanistan or Greenland for example is not a matter that really requires much discussion, while in Iceland, despite proposals in the 1900s, 1920s, and from the 2000s, the legacy is limited. The Reykjavik Harbour Railway of 1913-28 was a very short line built simply to move stone from two quarries for the improvement of the harbour breakwater and leaving the legacy of *Minør*, an isolated locomotive, on forlorn display, while *Pioner*, the other locomotive, is in a folk museum. There was also a hand-shunted farm railway at Korpúlfsstaðir and a diesel-operated light railway used to construct a hydro-electric power project.

Nevertheless, the phenomenon of steam locomotives rapidly became global, such that railways are part of modern human history on six continents, all of those of permanent human habitation, and should be considered accordingly. Their story contributes greatly to that of history as a whole, and the steam loco must be the starting point for presenting and assessing the history of rail.

The 1820s was a decisive decade for the development of rail travel and therefore for global history. Now, however, with many bold schemes for railing the world in disarray or at least serious difficulties, 2023 provides the opportunity to look anew at the history of rail. We move from the technological optimism, even triumphalism of its early decades, with the bold plans for development, plans that often paid scant attention to issues of terrain, demand and funding. The last century of rail's history is one of major and impressive expansion in routes and services, but also of competition with road and air, of often difficult trade unions and frequently poor management, of the crises of heavy industry in which rail freight was centred, and the weaknesses of the state-knows-best answers as well as of private provision. This then is the history of rail, but also one that is of wider relevance to the history of the last two hundred years.

The obituary in the *Times* on 16 December 1871 for George Hudson, 'the Railway King', a fraudulent British rail speculator, noted:

> It is impossible to deny that he did great things to develop the railway system in the North of England. He was a man who united largeness of view with wonderful speculative courage. He went in for bigger things than any one else. He took away people's breath at first, but he soon succeeded in persuading them that the larger the project and the bolder the scheme, the more likely it was to pay. He showed his confidence by investing more largely than anyone else.

The fifth son of a Yorkshire farmer who had been apprenticed to York drapers, Hudson (1800-71) epitomised the opportunities that could come from rail. Becoming wealthy, in part by inheritance, Hudson became a key man in York and chairman of the York and North Midland Railway Company, controlling over 1,000 miles of track by 1844. Financial manipulation could not protect him from the moves of rival companies, nor from the recession of 1846-7. This led to pressure on debt and substantial cash calls on shareholders, and in 1849 to a crisis in which – alongside straightforward fraudulent theft – it became clear that the statistics provided on traffic, revenue and expenditure were misleading. Capital had been used to pay dividends. As the *Times* of 10 April 1849 noted, the rail world was a 'system without rule, without order, without even a definite morality'. Hudson was obliged to flee abroad to avoid arrest for debt, being arrested in the end in 1865 when he returned to England. He was bust and busted.

This impropriety was different to contemporary failures of greater scale, such as Britain's High Speed Train 2. However much of this line is eventually built, it is hopelessly over budget, and will be only a fraction of the network originally promised. This failure, and those of a number of other rail schemes in recent years, for example the problems with, or delay or abandonment of, high-speed systems in Australia, Brazil and Germany, and of bold rail plans in West Africa, indicate the need today to contrast promise and execution. The failures and weaknesses of the present also provide a perspective in which to look at the past history, indeed pat history, of rail, both impressive and unsuccessful.

I am very grateful to Steve Bodger, Bill Gibson, Crawford Gribben, David Gwyn, Thomas Otte and Nigel Saul for comments on an earlier draft and to Enrico Cernuschi, Bruce Coleman, Richard Gaunt, Michael Gauvreau, Erik Goldstein, Lothar Höbelt, Hilton King, Nick Lewis, Jürgen Luh, Hiroshi Matsura, Jim Paugh, Murray Pittock, Maarten Prak, Geoffrey Rice, Kaushik Roy, Frédéric Saffroy, and Ulf Sundberg for their advice on particular points. This help is both valuable and valued. It is a great pleasure to dedicate this book to two good friends to Sarah and myself, with hopes for many more years of friendship.

WHAT WAS AT STAKE?

American Progress (1872) by the Prussian-born John Gast, the pictorial equivalent of the advice to 'Go west young man.' The train helps to shift the frontier.

'It was time for civilisation to take a trip south once more, travelling, as her wont is, in an armoured train.'

The Début of Bimbashi Joyce, a short story by Arthur Conan Doyle of 1900, describing recent successful British conflict with the Mahdists of Sudan.

The tombstone in Ely Cathedral is vivid, and a testimony to the confidence in Christianity of Britain, the birthplace of the Industrial Revolution. It is to two railwaymen who died in 1845 when their locomotive, travelling too fast, ran off the rails. There was no automatic speed-linked braking then. The tombstone carried 'The Spiritual Railway':

> The line to heaven by Christ was made
> With Heavenly truth the rails are laid,
> From Earth to Heaven the line extends,
> To Life Eternal where it ends.
> Repentance is the station then
> Where passengers are taken in,
> No fee for them is there to pay,
> For Jesus is himself the way.
> God's word is the first engineer,
> It points the way to Heaven so clear,
> Through tunnels dark and dreary here.
> It does the way to Glory steer.
> God's love the fire, his truth the steam,
> Which drives the engine and the train;
> All you who would to Glory ride,
> Must come to Christ, in him abide.
> In First, and Second, and Third Class,
> Repentance, Faith, and Holiness,
> You must the way to Glory gain,

Or you with Christ will not remain.
Come then poor sinners, now's the time,
At any station on the line,
If you'll repent, and turn from sin,
The train will stop and take you in.

This proved a very popular broadsheet ballad, bringing forward the traditional concept, seen particularly in John Bunyan's *The Pilgrim's Progress* (1678), of the journey through life to salvation but applying it to the world of rails, passengers, engineering, ticket classes, stations, and tunnels.

The history of rail has always had winners and losers, and it is appropriate to begin with an example from Britain, for the origins of powered railways are British. These deaths occurred at a time when Britain was leading in technological development and industrial capacity. That experience of rail created an example, a model, and a pattern for elsewhere, one that was all the more potent because it was that of the world's leading military power, source of finance and, already by 1845, very conspicuously the cause and creator of technological innovation and breakneck economic change.

The rise of rail was to be of infinitely greater importance in terms of human innovation than the beginning of human (and also chicken, sheep and pig) balloon flight in France in the 1780s, for such flight lacked economic practicality. Instead, rail meant the development of steam technology and its spread and implementation for profit and power. Steam not only literally expanded to help machines work, but also expanded both economies and the power and potential of states. Human horizons were transformed.

Steam was not only a matter of locomotives. As is too easy to underplay or even forget in a book on rail, steam power was also developing for maritime use. Indeed, although making change, the railway engine did not confront the issues of environmental pressures and maritime conditions faced by steamships. Furthermore, the steamship was linked to a growth in international trade to a degree that was far greater than rail, as well as transforming transport on internal waterways, both lakes and rivers. However, the steamship was less disruptive than the railway engine as the former meshed with an existing system of travel, including ports with developed facilities for trade. This was not the case with rail. Railroads along which horse-drawn wagons moved coal existed before the locomotive (moving) steam engine, but the steam locomotive revolutionised what was possible on rails.

The development of the railway engine provided the key technology for the rail revolution; and industrialisation supplied the necessary demand, capital and skills. The rapid feedback of innovations and limitations and speedy availability of capital produced a pattern of problems understood, confronted and overcome. The scale of rail construction and operations helped ensure the development of the relevant skills. As with other branches of industrial capitalism, the rail system required large numbers of trained (and motivated) employees able to provide the technical and administrative skills required. As later with the motor car, Britain had this skill base. Experienced and skilful manpower made projects more predictable, error less common, and investment (relatively) safer. Engineering education developed.

At the same time, Charles Dickens, a perceptive fixer of social change, was well aware that the railways relied on continual hard work and that they affected the health of the workers, which was true for both the construction of railways and their operation. Thus, in his novel *Dombey and Son* (1846-8), Mr Toodle is a stoker: "'The ashes sometimes gets in here" – touching his chest – "and makes a man speak gruff, as at the present time."' The hard grind of construction was captured in the workmen breaking the surface with pickaxes in Reginald Marsh's painting, *End of 14th Street Crosstown Line* (1936), a social realist work set in New York. Hard work to build the lines was one of the ways in which the railways touched the lives of those who never travelled, a feature even more widely seen with the standardisation of time. Management to a timetable based on the standardisation of time was a potent practice, both for the railways themselves and for the economy as a whole.

The organisational sophistication of railways was particularly impressive, both in terms of creating a system and, also, more obviously, of managing the works, trains, freight and passengers. The task was formidable. In 1848, Dickens referred to someone 'in the midst of enormous Druidical altars of other people's luggage, at Euston Square'. In Britain, the Railway Clearing House, established in 1842, led to standard rates and apportioned through revenues, ensuring that the apparent systemic confusion commented on by Dickens was in practice not the full story. Railways have frequently seemed, not least to passengers, to be a case of the former, but cannot operate without system.

Clearly, the railway increased the speed, regularity and reliability of transport. It offered a faster means than canal and road, as both were then horse-drawn transport and subject to all the factors involved in sustaining horses – feeding, watering, resting and reshoeing. Like rail, canal and road faced issues with construction and maintenance, but the train could provide passengers and freight with an all-day, all-weather service lacking with horse-drawn transport.

Rail helped drive forward the Industrial Revolution. The characteristics of rail improved the integration of production and consumption and furthered the development of the market; it became easier to dispatch salesmen, samples, catalogues, orders and replacements. Thanks to rail, it was easier to guarantee food supply to cities and railways were aligned with production schedules. Relative predictability, combined with only limited risk, distinguished rail from steamships, ensuring that insurance costs were lower for rail. Steamships still carried sails. The difficulties of applying steam technology at sea were compounded by the problem of providing sufficient coal and the extent to which carrying coal reduced the space available to transport cargo. The weather lessened the security of timetables for steamship travel. These difficulties would be reduced by the development in the late nineteenth century of the high-pressure steam engine, and the increase in efficient power it offered. America, Britain, and France were all early innovators in steamships.

One way to approach the long-term history of railways is to consider them in terms of their competition. The modern focus on passengers, and notably so in the West, ensures that this is generally seen in terms of cars versus trains. That is certainly an appropriate focus for some of the discussion of the last century and particularly the last seventy years in parts of the world, but it is not valid across the history of rail as a whole. Such a focus on cars underplays the role of freight; although looked at differently, humans are the most complex and profitable form of freight, one with very specific requirements and relatively few of the advantages of predictable bulk transport. Indeed, the contrasts between these types of freight are important to the profitability of rail services.

A longer-term perspective is provided by the relationship between water-borne and rail transport. Inland and maritime water-borne transport had cost advantages, especially, but not only, for bulk goods. Early horse-drawn railways sought to provide the same advantages, in imitation of horse-drawn canal barges. There were major problems with inland water travel, the water in some ways posing issues of provision later associated with coal for railways, notably regularity and thus predictability, but with coal having storage possibilities that were generally absent for water. Autumn heavy rainfall, flooding, winter freezing, spring snowmelt spate, and summer drought were all factors. In 1834, when the Parliamentary Bill for the construction of the Great Western Railway was in committee stage, some of the strongest opposition came from the Kennet and Avon Canal. The GWR directors lined up a number of speakers to complain about canal transport. Samuel Provis, formerly a freight carrier by canal between London and Bristol, told the committee that the fastest trip between the two cities was around three days, but that frequent seasonal delays, shortages of water in the canal in summer, and winter floods and frosts meant that the journey could take two to three weeks or longer. Richard Mills, a barge master from Reading, told MPs that the longest frost on rivers and canals he had encountered had stopped passage for nine weeks. (For the full story see *Iron, Stone and Steam: Brunel's Railway Empire* by Tim Bryan.)

These problems have become more pressing of late with climate warming and the consequent drop of water levels in rivers and lakes around the world, for example in the Colorado, Elbe and Po rivers. Inland waterways also suffer from all the problems of borders seen in the operation of long-distance rail links. More particularly, the use of hydro-power, from mills in the nineteenth century to hydro-electric plants in the twentieth on rivers such as the Dnieper, Nile, and Yangtze, have added major barriers to water-transport, requiring the adjustments of side-channels and locks. Indeed, some rail lines were a response to river obstacles, whether natural, as in rapids, or man-made, such as dams.

Maritime links, however, were different. They were not without obstacles, in the sense of shoals and storms, more particularly concentrated near the ports and, therefore, the start and end of voyages. However, steam could and then did counter many effects of the weather, and notably of calms when there was scant wind and also of adverse winds. Furthermore, the sea became the global commons. That had not been the case in the late seventeenth century, when there had been high rates of piracy and privateering across the world, including in the Arabian and Mediterranean seas and the Atlantic. Large-scale smuggling was also a problem, one that affected the profitability of established maritime trade. However, these rates were cut by naval action in the eighteenth century as well as, eventually, by free-trade policies in the nineteenth.

As a result, the nineteenth century was a period of expansion for maritime trade, when the profitability of individual voyages could be increased by a greater security that cut the need for protection, weaponry and crew and also for high insurance charges. The global commons was assured by the strength of the British navy, which protected not only the commerce of the leading maritime state and trader, Britain, but also that of the whole world. There was no equivalent on land, and this had a direct and major impact for rail once it moved beyond domestic markets, as we will discuss in chapter three. While Britain had the world's largest international rail system in the nineteenth century, this was owing to railways in its empire, an empire, the foremost in the world, that depended on a steam-powered navy.

By whatever means, better transport links helped to provide comparative advantages in cost and reliability. Regional specialisation increased because regions that could produce goods cheaply were now better able to compete in areas with higher-cost local production. This was crucial to economic development as division of labour was effective only with a high volume of production, and thus with a large market. In the early decades, this point might seem only relevant to domestic markets, but the ability of rail to ease transport to and from ports ensured a wider impact from the start, notably in Britain as an island built on coal, and greatly encouraged interest and investment in new rail links.

The consequences of rail were many and varied. Thus, in place of 'the mail-coaches which were whirling out of town' in *Oliver Twist* (1838) and knocking people down in *Little Dorrit* (1857), the train transformed postal services, which were organised, as before, from London. In 1840, instead of the earlier system of calculating the cost for each individual piece of post, a new, relatively inexpensive uniform charging system was introduced, and to that end, the Penny Black, the world's first postage stamp, was released. The scale, rapidity and cheapness of the new postal system of the 1840 Penny Post would not have been possible without rail links (as yet incomplete but clearly coming), particularly between the major cities. The number of letters delivered in the United Kingdom rose from 82.5 million in 1839 to 411 million in 1853. As a result of trains and steamships, it became possible at a distance to receive a reply on the same day on which letters were sent, thus contributing to a postal culture of speeded-up and reliable correspondence, one noted in W. H. Auden's 1936 atmospheric poem *Night Mail*, which described the London to Glasgow postal express. This postal culture was an important adjunct to literary forms, such as the plots in detective novels.

The combination of the train, the time and the post led to Dickens referring to 'Train-time,' the standardisation of time; the recovery of the railways from winter disruption prompted him to observe that the post had 'asserted itself triumphantly'. The sense of time and space changed as a result of the train, which offered a potent symbol of the human capacity to use new knowledge to remodel the environment and, unlike with steamships, to create totally new sensations and links. The train was a means of modernisation and a source, symbol and site of a new sensibility that was active in space and time.

Thanks in part to the train, local trends were eclipsed by metropolitan fashions. Railways meant the rapid circulation of news, notably in Britain of London newspapers across the country. Up-to-date daily news across the country became a reality, an aspect of the social revolution that was rail. Rail also offered the opportunity for migration, both domestic and international, individual and family.

The remodelling of the environment included underground travel. In 1862, William Gladstone, the Chancellor of the Exchequer, joined the directors of the Metropolitan Railway on the first run over the full length of their new London underground railway. This linked Paddington, the terminus for trains from the West Country, South Wales, and the South-West Midlands, to Farringdon in the City. The Underground had to fit into the new geography of the railway stations, but also made them more effective.

A key element in railway history was provided by the rapid diffusion of technology, both in the Atlantic world and more generally. From Britain, as discussed in the next chapter, there was an early spread to the European continent as well as to America and within the British empire. Whereas in Britain limited liability companies played the key role, this expansion of rail was frequently linked to a trend of rising state interventionism to promote economic development from the 1830s. This was particularly true on the Continent, with Belgium, France and Saxony (one of the German states) providing clear instances. In France, railway construction became the largest category of public works expenditure of the July Monarchy of 1830-48 and was seen by the government as important to modernisation.

Indeed, railways were in part a new version of older and sometimes then current systems of mercantilism. Designed by national governments to foster economic development and integration, railways were therefore regulated by national legislation. This ensured that in an age of increasing free trade, and notably so in maritime-based commerce, railway systems, despite the frequent use of foreign technology, expertise and capital, were also inherently protectionist. In one light, this meant that they could perform their inherent functional capability of integration within states. But an instructive contrast was that between Britain, where the absence of significant regulatory differences between England and Scotland ensured a more or less seamless rail system, and the situation that was to emerge in Australia, with incompatible track gauges between the states.

There were 20,000 miles of railways in the world in 1865, there were 300,000 in 1914, and about a million by 2020. The last figure is even more striking because of significant closures over that period. America saw about 100,000 miles of track torn up in the century from the 1910s and there were many line closures in Western Europe, notably in Britain and Belgium, as well as elsewhere, and indeed entire system closures in a number of countries, from Barbados to Lebanon. As a result, the last century of rail should be understood in terms of the coincidence of expansion and contraction. Placing an emphasis only on one, as is the tendency in the literature, is seriously mistaken.

Scale has always been a key theme in railway history, and in all respects. Thus, in the First World War, the London and North West Railway transported 325,000 miles of barbed wire and over twelve million pairs of army boots.

Railways continue to be a major force in modern transport ideas and practice. But the pattern of example has changed widely, notably away from Britain, to in particular within and diffused from China. Rail also is now presented as offering greener alternatives to air travel as well as to road transport. Although rail passenger transport declined in America in the second half of the twentieth century and became proportionately less important in Europe as road transport rose, rail still remained particularly significant for freight, and notably long-distance freight. In the late 1990s in America, rail provided 1.2 trillion tonne-miles of freight transport compared to 900 billion tonne-miles for road. Both were formidable figures reflecting the synergy between economic demand and transport provision and the possibility that profit could be obtained from both forms of transport. Where car ownership was lower and air travel less important, rail retained a major role in passenger travel. At the end of the twentieth century, Indian Railways sold 4.5 billion tickets annually. Moreover, authoritarian states maintained a focus on rail. Thus, alongside cuts in networks and services in many countries, they continued to expand in others, notably China.

A standard approach to the history of railways is that of technological capitalism. Crucial factors in growth and sometimes decline, are the ability and freedom of capitalists in and from liberal economies, notably Britain, to use capital and pursue profit. Repeatedly, this was a key element in the development of rail and in the choices made. In this account, the return on investment is a crucial driver, the availability of that capital is a fundamental enabler, and the desire for market share a significant motivation. Yet, in practice, the state was also important, both as an active player and in terms of the context of operations and the nature of regulation.

In authoritarian systems, the situation was obviously totally different to those of free-market capitalism, because goals were set and assets deployed in terms of values pursued and defined by the state. At the same time, states were not monoliths and the level of control desired varied greatly. So did its effectiveness. Thus, in China under the Communist regimes from 1949, there was major disruption for the rail system under the Great Leap Forward of 1958-62 and the Cultural Revolution of 1966-76, but very impressive growth thereafter.

As an instance of a factor that tends to be underplayed owing to a stress on geographical networks, the role of rail in labour relations remains important, as in Britain and France. This role has been transformed by the spread of automation and other changes, such that the number of workers on American railways fell from a peak figure of nearly 2.1 million in 1920 to 0.78 million in 2019. Computers now handle freight movements as well as control locomotives and lights. Satellites are part of the control and communication systems, which engenders a new type of vulnerability. At the same time, rail unions have tended to resist moves to change working practices, notably in Britain and France. As a result, the unions can appear as a conservative element in the story.

The reality of tensions underlying what might otherwise be an unproblematic account of development and progress can be amplified by considering the impact of the railway on natural and human environments. Railways were to be seen as aspects of a threatened past when networks and services were cut in many countries in the late twentieth century, and notably so in Britain in the 1960s, although the same process generally caused less alarm in America. The initial impact of rail, however, was far more severe for those deprived of their lands, as with native peoples in the Americas in the nineteenth century who suffered the seizure of their land by the rail companies. The transcontinental railways proved particularly disruptive, in Siberia as well as North America, although that element of the former has attracted less attention. Modern railway schemes are highly disruptive, both in human and ecological terms, as in Tibet and on Java.

While shot through with the commercial interest of particular companies, the role of the railway was strategic and logistical in the broadest sense, in that, like Roman and Inca roads and Chinese canals, it helped in the development of the economic links that sustained and strengthened the major powers. For example, the railway was fundamental (and believed to be so) in integrating the frontiers of settlement with the world economy. This integration was important in the spread of cultivation and ranching, with the cattle being driven to railheads, and also in the exploitation of mining opportunities. The combination of railways, steamships, credit and trade helped ensure that the 'logistical space' of most states was transformed.

The discussion of transport links can ignore the interrelationship of systems too often presented as competing, for example between railways and canals, and between seaports and railways. The standard focus is on the supply-side, that of railway links, but, as with industrialisation, this can lead to an underplaying of the significance of demand factors. They were important to the hopes on which the provision of new links were based, and the related financing, and then to the viability of services once established. As this book will show, these links, demands and services were frequently a matter of political as much as economic rationales.

Demand can be shown in part by data on usage; but that data does not indicate *potential* demand, which was a matter of economic hopes and social assumptions. Thus, among much else, the history of rail was a history of economic experience and hope, as much as of political decisions, and this remains the case looking into the future. A classic instance of demand driving rail provision was, and continues to be, the social assumptions and planning (individual and collective) considerations bound up in commuting and suburbanisation, which, to underline the role of perspective, can also be presented as sprawl. The potential for profit enjoyed by entrepreneurs, both transport providers and property developers, did not lessen the degree to which there was a popular demand for housing of a certain availability, space, location and cost. To suggest that only one element was at play would be to underrate the complexity of rail, a complexity that will emerge repeatedly in what follows.

2

THE EARLY DECADES OF STEAM

The British General Francis Rawdon Chesney, the explorer who championed a route to India via train across Turkey and steamship on the Euphrates River in the 1830s.

British technology conquers the world. The picture is a clear one. Beginning in Britain, steam-powered railways transformed economies, societies and states, with Britain the key presence in an astonishing leap from the north-east of England across first the country and then the world. And thus our story would be one of achievement, triumph, transformation. Well, yes and no. We need to be more sophisticated in our approach, for rail is the history of the modern world, one of success and failure, with both spectacle and expedience in each. If the rail of today, as discussed in the last two chapters of the book, is one of debacles and overruns as much as high-speed services or terrain bridged and tunnelled, of non-performance as much as achievement, so also in the past. So let us begin our account of the early decades with that of a bold project never brought to fulfilment, with the dual sides of ambition and implementation that are accordingly offered.

From early days, some plans for rail were very bold. At first, as advanced from the late 1820s, the British idea of a steam route to India via the Euphrates River involved a railway across Turkey to the river, then continuing with a steamship service on the Euphrates to the port of Basra and then another by sea down the Persian Gulf and across the Arabian Sea to Bombay (Mumbai). A key British protagonist, Francis Rawdon Chesney (1789-1872), explored the route in the 1830s and subsequently supported the Euphrates Valley Railway Company set up in 1857. However, the problems of the project ensured that the focus in the 1840s and 1850s was on the steamships on the Euphrates, which took the British maritime presence in the Persian Gulf into the interior, and not on the railway. Moreover, the emphasis on the route to India avoiding the long haul round southern Africa came to focus on a Suez Canal.

There was also interest in a Euphrates railway from Indian rail circles, notably William Patrick Andrew (1807-87), a Director of the East Indian Railway, and the founder of the Scinde Railway Company, established in 1855 to build a line from Karachi to Kotri linked to a steamship service on the Indus. He wrote a series of geopolitical rail works, notably, *Indian Railways. As Connected with the Power and Stability of the British Empire in the East, the Development of its Resources, and the Civilisation of its People; with an analysis of the projects now claiming public confidence* (1846), *The Scinde Railway and its relations to the Euphrates Valley, and other routes to India* (1856), *European interests in the Euphrates Valley Route* (1861), and *The Euphrates Valley Route to India in connection with the Central Asian Question* (1873). Andrew became President of the Euphrates Valley Railway Company, which sought to gain a concession to construct a first section from Izmir on the Aegean to Aydin, and presented itself as a British alternative to the French-dominated Suez scheme.

British governmental financial backing for the Euphrates Valley Railway Company was sought in 1857, but without firm financial support from there or the Turkish government, the idea of a rail or rail-river route to India across South-West Asia lacked viability, with British merchants preferring the Red Sea. Indeed, a railway from Alexandria on the Mediterranean to Suez was floated by these merchants in the 1840s and built by Robert Stephenson in 1852-8, who was also an opponent of the idea of a Suez Canal. Publications in favour of the Euphrates route, for example by William Beaumont Selby in 1864 and Thomas Chenery, later editor of the *Times*, in 1869, therefore lacked credibility. That the idea for a Euphrates route, however, had been advanced so speedily showed how rapidly rail had gripped the imagination and, less positively, without much attention to economic or political practicality.

As well as leading to a rethinking of global links, as in this case, rail had produced a new Iron Age, and thus contributed greatly to industrialisation. It was unsurprising that Britain, the country of coal and iron, or at least coalmining and ironworking, led the way with the technology and practice of rail traffic. Without steam locomotion, wagonways had existed for many years, with horses drawing wagons along wooden, and from 1767 cast iron rails, especially from the collieries to the coal-loading staithes on the Rivers Tyne and Wear in North-East England, but also elsewhere. Other products, such as stone, were also carried.

It was no surprise that the North-East of England was the forcing-house in the creation of rail use. British coal production had risen steadily from the sixteenth century. It was widely distributed across a number of coalfields, several close to the sea, but in 1700 the North-East had nearly half the national output of about 3 million tons. It was also the crucial source of coal for London and intermediate ports, such as King's Lynn and Great Yarmouth, with the coal shipped from the Tyne and, to a lesser extent, the Wear. The average annual amount of coal shipped from the Tyne rose from just over 400,000 tons in the 1660s to well over 600,000 by 1730-1, and to nearly 800,000 tons in the 1750s.

The movement of this coal was the key basis for railway developments, which initially did not involve locomotive steam engines, although stationary steam engines were used to pump water out of pits. Wagonways were developed to link coalfields to riverside wharves. The horse-drawn wagons ran on wooden wheels, which were later flanged (giving a protruding rim for strength and guiding). Horses were also used to provide the power on canals. Indeed, they linked rails, roads and canals. In 1725, Thomas Coryat, who was in the party of Edward, 2nd Earl of Oxford, an inveterate traveller, observed rail from the mines near Chester-le-Street, County Durham:

Towards Newcastle we pass over two way leaves [rights of way] which cross the great road. These way leaves are an artificial road made for the conveyance of coal from the pit to the staithes on the riverside; whereby one horse shall carry a greater burden than a whole team on a common way... the loaded cart goes upon one, and the empty one returns upon the other. The whole length of these two way leaves from the coal pits to the place from whence the coals are loaded into the lighters or keels at Sunderland [on the River Wear], is five miles.

In 1725-6, the earliest known stone railway bridge in Britain, Causey Arch, was built for the movement of coal across the Causey Burn towards the wharves on the River Tyne. It had the largest span of any bridge built in Britain since Roman times, and the architect had to work from Roman models. After the formation of the Grand Alliance of leading coal-mining families in the North-East in 1726, a process of sharing and rationalising existing wagonways and of improving the system led to an increase in the length of wagonways and thus in their efficiency. This was to be more generally the case subsequently with railways.

It was not until the application of steam power that such railways could develop into anything other than feeders to existing water links and become a long-distance network of their own. Steam power helped not only on level terrain but also to confront slopes, and the latter was obviously a key advantage over waterways. At the same time, there was a continued use of non-steam railways in some areas. Thus, in the Carrara marble quarries of Italy, blocks of marble were, until a steam railway was introduced in 1876, moved out of the mines and down the mountainsides on wooden runners. These were guided with ropes along wooden tracks into the valley for loading onto carts pulled by oxen for onward movement to the railway station at Avenza, opened in 1866 on the main line, and thence to the port of Carrara.

In Britain, James Sharp, an active promoter of profit from novelty, in about 1770 produced *Rolling Carts and Waggons*, a descriptive advertisement in which he advocated rollers sixteen inches wide for carriages and wagons rather than narrow wheels that caused ruts. Sharp argued that his rollers would approach the efficiency of 'rail'd roads,' on which one horse can draw four tons 'because the road is made a part of the mechanism, which every road ought to be'. Reflecting the early development of the metallurgical industry in Britain, rails and wheels, meanwhile, moved from wood to more durable iron. By the 1730s, iron bindings were being tried, and by the 1780s cast-iron wheels were in general use.

As opposed to private lines, the horse-drawn Lake Road Rail Road, the world's first public railway, began operating in 1798 in order to carry coal to the Aire and Calder Navigation. It was followed by the Surrey Iron Railway which operated between a Thameside dock at Wandsworth and Croydon, south of London, from 1803. A toll railway on which goods' hauliers operated their own horses and wagons, it carried goods, notably coal, and had a length of eight miles. However, the opening of a canal between Croydon and London in 1809 meant that the line closed in 1846. The line was also redundant as a result of the potential offered by more powerful steam locomotives, which were too heavy for the cast iron plateway of the Surrey Iron Railway. Weight and its impact were key engineering issues. Steam locomotives changed the situation, not least by making long-distance movement possible.

In South Wales, horse-drawn tramroads became more common from the 1780s. In 1802, George Overton built a tramroad between the Penydarren ironworks and Abercynon on the newly built Glamorgan Canal in South Wales upon which Richard Trevithick tried the first steam railway locomotive engine, essentially a mobile beam engine, pulling ten tons of iron and 70 men, although owing to its weight breaking the rails, which was always a problem with heavy loads. Trevithick, a Cornish mining engineer, in the late 1790s improved boiler technology to produce a high-pressure steam able to move a piston, rather than relying on a low-pressure condensing engine, as was the established means. Dispensing with the condenser ensured that a smaller cylinder could be used, and this saved weight and space. In 1801, he built a steam road locomotive, *Puffing Devil*, in 1802 an effective high-pressure steam engine, in 1803 the London Steam Carriage, and in 1804 the hammer-driving stationary high-pressure steam engine he had built for Penydarren in 1802, with the wheels added in 1803, made its journey. Trevithick pressed on, providing the designs in 1804 for a locomotive for Christopher Blackett who owned the Wylam colliery. Built at nearby Gateshead, it was probably the first locomotive to have flanged wheels but was too heavy for the existing rails. In 1808, Trevithick built another locomotive, *Catch Me Who Can*, that was displayed in a 'steam circus' near Euston, with the admission of one shilling including a ride along the circular track. This did not prove a great success, and Trevithick moved on to other initiatives with steam power.

The next step forward was taken by Matthew Murray, who in 1812 designed and built *Salamanca*, the name a tribute to Wellington's recent crushing victory over the French in Spain. This was the first commercially viable steam locomotive. Born in Newcastle, Murray was active in the 1790s in new machinery for flax-spinning and moved on to improve steam engines, an example of the ready transfer of expertise that was important to early rail development. He took Trevithick's work on high-pressure steam further by using two cylinders rather than one, and in 1811 also patented a toothed wheel and rack rail system. Murray made four locomotives used on the Tyneside coal wagonways, benefiting from the development of malleable iron rails in place of the cast iron ones that could not take the same weight. As a reminder that the story of progress should attract caveats, two exploded killing their drivers, the other two became unreliable and the Middleton Colliery turned back to horse-drawn wagons.

Steam technology was spreading. Thus, steamships were introduced to carry passengers in the Thames estuary in 1815. It was in the 1810s that George Stephenson acquired his expertise in steam-driven machinery, designing his first locomotive in 1814: *Blücher*, named after the Prussian general, was designed to haul coal on Tyneside. Locomotive technology achieved a breakthrough in the 1820s. The development of the locomotive from the stationary steam-engine provided the technology for the rail revolution, and industrialisation supplied the necessary demand, capital and skills. That this was a postwar decade was also significant, as British capital and resources had been very heavily engaged with the war effort against France from 1793 to 1815. Stephenson built the eight-mile Hetton Colliery Railway in 1820-2. The more famous Stockton and Darlington Railway followed in 1825, opened with a ceremonial journey from Witton Park colliery to Stockton. Commercial extraction of coal from the Witton Park Estate, near Bishop Auckland, had begun in 1819, and the railway increased its profitability.

Economic considerations and financial return were foremost for the early railways. Thomas Meynell, a wealthy merchant who was a leading promoter of the Stockton and Darlington Railway, had argued that a railway was preferable to a proposed canal, as it was likely to yield a better return and would be less expensive to build. The 25-mile-long line was designed to transport coal from the coalfields near Bishop Auckland to the port of Stockton, carrying 10,000 tons in the first three months and leading to a fall in the price of coal in Stockton. Again, a port link was crucial. The Stockton and Darlington was extended in 1830 to Middlesbrough, which became a major industrial centre, and a suspension bridge took the line across the River Tees.

Meanwhile, Stephenson had received approval in 1826 to tackle the Liverpool and Manchester, but faced the challenge presented by rivers, valleys, hills, and the waterlogged parts of south Lancashire, notably Chat Moss, a four-mile stretch of bog that swallowed the tracks. He overcame the bog by floating the track on tree trunks and shingle across its length. The other natural obstacles ensured that the line required 63 bridges to traverse the terrain. Each increased costs, but linking the two cities and opening the railway in 1830 was a great prize and very newsworthy. As with the earlier construction of canals once they broke away from being a matter of enhancing rivers, railways were projected in a fashion separate to existing transport routes. That offered possibilities in terms of a relative flexibility, but also constraints with reference to the attitudes of landowners as well as terrain. The Liverpool and Manchester Railway was the world's first steam-powered, inter-urban railway designed to transport both passengers and goods, notably raw cotton shipped into the rapidly growing port of Liverpool and turned into textiles in Manchester's mills.

Railways offered new links and cut journey times for both freight and passengers. With the benefit of a multiple-tube boiler and the use of the already developed blast pipe pulling air through the fire, the *Rocket* locomotive, designed and built by Stephenson in Newcastle in 1829, could travel at 30 miles an hour. The following year, *Rocket* won the Liverpool and Manchester Railway's locomotive trials at Rainhill, trials that emphasised speed as the intention was to carry passengers. Direct drive from the cylinders and pistons to the wheels increased efficiency, as did an engine design that boiled water more rapidly. William Huskisson, a politician and local MP, formerly President of the Board of Trade and Colonial Secretary, was fatally wounded by the *Rocket* on the 1830 opening day, the first prominent individual killed by a train.

There was still significant competition for new transport systems, however. In part, this was because rail did not arrive in a period of archaic and inefficient forms of transport. Instead, there had been a transport revolution in the eighteenth century, one of improved roads and new canals. By 1770, there were 15,000 miles of turnpike road in England, and most of the country was within 12.5 miles of one. This set a challenge, standard and model for rail. Although turnpike trusts, authorised by Parliament to raise capital and charge travellers in order to construct turnpike roads, reflected local initiatives, a national system was created. In addition, travel was made faster and more predictable by the development of stagecoach services, better coach springs, and investment. As a result, journey times and therefore operating expenses fell rapidly. Canals cut the cost of transporting bulk goods. By 1790, the industrial areas of the Midlands were linked to the Trent, Mersey, Severn and Thames. This was not new technology, for canals went back to Antiquity, but, prefiguring rail, the rate of canal construction reflected demand from a rapidly burgeoning economy, the availability of investment, and a sense that change was attainable and could be directed. Canals made Britain's maritime trading system more effective by extending the range and easing the operation of coastal shipping.

Indeed, for several decades the competition between railways and canals was in part to involve the issue of access to coastal shipping. The ability of the latter to play a role in domestic commerce was enhanced by the degree to which major waterways, such as the Tay, Forth, Tyne, Wear, Tees, Humber, Ouse, Thames, Medway, Severn, Wye, Mersey, and Clyde, went inland. This created specific problems for land transport, and, more particularly, an especially problematic environment for railways. The ferries used by carts, carriages and passengers, for example across the Severn at Aust and the Forth at Queensferry, militated against rail dependent on expensive bridges and tunnels. Those estuaries were crossed for rail, by tunnel and bridge respectively, long before road bridges were constructed. In contrast, the Humber was eventually to be crossed in 1981 by a road bridge, but not by a rail one as suggested from 1883, nor, as also envisaged, a rail tunnel as originally proposed on a number of occasions from 1872.

In engineering, economic and fiscal terms, rail in Britain had to adapt to this water environment and economy more than other rail systems of comparable size, although Japan was to confront the issue of being comprised of several islands. The opportunities, however, were in linkage to this water economy, enhanced by Britain's maritime and imperial position. Railways and steamships were frequently depicted as co-existing by landscape artists.

The transport revolution of the eighteenth century continued into the nineteenth. The *Taunton Courier* of 23 January 1828 referred to the establishment of a tri-weekly coach service to Bath, connecting there for London:

> A regular and cheap communication to the markets of the metropolis being equally important to the manufacturer and agriculturist, for the disposal of their produce, as it is to the tradesman and shopkeeper, for the purchase of their stock, we trust and feel confident, that the public will support an undertaking which has been begun.

Taunton railway station opened in 1842 as part of the Bristol and Exeter Railway completed in 1844, with, subsequently, a major direct line from Reading, opened in 1906, becoming the leading route from London to Devon and Cornwall; competing with the line from London, Waterloo via Salisbury and Honiton opened in 1860. Part of the history of rail was a matter of the changing relationship of routes, both rail routes themselves and rail and non-rail routes, and the resulting hierarchy of services.

The canal system did not expand greatly in the early nineteenth century, in part because most of the clearly profitable opportunities had already been exploited, which provided investment for rail; but there was still fresh construction such as the Lancaster Canal (1819) and the Caledonian Canal (1822). The engineering feats of canals provided examples of problem-solving that were to be important to rail, as with Thomas Telford's cast-iron aqueduct at Pontcysyllte, built in 1805, which carried the Ellesmere Canal over the River Dee at 127 feet.

To meet the competition from rail, canal companies drastically cut tolls in 1840. This was of value to freight-shippers but not passengers. The use of steam tugs instead of horses speeded up canal transport. The *Glocester Journal* noted on 9 April 1836:

> The formation of a Steam Boat Company, for the purpose of facilitating the passage of vessels bound to or from this port, is a matter of such paramount importance to the mercantile classes connected with Gloucester, that we feel it is only necessary to direct attention to an advertisement which appears in an adjoining column.

Instead of canals, it was land transport that improved most in the early nineteenth century with important developments in many regions before the steam railway reached them. Prefiguring rail, there were smoother and more level roads, and thus an ability to pull heavier loads. Robert Newman, an Exeter MP of 1818 to 1826, told a House of Commons Select Committee that: 'Since the roads have been improved … a very large amount of the economy of the county is daily sent from Devon to the Metropolis.' Bridge improvements also benefited rail. The Union Chain Bridge, opened over the Tweed near Berwick in 1820 for the local turnpike trust, was the first British suspension bridge able to carry loaded carriages. Bridges replaced ferries, for example in North Wales and South Devon. The transport revolution of canals and improved roads provided an active background for rail, creating expectations from the new system for economic development, integration and efficiency.

Initially, in Britain, and on the pattern of the North-East of England, the railways were mostly small-scale, independent concerns providing local links. The movement of coal was crucial to these lines. Thus, the Leicester and Swannington Railway of 1830 was designed to move coal to the expanding Leicester market and to undercut canal-borne supplies from Nottingham and Derby. The company paid an 8 per cent dividend in 1839. Rail really mattered as the means to move coal, the fuel of industrialisation, one that had a far greater calorific value than wood and was more readily transportable. Indeed, it is unlikely that rail would have developed as it did had wood remained the main fuel. This also helped explain the early development of rail in Britain as the transfer from wood to coal was furthest advanced there for industry and residential heating.

Yet, the movement of passengers also rapidly became significant, and lines such as the 1838 Carlisle-Newcastle one, were important for more than local reasons, as they provided regional links. Rail increasingly played a role in meeting and encouraging a range of demands, notably transporting passengers and mail. With time, bolder trunk schemes were advanced and financed and existing lines were linked to create long-distance networks.

A new Iron Age was in progress. Completed in 1823, the 50-foot-long Gaunless Bridge on the Stockton and Darlington Railway was one of the first railway bridges to be constructed of iron and the first to use an iron lenticular truss (though it was only designed to take the weight of horse-drawn wagons). Aside from new bridges, wooden bridges were replaced by iron, as on the North Midland Railway at Belper. Existing ironworks began to produce for the railway. The Britannia Foundry at Derby came to make railway bridges and turntables, carriage wheels, locomotive tenders and steam engine castings. The Foundry was linked by sidings to the Great Northern Railway, and another site for the Foundry linked to the Midland Railway system was built. Train works were opened across the country, including in Newcastle, Gateshead, Crewe, Derby, Swindon and Wolverton.

The belief in the beneficial impact of the train and the atmosphere of boosterism that surrounded the development of rail was captured (and gently mocked) in Dickens' *The Uncommercial Traveller* (1860). The traveller was pressed by the landlord of the Dolphin's Head to sign a petition for a branch line: 'I bound myself to the modest statement that universal traffic, happiness, prosperity, and civilisation, together with unbounded national triumph in competition with the foreigner, would infallibly flow from the Branch.' In *Middlemarch* (1871-2), the novelist George Eliot has Caleb Garth, the wisest and finest character in the book, remark 'Now my lads, you can't hinder the railroad: it will be made whether you like it or not.'

Change proved rapid and dramatic, the poet Alfred, Lord Tennyson writing in his poem 'Locksley Hall', composed in 1835 and published in 1842:

Forward, forward let us range,
Let the great world spin for ever down the ringing grooves of change.
Thro' the shadow of the globe we sweep into the younger day;
Better fifty years of Europe than a cycle of Cathay.

Tunnels were blasted through hills, such as the Kilsby tunnel (1834-8) between London and Birmingham. With gunpowder, tunnel construction, like that of cuttings, was achievable but it was costly, particularly the movement away of rubble. The Woodhead tunnel (1839-52) was necessary for the route between Manchester and Sheffield. A tunnel under the Severn was completed in 1886.

The geological strata were highly significant: igneous rocks, such as granite, were the hardest, sedimentary, such as sandstone, the easiest, and metamorphic in between. Alongside the key issue of gradient, this ensured that the shortest route from Exeter to Plymouth, across granite Dartmoor, was not followed. Furthermore, as another instance of the significance of geology, it was necessary to brick-line tunnels in porous strata, whereas impermeable rocks blocked water. The problem of low-lying waterlogged ground was greater as stable embankments had to be constructed, a matter of engineering, labour and cost.

Between 1830 and 1868, about 30,000 bridges were built in Britain, a very clear and expensive demonstration of the process and problems of linkage. Major bridges included Robert Stephenson's Britannia Tubular Bridge across the Menai Straits en route to Holyhead, which took from 1846 to 1850 to build, and the bridges across the Tay (1877) and Forth (1890). The overall cost of construction was formidable: the London to Brighton line opened in 1841, including the spur to Shoreham, cost £2,569,359.

Although it remained very important, not least as a feeder to rail services, the horse ceased to define the possibilities of land travel. As a result, and having more of an impact because there had been no comparable transformative change, unprecedented speeds of travel became possible, and then commonplace. This was now part of a continuing process that itself was highly significant. By 1850, speeds of 35-40 mph were normal in Britain. This was greater than the early rail speeds, and there were comparable and rapid improvements in carriages, stations and railway safety.

The new sounds and sights contributed to a powerful sense of change, which was overwhelmingly seen by commentators as progress. The *St James's Chronicle* of 30 March 1847 was far from alone in considering the impact of rail travel on the human body. It was widely believed that it brought on labour for pregnant women, but concerns did not stop travel. That January, Dickens, a writer fascinated by the impact of rail, used the comparison of 'Railroad speed', and, that February he had the good luck to catch the express train at Folkestone for London, the journey only taking two hours twenty minutes, although in part by cutting down on intermediate stops such as Cloisterham (Rochester), as mentioned in his novel *The Mystery of Edwin Drood* (1870). In Dickens' *Bleak House* (1852-3), Mrs Rouncewell and Mrs Bagnet leave Lincolnshire for London by carriage:

Railroads shall soon traverse all this country, and with a rattle and a glare the engine and train shall shoot like a meteor over the wide night-landscape, turning the moon paler; but, as yet, such things are non-existent in these parts, though not wholly unexpected.

Preparations are afoot, measurements are made, ground is staked out. Bridges are begun, and their not yet united piers desolately look at one another over roads and streams, like brick and mortar couples with an obstacle to their union; fragments of embankments are thrown up, and left as precipices ... everything looks chaotic, and abandoned in full hopelessness.

The railway reached Lincoln in 1846, but much of that large county with its relatively low population density was not served until later, the Grantham to Boston line opening in 1857-9, with the section to Skegness following in 1873.

Low government borrowing (and lower yields on gilts) after 1815 helped railway investment and development. By the 1830s, railway shares had become the great and widely purchased alternative to government stock. The Jane Austen world invested mostly in gilts, but the Dickens/Trollope world largely in railways which usually, although certainly not always, produced higher dividend yields.

The pace of development saw 54 Railway Acts passed by Parliament in 1825-35, and another 39 in 1836-7 alone. Speculation, both sensible and less so, was attracting liquidity to the railways, and railways became the prime form of domestic and international investment, although the Bristol and Exeter Railway found it difficult in 1836-7 to get subscribers to pay for the shares they had committed to purchase when floated in 1835. By 1841, 1,696 miles was complete and the authorised capital of rail companies was £78 million; by 1846, the figures were 3,036 and £296 million, and the more capitalised nature of the industry was linked to the amalgamation and expansion of the system, so that in 1845-6, amid the 'Railway Mania,' the building of another 7,000 miles was authorised by Parliament.

The public British financial markets owed much to the Joint Stock Companies Act of 1844, although they were limited until the, for then revolutionary, Limited Liability Act of 1855. This legislation was of fundamental importance to the creation of capital markets and was copied later by other developed nations. Limited liability lessened the nature of risk and contributed to faster growth.

Alongside long-distance routes, commuting into London rapidly developed as an extensive network spread over nearby areas. Aside from suburbanisation linked to major long-distance routes, there were also lines that were more specifically suburban and regional. Thus, floated in 1831 and with an Act of Parliament obtained in 1833 and completed in 1838, the London and Greenwich Railway was the first steam railway in London and the first entirely elevated railway; the key element was a viaduct of 878 brick arches. This railway rapidly became very busy; although the high costs of building the line ensured that the company was not profitable. Other commuter lines followed including to Croydon in 1839, to Margate in 1846, and to Southend in 1856. By then, the tolls on turnpikes no longer appeared viable and, in 1857, the Toll Reform Committee recommended abolition within six miles of Charing Cross in London. Their abolition rapidly followed. The major rail lines also had a great impact on what became London suburbia, opening up areas for development. Thus, in 1838, the line to Southampton reached what is now Surbiton, leading to the building of housing estates around the station.

Alongside increased specialisation of function so that housing was separated from other activities, as well as the clearance of rookeries (slums) in city centres, suburbanisation played a big part in the decline of population in the central areas, not least the City of London, from the 1850s onwards. The suburbanisation was to be a continual feature of rail passenger developments, and notably so when combined with loose planning restrictions and easy access to land purchase. At the same time, as in other countries, the suburbanisation was much denser, and thus less environmentally disruptive, than that which was to follow with cars.

Within cities, commercial patterns began to change, as districts were demolished to accommodate the lines, goods yards, and centrally located terminus structures. Street patterns were focused on the new railway stations. The major ones, such as Isambard Kingdom Brunel's Paddington and, later, Gilbert Scott and W. H. Barlow's St Pancras, were designed as masterpieces of iron and glass, in effect versions of the Crystal Palace built for the Great Exhibition in 1851. The stations each also had large railway hotels, such as the Great Western Royal Hotel at Paddington, opened in 1854. In a piece of 1860 decrying 'Refreshments for Travellers,' Dickens had an interesting reflection on the new impersonality of society with reference to '... the great station hotel.... Where we have no individuality.... We can get on very well indeed at such a place, but still not perfectly well; and this may be, because the place is largely wholesale, and there is a lingering personal retail interest within us that asks to be satisfied.'

The railways needed a standard time for their timetables, in order to lessen the risk of collisions and to make connections possible, thus ensuring that railways and timetables could operate as part of a system. This characteristic was important to effectiveness and profitability. Standardisation became the norm and was seen across the world. It was more significant for trains than for steamships. In place of the previous variations of time in Britain from east to west, with the sun, for example, overhead at Bristol ten minutes behind London, the railways adopted the

Greenwich Observatory in London standard as 'railway time'. In 1840, the Great Western Railway to the West of England became the first railway to adopt London time and by 1847 most British rail companies had followed suit. From its offices on the Strand in London, the Electric Telegraph Company communicated Greenwich Time from 1852, the entire process reflecting the centrality of London. More generally, the fixing of time and time-based practices were very important in changing the nature of the world of work. Clocks were kept accurate by the electric telegraph that was erected along railway lines largely to that end. The electric telegraph was patented in Britain in 1837, with an electromagnet utilised to transmit and receive electric signals. The new invention was initially used largely by private companies to transmit information about trains.

The construction of networks, especially rail construction, was experienced as highly disruptive, which appealed to some but troubled many. This disruption was true of the natural environment and of the built one and looked toward the present situation. Human experience was challenged from the aesthetic to the practical. Dickens captured in his article 'Dullborough Town' (1860) the train as a cause of lost innocence as well as a source of new experiences, and recorded the extent to which the sights, smells, and much else of life, were transformed, and created anew, as the country modernised:

The Station has swallowed up the playing-field. It was gone. The two beautiful hawthorn-trees, the hedge, the turf, and all those buttercups and daisies had given place to the stoniest of jolting roads... The coach that had carried me away, was melodiously called Timpson's Blue-Eyed Maid, and belonged to Timpson at the coach-office up-street; the locomotive engine that had brought me back, was called severely No. 97 and belonged to SER [South

Eastern Railway], and was spitting ashes and hot-water over the blighted ground.

Similarly, in Frank Norris's *The Octopus: A Story of California* (1901), there is a reference to a quiet station: '... on the switch below, a huge freight engine that lacked its cow-catcher sat back upon its monstrous driving-wheels, motionless, solid, drawing long breaths that were punctuated by the subdued sound of its steam-pump clicking at exact intervals.'

The controversial nature of the expansion of the rail system was noted in Dickens' novel *The Mystery of Edwin Drood* (1870), where Cloisterham (the fictional Rochester, a city Dickens knew well) lacked a railway and Mr Sapsea said there never would, or should, be one:

'And yet, marvellous to consider, it has come to pass, in these days, that Express Trains don't think Cloisterham worth stopping at, but yell and whirl through it on their larger errands, casting the dust off their wheels as a testimony against its insignificance. Some remote fragment of Main Line to somewhere else, there was, which was going to ruin the Money Market if it failed, and Church and State if it succeeded, and (of course), the Constitution, whether or no; but even that had already so unsettled Cloisterham traffic, that the traffic, deserting the high road, came sneaking in from an unprecedented part of the country by a back stable-way.'

There was massive destruction involved in the building of stations and lines, with trains the strong 'iron monster.' Dickens discussed this destruction in his account of north London: Camden Town and nearby areas was transformed by the building of Euston, King's Cross and, later, in the gap, St Pancras stations, and their extensive supporting marshalling yards and lines. This was the biggest concentration of major stations and railway facilities in London and the country and was not matched elsewhere. In *Dombey and Son* (1848), Camden Town is the epicentre of change:

> The first shock of a great earthquake had ... rent the whole neighbourhood to its centre... Houses were knocked down; streets broken through and stopped... Everywhere were bridges that led nowhere ... mounds of ashes blocked up rights of way, and wholly changed the law and custom of the neighbourhood ... the yet unfinished and unopened Railroad was in progress, and, from the very core of all this dire disorder, trailed smoothly away, upon its mighty course of civilisation and improvement.

Alongside spectacle and class distinction, railways also provided material for the language, as with Dickens' 'the course of true love is not a railway.' In *Great Expectations* (1861), 'Joe's education, like steam, was yet in its infancy.'

At the same time, the nature of the new network inevitably posed problems. Dickens found this in 1862 when travelling from Leamington Spa to Cheltenham via Birmingham, where he was stranded for an hour. He discussed this in terms of 'cross-Railway-travelling'. It remains the case today, and for many junctions he would now be considered fortunate that it was just an hour. This situation was also true of contemporary France.

More seriously, there were accidents. Near Chester in 1847, there were five deaths and nine serious injuries as a train fell through the newly constructed bridge into the River Dee. The Staplehurst accident of 1865 affecting the Folkestone express was due to mistimed plate repairs: ten were killed and 14 seriously injured, although not Dickens, who helped tend the wounded. This was death in the midst of life, and not the prepared death that Victorians commonly discussed. The accident, about which he wrote powerfully, noting the role of chance, led Dickens to become more nervous about travelling. He disliked the rocking of carriages, which led him to advise against the Leicester to London express in 1867. More generally, as part of the educative process of travel, passengers had to adjust to risks such as putting their heads, arms or elbows out of windows, jumping from moving trains, as did pedestrians (and animals) near tracks, or on the edge of platforms, or on crossings. As later with cars, it was necessary to establish and learn rules.

The building and operation of railways attracted fraud, notably by George Hudson, the 'Railway King', whose speculative schemes contributed to the financial crisis that hit hard in 1847. Dickens had referred to him as 'the Giant Humbug of this time, and not a pleasant illustration of our English Virtues'. Like most issues of planning involving vested property interests, the emergence of railways, with their attendant companies, boards of directors, agents, surveyors, promoters, shareholders and speculators, encouraged both advocates and opponents for particular proposals. The number of railway bills and the number of committees to investigate proposed new lines (particularly committees of the House of Lords) was a major occupation of the 1830s and especially 1840s. Some MPs, like Hudson and Trollope's fictional Melmotte, were railway entrepreneurs who entered Parliament; but many other MPs were involved as directors, lobbyists (unpaid or otherwise) and, in some cases, opponents. Some aristocrats disliked lines crossing their prized acres or spoiling their view. As far as rail plans were concerned, politics hardly mattered in the sense of political parties, but very much did so in the case of private or corporate interests. Some parliamentary boroughs wanted lines. In contrast, the City of London kept the early lines outside its boundaries, as did the wealthy of the West End. Engines and stations were unattractive in terms of social and environmental amenity. But the likely profitability of lines attracted some, including City bankers who helped to promote the companies.

All these interests had influence in Parliament, some of the individuals involved were members of one House or the other, and every new line required a private Act of Parliament for both the company's incorporation (until general legislation facilitated the formation of joint-stock companies with limited liability) and the construction of the line. It meant that, unless all the interests were squared beforehand, a railway Bill could be defeated or at least held up in Parliament. Most of the negotiation went on off-stage, but some debates on the Bills reveal the underlying tensions. On the whole, the aristocracy and other big landowners did very well out of the process.

Dickens followed up the Staplehurst accident of 1865 by writing: 'Every day of my life, I think more and more what an ill-governed country this is, and what a pass our political system has got to. How has this enormous Railway No-System grown up without guidance, and now its abuses are so represented in Parliament by Directors, Contractors, Scrip Jobbers, and so forth, that no Minister dare touch it.' In practice, however, there was regulation, with the Railway Department of the Board of Trade established in 1840 and Railway Regulation Acts passed in 1842 and 1844. 'Parliamentary trains', those, referred to by Gilbert and Sullivan in their operetta *The Mikado* (1885), operated to comply with the Railway Regulation Act of 1844, which obliged train companies to provide inexpensive rail transport for the less affluent: 'The provision of at least one train a day each way at a speed of not less than twelve miles an hour including stops, which were to be made at all stations, and of carriages protected from the weather and provided with seats; for all which luxuries not more than a penny a mile might be charged.'

Thereafter, however, government control did not increase until the Regulation of Railways Act of 1868, and the opportunity for a government-guided rail network, avoiding over-capitalisation and competing lines, was not taken.

Meanwhile, services from London had reached Birmingham in 1838 (with part of the line opened in 1837 to facilitate travel to London for Victoria's coronation), Southampton in 1840, Exeter and Oxford in 1844, Norwich in 1845, Ipswich and Bury St Edmunds in 1846, Plymouth and Portsmouth in 1847, Banbury and Holyhead in 1850, and Truro in 1859. Glasgow and Edinburgh were linked by rail in 1841. Birmingham and London, however, remained cities uncomfortably divided between railway companies and their respective stations. So, also, for other such cities, for example Boston and Paris. In contrast, some large cities had individual main stations; again, a contrast seen today. One of the problems with the current HS2 project is that it requires a separate major station in Birmingham.

Railways hit canal business and in some cases, railways directly replaced canals. The opening of the Buckinghamshire Railway in Oxford in 1851 brought severe competition to the Oxford Canal Company. In the year ending 1 October 1853, the canal carried 24,079 tons of coal to Oxford against the railway's transportation of 51,608 tons. In Plym Bridge Woods, the railway was built on the canal towpath to bring stone and peat from Dartmoor to Plymouth, the stone used for building and the peat for fuel. Similarly, the canal from Carlisle to Port Carlisle closed in 1853 and was converted into the Port Carlisle Railway. The railway also hit river traffic: the opening of a service to Barmouth in 1867 wrecked the carriage up-river to Dolgellau: 167 ships entered and left the port in 1866, but only eleven in 1876. But for the railway, more freight within Britain would have gone by steamships.

Instead, they were linked to railways at ports, such as Hartlepool, Lowestoft and Penarth, and the two developed together.

Yet, even in the 1850s when the rail network was becoming well-established, sea-borne coal was far more important to London than that brought across land: in 1855, 3 million tons came by sea, compared with 1.2 million tons by rail. The ease of moving coal by sea was facilitated by the use of large steamships as well as the mechanisation of unloading. Only in 1869 was coal brought by sea to London matched by that moved by rail. Railways linked to ports were also very important for fish, with fresh fish moved rapidly to the major urban markets, so that the Lowestoft-Ipswich line opened up large-scale haulage to London. At the same time, such lines also moved coal. That line ensured that coal could be moved to Woodbridge, a port nine miles up the River Deben, and therefore started to take the seaborne coal trade away from the port. The routes of fish trains included Aberdeen, Hull and Southampton to London, Hartlepool and Hull to Manchester, as well as Grimsby to South Wales, and other routes.

The prospectuses for new lines clarified what was thought desirable. That of 1845 for the London and Manchester Direct Independent Railway, with a branch to Crewe, claimed that it would offer an important route to Scotland, adding: 'not by means of a route made up of circuitous segments of various undertakings, already overworked with a patch of new railway between, to make up a solicitor's line, but by one continuous railway'.

The prospectus for the London and Holyhead Direct Railway noted: 'The line will be, for the most part, of easy construction, as abundance of building materials exist over a part of the line.' This was important due to the need for a firm railbed. Ballasting was significant and had to be consistent.

Railways were all-weather, and therefore transformed links and had better financial yield than if had they been only seasonal. The necessity for tunnels and bridges meant that the relevant technology, expertise and finance were crucial. On 29 August 1850, in one of the public displays of ceremony that the era greatly loved, Queen Victoria opened the Royal Border Bridge over the River Tweed at Berwick. Designed by George Stephenson's son Robert (1803-59), one of the greatest engineers of the day, this viaduct of 28 arches cost £253,000 and is still impressive today, the height of the bridge and the curve of the approach providing a fine vista. This was a man-made vista, as those of Victoria's reign increasingly were, and notably so with the railway. The bridge provided the last railway link between London and Edinburgh, one that enabled Victoria to go to Balmoral, her palace in the Scottish Highlands, whereas George IV had gone to Edinburgh by sea. Robert was to be buried in Westminster Abbey, a recognition of the importance of engineering.

Far less prominence and recognition were given to the labourers. Many were Irish, a large number of whom had responded to the crisis caused by the Great Famine of the late 1840s and fled to England and Scotland. They were particularly important in construction projects, such as the railways.

Best practice for rail developed through trial and error, although both involved political and social as well as financial considerations. Thus, a stationary engine house was built at Camden Town for the London and Birmingham Railway. The engine, which pulled trains by rope up the incline from Euston to Camden Town, was only used for six years, until 1844. It has been said that early locomotives were not powerful enough to haul trains up the slope, especially as it had to rise high enough to pass over Regent's Canal near Gloucester Road, but this was not the case. Instead, Parliament had not allowed the railway company to operate steam locomotives close to the city, a restriction that was soon relaxed and then ignored completely.

Adapting to regulations but also adapting regulations were both key aspects of the development of rail systems, not least in experience and expertise. The learning curve had to be a steep one, as an entire infrastructure had to be designed and operated, as had the relevant organisational structure, operating systems including timekeeping, and finances.

Early rails were not strong enough for heavy steam locomotives, but wrought-iron rails, less brittle than cast iron, were rolled successfully from the 1820s, while the far more resilient steel rails were introduced from the late 1850s. These created a permanent way that could bear heavy weights. This made it possible to invest in more powerful locomotives that were able to pull heavier loads and engage with more difficult gradients. As a result, more freight or passengers could be carried on individual trains, thus raising the efficiency and capability of the system. The availability of fresh investment capital interacted with the determination to seek and apply technological advantages.

The British innovation spread rapidly, with British expertise and finance playing major roles. The gold rushes of mid-century, that in California from 1848, Australia in 1851, and New Zealand in 1861, increased the money supply and ensured that credit was plentiful and cheap, which helped ensure both public and private investment, and both international and domestic finance.

The Italian and Austrian Railway Company that proposed in 1845 a line from Verona to Ancona had British directors and Isambard Kingdom Brunel as engineer. The prospectus stated: 'Railways from Vienna are now in progress towards Russia,

Poland, Prussia, and Hamburg; and thus the railway system will speedily be spread throughout the whole continent of Europe.' The use of British expertise and finance was even more the case in the British empire, particularly Canada, India and the West Indies. In the last, there was especially significant development in Barbados, Jamaica and Trinidad. In each case, the money provided was largely raised in London and the prospectuses emphasised what were seen as the bases for profit. They included the flatness of the line, as steep inclines were hard to work, as well as access to sources of product and to ports. As such, rail was part of a global economic-fiscal system, that of free trade and investment flow within the empire. The 1845 prospectus for the City of Toronto and Lake Huron Railway sought £500,000 for its projected 120 miles and declared that it would shorten the route to Chicago by cutting out the need to traverse Lake Erie by ship, with all the problems that entailed of storms and winter freezing. As in this case, railways were linked to colonial development, indicated in the prospectus:

> The most certain and effective means of establishing an enlarged system of colonisation consist in the judicious investment of capital within our colonies, for the purpose of extending trade and facilitating the communication of the colonist with rich and abundant markets... There are no engineering difficulties, there being a gradual ascent from Toronto, for the distance of thirty miles, and the remainder being almost a dead level... Land, which in English lines forms so prominent a feature of the expense, can be purchased in Canada for a very inconsiderable sum.

So also with the 'informal empire' where British economic power was considerable, notably Latin America, particularly Argentina but also Uruguay, Brazil, Chile, Peru, and Cuba. In

Anthony Trollope's novel *The Way We Live Now* (1875), the shady financier (and MP) Augustus Melmotte seeks in London to ramp up the share price of a company that is to be floated to construct a railway line from Salt Lake City to Veracruz, Mexico's leading port, the South Central Pacific and Mexican Railway. The fraudulent scheme collapses.

Most companies were not fraudulent – but were overly optimistic about profits. Their finances were often precarious, and the refinancing involved frequently cut corners. Capital markets and banking developed in part to finance railways, both domestically and internationally. Yet, these markets and banks were also affected, at times disastrously so, by the difficulties in turning investment and operating costs into yield and profit, repaying debt and paying dividends. Profitability was an issue whether or not there was a state role. Indeed, the latter posed particular problems in the form of investment in rail being challenged by other calls on public expenditure.

France is a larger country than Britain, but although it had coal, notably in the north-east, it was less widely available than in Britain or Belgium. Nevertheless, the situation was very different to the Netherlands, where the absence of mining prior to 1907 was a bottleneck for the early development of railways and industry in toto. In France, with the development of the metallurgical industry and the use of the coal and iron resources available, an impressive railway system was created, albeit not as rapidly as in Britain. The first railway opened between Andrézieux and Saint-Étienne in 1828 in order to move coal to river barges. A passenger line between Paris and Saint-Germain followed in 1837, with the money raised by bankers as a joint-stock enterprise. In 1838, a Ministry of Public Works was established in part to regulate the railway companies. Railways were seen by the government as a way to help prosperity, enable the movement of grain, and deal with food riots such as those in 1838-9. However, a financial crisis in 1839 led to bankruptcies that ended the railway boom. This caused the government to change direction and become willing to provide the financial support hitherto not made available. As a result of earlier government caution, there were far fewer miles of track completed in France than in Britain by 1842 – 300 to 1,900. In contrast, a government plan of 1842 saw the government agree to contribute heavily to the construction of several major trunk lines, and by 1848, 2,000 miles of track were in operation. Only 274 million francs had been spent by government and private investors by 1841, but 793 million was spent between 1841 and 1847, of which 618 million was spent in 1841-7.

The great breakthrough in France occurred in the 1850s and 1860s, not only with more mileage, but also the establishment of a network, which, as in Britain, was crucial. However, in France, as in Britain, this was not yet a truly integrated network due to the multiplicity of companies and a system converging on Paris. This was comparable to the British focus on London, although in Britain there was also a greater attention to links to the ports. French convergence on Paris created major problems for links between the regions. Costs increased because of the need to take longer, often far longer, journeys via Paris, which contrasted with the situation in both Germany and Britain. In the 1850s and 1860s, the emphasis in France was on private finance rather than the state: the latter had provided 28.7 per cent of railway spending in 1830-48, but only 8.9 per cent in 1851-70. Instead, government dividend guarantees helped encourage private investment.

This encouragement ensured that railway concessions were actively pursued by financial interests, notably the *Crédit Mobilier*, established in 1852, and the Rothschilds. Involving

French interests, this process extended outside France, for example in French North Africa (Algeria), Spain and the Balkans, for which Baron Moritz von Hirsch, who moved to Paris, established the *Chemins de fer Orientaux*, its headquarters in Paris from 1869 to 1878. There was no relation to the French bank, but in 1864-7 the *Crédit Mobilier* of America was involved in a scandal that saw inflated costs to build the Union Pacific Line with the excess lost through corruption.

In France in 1871, over 23,000 kilometres (14,000 miles) were in operation and by 1914, 60,000 kilometres (37,000 miles), about a third of which were narrow gauge. Railways changed the local, regional, and national geographies of France, not least as towns that had been important for river trade and/or as bridging points or road junctions were bypassed. Coal was increasingly moved by rail, rather than canal, but a very different use of rail was made by the wealthy, who travelled to new recreational destinations such as the seaside resorts of Deauville, Le Touquet and Nice.

Rail was also introduced to France's colonies. In Algiers in 1862, a station was opened in the centre of the city close to the port, and a system developed in the coastal parts of the colony. It was part of the imposition of colonial control and the related reorganization of links and networks.

Germany had coal and iron, but when rail began it was divided into numerous states. In 1828, the poet Goethe observed that he 'was not uneasy about the unity of Germany ... our good high roads and future railroads will of themselves do their part.' Early railways had mostly run within states, and only short distances at that, notably from Nuremberg to Fürth (1835), Berlin to Potsdam (1838), Brunswick to Wolfenbüttel (1838), and Leipzig to Dresden (1837-9). There was an initial dependence on British expertise and technology, with a British-made locomotive used in 1835 for the Nuremberg to Fürth line. German expertise developed very rapidly, however, as with Franz Anton Ritter von Gerstner who became an important railway engineer in the 1830s and was commissioned by the Russian government to oversee the building of a line between St Petersburg and Moscow.

There was a political counterpart to rail-building in Germany with attempts to organise a *Zollverein* (Customs Union) in order to overcome toll barriers between states, foster unity, notably under Prussian leadership, and provide protection against British industrialisation. In 1834, the *Zollverein* came formally into existence as the result of the merger of existing attempts, but other states only joined later, including Hanover and Oldenburg, both in 1854. Rail has to be understood in part in terms of these political strategies.

The 1840s saw major expansion. The first 'international' mainline joined Magdeburg in Prussia to Leipzig in Saxony in 1840, by when there were nearly 1,000 kilometres of track. Frederick William IV of Prussia (r. 1840-61) was a great enthusiast for rail, and the Prussian system grew rapidly, in part in order to counter fears about the strategic threat posed by French rail construction toward Germany. The Cologne-Minden railway, opened in 1845-7, helped industrialise the Ruhr and link Prussia to its Rhenish possessions. In 1846, the Berlin-Hamburg railway provided a key link from Prussia to a North Sea port, and thus access to the Atlantic, as well as another international mainline within Germany. As with Britain and Belgium, Germany benefited hugely from already being a major source of coal and iron production, and these increased greatly, with the railways moving the very products on which they relied. In the same way, Germany rapidly moved into steel production. The Germans also quickly developed the necessary railway skills and works, although funding the system helped cause serious political difficulties in

Prussia in 1847, leading to the convening of what was known as the Union Diet.

At the same time, rail served a range of political strategies. In 1848, well-disciplined Prussian forces, benefiting from the use of railways, put down poorly led uprisings in Baden, Hesse and Saxony. Separately, Austria and Prussia developed their networks for a conflict along their common border in Silesia. The Prussians benefited in their wars with Austria in 1866 and France in 1870-1 from the use of planned rail movement to make army mobilisation a rapid and predictable sequence that greatly facilitated the concentration of forces. Uniform speed by all trains was employed by the Prussians in order to maximise their effectiveness, and military trains were also of standard length. Rail use was planned and controlled by a railroad commission and by line commands, creating an integrated system that was linked and made responsive by the telegraph. This was an instance of a key element of railway development, the multiplication of capability by means of the integration of technologies, and also of the reliance of logistics on information and its rapid dissemination. Furthermore, the number of locomotives was kept high in order to cope with a wartime rise in demand, a practice that was at marked variance with the peacetime need to even out demand in order to make the most effective use of locomotives and rolling stock. The crucial point, which Helmuth von Moltke the Elder, the Chief of Staff, seems to have understood and carried out intentionally, was to make mobilisation, followed by concentration and then invasion, part of the same seamless movement – ideally, all the way through to the final battle.

This Prussian capability took on greater value in 1870 given the inadequate French response, part of the standard pattern in which capability emerged in part in relative terms. Although the French had a better railway system, they made worse use of it.

The French tried to combine mobilisation and concentration, and, instead, created chaos, in part due to a badly managed focus on effort in a small area. French mobilisation and subsequent operations also suffered greatly from the concentration of the rail system on Paris. This made it harder to move troops and supplies. From the early frontier battles through to that of Sedan, French units were crippled or paralysed by logistical problems. Furthermore, once Paris was surrounded by German forces in late 1870, it became far harder to support the disparate French units that elsewhere sought to maintain resistance.

Yet, in 1914, once the fighting began in the First World War, it was to be the French use of rail in order to move troops that proved more effective than that of Germany. Being on the defensive then, the French proved able to use their own rail network with greater success, as the Soviets were to do when attacked by the Germans in 1941.

Starting later than Britain, the Germans developed a rail network of greater scale:

	Britain (km)	Germany (km)
1860	16,798	11,089
1880	28,846	33,838
1913	38,114	63,378

In part, the contrast arose from the far greater size of Germany and in part from the more significant role of maritime trade for Britain, both coastal (not least in coal movements) and international. Nevertheless, the developing contrast between the two states, which was also seen in iron and steel production, was instructive.

Lines into the Austro-Hungarian empire (Austria for short) were an aspect of the degree to which German activity and initiatives did not stop at the border of what would subsequently be described as Germany. Yet, although the Germans were to build railways in the colonies they seized from the 1880s on, principally in Africa, as well as in the Balkans and Turkey, there was no equivalent to the scale of British or French overseas construction, and notably that of Britain in India and Latin America. The German focus on railways in Germany itself was partly responsible.

The year 1839 saw the first Italian railway when the Bourbons of Naples opened one from Naples to Portici, linking the royal palace to the sea; whereas in Piedmont, the first, from Turin to Moncalieri, did not open until 1848. However, thereafter, growth was largely in the north of Italy. Count Cavour, Prime Minister of Piedmont in 1852-9 and 1860-1, and a keen and ambitious moderniser, was able and willing to borrow heavily to develop a rail system in Piedmont, the most industrially developed part of Italy. Cavour, who looked to Britain and France, also had a strategic sense, both economically and politically, aiming in particular to use rail to link inland Piedmont with Liguria, specifically the port of Genoa, which it had acquired in 1814 as part of the Congress of Vienna settlement. Begun in 1845, the first leg was opened in 1848 and the line completed in 1853. This included the Giovi Tunnel in the Apennines, and aside from hard labour and much cost, the line involved purchase of the *Mastodonte dei Giovi* (Mastodons of Giovi), a double steam locomotive – two locomotives coupled back-to-back under one driver. They were designed by the Stephenson workshop in Newcastle and could haul trains of 150 tonnes on a slope of 3.6 per cent at 7.5 mph.

This line competed with the rail links being developed to the east in the then Austrian-ruled part of Italy, notably from Milan to Venice and still further east, from Vienna to the port of Trieste.

The 1845 plan for a line from Verona to the Papal port of Ancona was part of this geopolitical linkage, because the Papacy was aligned with Austria against Piedmont and the related idea of Italian unification. There were fond hopes that Trieste might come to rival Hamburg as a commercial outlet.

Yet again, it was important to access ports from the interior. Rail offered a major alternative to rivers in this respect, as the ports selected could be those that were not necessarily linked to rivers or navigable rivers. In addition, rail could cross the watershed of rivers, as from Turin to Genoa, Verona to Ancona, and Vienna to Trieste, and thus provide valuable flexibility. Tunnelling made this process of crossing watersheds easier, although lines through passes were less expensive.

With politics to the fore again, the situation in Italy was very much affected by conflicts between Austria and Piedmont. In 1848-9, the latter was defeated, but in 1859, in contrast, French intervention with troops moved by rail and steamships helped Piedmont to victory over Austria, a process that was completed by further expansion in 1860-70, after which most of modern Italy had been acquired. By 1866, meanwhile, the entire peninsula was connected by rail, and the network in northern Italy was impressive. Railways were described as the laces that held the Italian boot together. In 1899, a boat-train service by ferry across the Strait of Messina began.

The Alps limited the rail links between Italy and its neighbours. More generally, railways initially were built within countries. If the proximity of states in Western Europe, and notably so in the German lands, encouraged links between them, these were still sensitive both politically and economically. As a result, politics were even more to the fore in these cases than in those within states. Nevertheless, there could be state political and economic reasons to support international links that might also appear commercially desirable at the company level. A mixture of these motives can be seen in rail-related diplomacy in 1850-1. The Bavarian-Württemberg agreement of 1850 was designed to provide a line from Munich to Stuttgart, and to ensure that Württemberg was part of the non-Prussian rail system that was being established. In 1851, Austria, Prussia's major opponent, and Bavaria agreed to build railways to join at Kufstein, which for the Bavarians were designed to provide a connection to the Austrian Adriatic port at Trieste. As a reminder of the range of geopolitical factors involved in rail links, again a factor that lasts to the present-day, the Munich-Innsbruck line was important to Austria because of the link between Rosenheim in Bavaria and Salzburg, which provided a quick connection to the west of Austria avoiding the issues posed by Bavaria's Berchtesgaden salient.

The British example of railway construction was rapidly copied not only in Western Europe and the British empire, but also in America. This process was encouraged by the diffusion of British technology and the availability of British investment capital, as seen with the Baltimore and Ohio Railroad, an American trailblazer. There was a curious phenomenon in Pennsylvania of a rail and water link with boats on wheels, which was an indication of the hybrid forms attracting attention in a period of transition; but trains and steamships won out. Paintings in which both appeared included David Johnson's *The Hudson River from Fort Montgomery* (1870) and George Bellows' *North River* (1908).

The opening of the American interior for rail was powered by its extensive forests. For the Americans, this was not just a matter of the crossties (rail ties) for the tracks, but also the use of wood from the charcoal required for the iron for the rails (the last charcoal furnace closed in 1945). In contrast, charcoal furnaces were uncommon in Britain after the early nineteenth century.

With its rapid industrialisation and build-up of capital reserves and borrowing capability, Massachusetts saw an early adoption of railways, such that in 1830-1, after first thinking of horse-drawn rail lines, the legislature chartered three private steam railway companies. This ensured a competition that helped provide opportunities for investment while also acting as a restraint on costs. By 1850, more than $50 million had been invested in New England railways, which made them the largest private companies in the country. As in Britain, traffic was sufficiently heavy and capital plentiful enough to enable investment in a far-flung system; and not only in New England where it first concentrated. Furthermore, the degree to which the canal system was limited, not least as a means to go beyond the Appalachians, would encourage investment in railways.

Railway competition extended to that between ports acting as outlets for the interior, notably Boston, New York and Baltimore. The Erie Railroad reached Lake Erie in 1851, providing New York with a link that thwarted Boston's hope of channelling trade from the Hudson River and the Great Lakes east via Massachusetts to the Atlantic at Boston.

Railway companies were pioneers of large-scale managerial enterprise, which was to be important to American history. Indeed, they were to help foster this enterprise, and particularly so because rail remained outside state control, a pattern that has remained dominant in peacetime. Nevertheless, there was an important degree of government-private co-operation. Thus, although early railways primarily involved private enterprise, there was also, usually, the purchase of rail securities by states, counties and cities, as with Massachusetts and the line from Boston to the Hudson Valley at Albany. Subsequently, as another instance of governmental involvement, the army was to play an important role in surveying alternative routes for transcontinental railways, and military engineering skills were to be significant to the management and development of rail companies.

In America, as elsewhere, time was one of the key managerial issues. There were many time standards, and trains had their clocks set by the time at the main departure station, which caused problems with the use of differing time standards by trains on the same line. This practically ensured a large number of crashes. To cope with this, from 1849 the New England train companies used time standardised by the Harvard College Observatory, whose head, William Bond, was Boston's leading clockmaker. From 1851, the time signals were sent by telegraph from the Observatory to Bond's Boston shop, from where the rail companies took the time. This became compulsory after an 1853 crash on a blind curve near Pawtucket, Rhode Island. The telegraph was important to timetabling, and the synchronisation of time followed the rail lines. Far more than the fixing of time was involved, as railways struck Americans as providentially designed and a means to power and profit, and they were certainly presented as such, indeed as part of America's 'Manifest Destiny' to expand.

3

SPANNING THE CONTINENT AND
OTHER ADVENTURES OF RAIL

Railways fired up the imagination of projectors, politicians and the public, and the toil of engineers and workers. And these achievements can be readily seen to this day. Thus, the deep ravines on the Volcanic Plateau on the North Island of New Zealand were traversed by spectacular steel viaducts, and the Raurimu Spiral, built between 1905 and 1908, is still one of the engineering marvels of rail construction.

On a different scale of achievement, the 'Cosmopolitan Railway' was a striking instance of the hopes for rail that flourished from the start and became far bolder with time. It was the brainchild of an American, William Gilpin (1813-94), who was typical of the projectors of the age, projectors who were to be crucial to the history of rail, both in envisioning lines and in financing them. It was as if they prospected for rail. Americans were particularly active in this sphere, and not only in America. Initially serving in the army (1836-8), Gilpin became committed to the development of the frontier and in particular to Colorado, the subject of *The Central Gold Region. The Grain, Pastoral, and Gold Regions of North America. With Some New Views of Its Physical Geography;*

Works drawing of the Garratt K1 designed by Herbert William Garratt and built in 1909. Garratt's articulated layout kept the boiler and firebox away from the running gear. The advantages were tremendous, with power output practically doubled in comparison with 'rigid' locomotives.

and Observations on the Pacific Railroad (1860). This linked American Manifest Destiny to global progress, the two to be joined by a transcontinental railway and its extension to a line across the Bering Strait in order to make western America central to a world in which Asia was to be joined to America and, via the latter, Europe. Denver was to be the capital of a new civilisation, with all the great cities of the world along that latitude linked by rail. In turn, Gilpin, an endless self-inventor, was, as Governor of Colorado in 1861-2, active in that stage of the Civil War as well as a land speculator of highly dubious morality.

Gilpin continued thereafter to advance his views, including in *The Cosmopolitan Railway: Compacting and Fusing Together All the World's Continents* (1890) in which he devoted much space to the civilisational potential of rail – 'The Railway as a Factor of Progress' – and referred to Denver as 'the railroad centre of the West'. The prose was rich:

> Never, except by such cataclysms of war as the superior intelligence of mankind forbids us to anticipate will London, New York, and Denver be blotted from the face of the earth, as were Carthage, Corinth, and Palmyra. On the banks of the Thames and the Hudson, and at the base of the Rocky mountains, will stand for many a century to come those great commercial emporia, sending forth their richly freighted argosies and rail trains to every quarter of the globe. The empire of monarchs may pass away, but the empire of commerce will remain as long as this solid earth endures.

In practice, Gilpin, like other visionaries, was greatly overegging his account, both in the description of the current situation and the discussion of future possibilities. It was wrong for Gilpin to say that the American rail system was 'drawing nearer and nearer toward' the Bering after the purchase of Alaska from Russia in

1867. A dubious prospectus for the future rested on questionable accounts of past and present:

> To the very existence of civilised communities the railroad has become almost as much a necessity as is the circulation of the blood to the individual. Not only do we depend upon it for the means of locomotion, but for almost everything that we eat or drink or wear. And in no country in the world do people rely so much on their railroads as in the United States, where in the more thinly populated sections coal for fuel and lumber for building are often conveyed by rail hundreds of miles from the place of production. But perhaps their greatest benefit has been in the opening up for settlement of vast and fertile regions, before unpeopled except by savages and wild beasts ... converting, as at the touch of a magic wand, what was before little else than a desert, or at least a pasture ground, into a region abounding with grain and fruit ... and giving especially to Colorado and California a commercial and industrial development such as has never before been witnessed in the lifetime of a single generation.

Four years later, Gilpin was killed by being run over by a horse and buggy in the erstwhile capital of the future, Denver. The idea of a Siberian-Alaskan rail link, by bridge or tunnel, was revived by rail planners and futurists on a number of occasions, including the 2000s and 2010s, but never brought even close to fruition.

The triumph of the new in the shape of the drama of rail apparently provided a clear demonstration of human progress, with bridges, viaducts and indeed locomotives themselves signs of this new potency and of the change this could effect. This was civilisation in process, and, the key enabler, technology as progress. As a result, there was a repeated appearance of relevant images, not least with photographs capturing success such as the driving in of spikes when lines were joined. These photographs were often reproduced on postcards and in newspapers and magazines. Film subsequently was to take on this task.

In reality, there was no comparable publicised record of failures, which included significant cost overruns and major delays. The only comparable public record was of accidents, which, indeed, attracted extensive coverage as well as much speculation over causes. In part, the latter offered the public education about the possible limitations of rail.

Bridges could dramatically alter local, regional and even national geography. And the process was not without serious problems, both in general and in many individual cases. The Tay bridge, completed in 1877, was a triumph of Victorian technology, specifically iron-working. Nearly two miles long and consisting of 85 wrought-iron lattice-girder spans resting on cast-iron columns, it was designed by Thomas Bouch. He was knighted by Queen Victoria when she crossed it in the summer of 1879. On 28 December 1879, 74 people died when part of the bridge collapsed during a storm as a train was crossing. The resulting inquiry highlighted problems in design, construction and maintenance, for which much of the blame fell on Bouch.

This is a reminder both of the problems that were an aspect of Victorian engineering achievements, and yet also of their ability to learn from mistakes. This process was necessary, as railways were at the forefront of new techniques including construction, maintenance and working practices. The replacement Tay Bridge (1887) was better built and did not collapse.

New systems developed to span countries and then continents. There was also an intensification of existing networks in Europe, eastern America and India, and the establishment of systems in new areas, notably East Asia. Alongside the reduction in cost of land transport and the capacity to move large quantities of freight long distances, came the opening of areas to economic development and growth.

There were other aspects that can be overlooked, but that also deserve attention. The sense of time and space changed as a result of the train, which offered an explicit emblem of the human capacity to use new knowledge to remodel the environment and to create new sensations and connections. Thus, the train was a means of modernisation and globalisation, indeed Westernisation, and a source, symbol and site of a new sensibility that linked humans to machines. This situation suggested a new aspect to evolution, one that was forward-looking, and framed and effected by humans, rather than being the more challenging relationship with other species discussed by Charles Darwin. Indeed, the machine-characteristics of the railway and steamship transport revolution implied a new stage of the sociological progression outlined by late eighteenth-century Enlightenment writers such as Adam Smith, Edward Gibbon and William Robertson. Machines of this type appeared to move mankind beyond the urban-industrial situation that was the last stage of that model, because their capacity was so much greater, not least in creating new global links.

At a more mundane level, rail brought a new speed to news and changing fashions. Local trends and towns were thereby eclipsed by metropolitan fashions. A different form of shaping was provided by tourist guidebooks, first for rail and then for road travellers. Guidebooks offered an important means to define and represent national and regional identities, and presented their information accordingly.

As with other branches of industrial capitalism, but more so given its scale, range, and extent beyond the factory, the rail system required large numbers of trained (and motivated) employees able to provide the technical and administrative skills required, skills that varied considerably in their sophistication. The major growth of engineering education provided the technical manpower, as did the expansion of the educational system as a whole. Experienced and skilful manpower made projects more predictable, error less common, and investment safer. Helped by improved transport and emigration, engineering experience was readily available around the Western world, and was rapidly spread to other states. That process was encouraged by the association of Westernisation with modernisation. Engineering skills were essential for the construction of rail systems and also for their operation. Aside from staffing of a new type, including engineers and stationmasters, railways needed advertising and booking and payment systems.

The railways were ultra-modern, with customer service and a system of work designed so that employees would respond rapidly and predictably to orders. The world of railway work, with its labour discipline, quasi-military uniforms (thus enforcing corporate identity), and well-regimented hierarchy and command systems, reflected a labour process and organisation ethos that was very different to traditional ones. Aside from the harshness this discipline could entail, with staff readily dismissed for infringements, there were also numerous rail workers killed or injured in construction and in maintenance accidents. It was difficult to introduce and enforce the necessary safety matrix. More positively, there were also major improvements in the technology, including the introduction, improvement or spread of greater steam-engine efficiency, braking mechanisms, signalling, and steel rails.

Yet, in a fashion that is still instructive, railways were also very vulnerable to economic downturns. In part, this was because their expansion, much of it very speculative, was largely financed by high rates of debt, which ensured that many companies failed when there were major financial crises, as in 1837, 1857, 1873, 1893 and 1929. This reliance on entrepreneurial capitalism was very much the case in Britain and America, but also seen where it was necessary to import the relevant finance and expertise. These crises owed much to the specific problems of railway investment. This was particularly the case in America in 1873.

As well as being a cause of financial crisis, railways were a symbol of integration and convergence, encouraging a more joined-up economy. They were dramatic statements of a new power, as with major stations, for example in Madrid. Yet, the extent to which foreign capital played a role, as for example in Spain, where railway construction developed rapidly after the Railway Act of 1855, and also in Argentina, reflected the great power of international capital and of the related British-dominated international economic order. Railways were also a major cultural symbol and practical help to imperial power, as for the British in India.

The organisational sophistication of railways was particularly impressive, both in the creation of the system itself and also, more obviously, in managing the works, trains, freight and passengers to derive revenue, limit costs and ensure profit. Management produced and consumed information, and institutions, such as the Railway Clearing House in London, required reliable data in order to apportion through-revenues and thus produce a clear return from a system with many companies. Without such an apportionment, profit was uncertain, investment discouraged, and litigation between companies likely.

Thomas Edmondson, a stationmaster on the Newcastle and Carlisle Railway, developed what was to become the standardised type of ticket, first, in place of hand-written paper bills as tickets, a piece of cardboard pre-printed with journey details, and then a machine to print tickets in batches complete with their serial numbers. These machines were operated by railway companies on a royalty basis. The Railway Clearing House ensured that the system came into general use. These tickets were last used by British Rail in 1990, being replaced by computerised systems. The Edmondson tickets were also used in Europe and further afield.

The potential and practice of rail created issues of control and communication in many spheres, notably in business organisations. Established localised structures and processing methods were judged inadequate for rail, which was definitely the case with mergers and takeovers. This general situation led to pressure for the development of organisational messaging and business communications through the telegraph, and for wider systems of resource pooling and networking. More generally, innovations in economic, technological and processing control stemmed from the problems, opportunities and capital requirements created by the new rapidity of production and communications centred on rail. If, for example, the far more resilient steel rails introduced from 1857 created a permanent way that could bear heavy weight, making it possible to invest in more powerful locomotives able to pull heavier loads, reaching the resulting capability of the system required investment, organisation, management, prioritisation and sales. Thus, technology was only part of the story.

So also with factors such as cost structures, and the assumptions as well as market-knowledge and testing they reflected. Quantity, in particular, was not necessarily synonymous with profitability. In Guy de Maupassant's novel *Bel-Ami* (1885), the protagonist, Georges Duroy, catches the Paris express at Cannes: 'It had only five carriages – a real express train.' This was an acknowledgement of the greater speed enjoyed by shorter trains and the related higher charges which could only be afforded by a few passengers. In turn, the high price made it unnecessary to have so many passengers.

The rail system was linked to the major expansion in the press, as railways moved newspapers round the national spaces. *Besley's Devonshire Chronicle* of 25 January 1847 noted that Queen Victoria's Speech opening Parliament in London had arrived in Devon by express train. The combined impact of the railways and the telegraph in speeding up communication amounted not merely to an improvement but to a transformation: the railways transformed physical contact and the telegraph mental interplay.

This took place in many ways. Whereas stagecoaches were bumpy, crowded and poorly lit, trains, if adequately lit, were more convenient for reading, and it became a normal activity for passengers. This was true both for distant journeys and for commuting. As a result, entrepreneurs such as Louis Hachette in France and W. H. Smith and John Menzies in Britain developed from the mid-century networks of railway bookstores, helping to create as well as satisfy a new market. In 1852, Hachette reached an agreement with seven French rail concerns to establish station bookstalls. They sold travel guides for passengers as well as novels. Such bookstores revolutionised the sale of books and they retained a crucial role until recent years when newspapers became increasingly read on the internet. In turn, this created new technological requirements for trains, those for wifi reception and charging points. Aside from selling books, railway stations were also used by circulating libraries to display and lend books and to organise their distribution, as in Britain by Charles Mudie (1818-90), the founder of Mudie's Lending Library and Mudie's Subscription Library.

The mass-produced new train timetables provided opportunities for publishers. Though timetables posed problems of comprehension, both of the display of complex information in print and at stations, and for those whose literacy was limited. Samuel Wilberforce, Bishop of Oxford and then Winchester from 1845 to 1873, joked that the book beginning with B that every bishop needed was Bradshaws, the railway timetable, and not the Bible. In Transylvania, the fictional Count Dracula has a Bradshaw as a preparation for his settlement in Britain, which helped characterise him for British readers as a meticulous planner.

Meanwhile, in America, the financial Panic of 1837 had discredited state borrowing and helped ensure that transport improvement was left to the private sector, which had to spend the 1840s repairing its credit before expanding greatly. There was then a massive expansion in the rail system and in the assessment of its benefits. Across a longer timescale, railways were to provide a key aspect of counterfactual (what if?) discussion in American history. Robert Fogel's study of railways in the American Industrial Revolution, *Railroads and American Economic Growth* (1964), focused on what would have happened had there been no railways but only roads and canals, both of which would therefore have attracted much more investment, a point that is also valid when considering transport investment today. Arguments that in America the benefit amounted to only 4 per cent of national income and in Britain to just between 7 and 11 per cent, met contrary claims that the removal of a key factor can change the situation so dramatically that one is not talking about the same situation. In practice, accurate quantification of such factors is elusive.

The railways, which expanded greatly in America in the 1850s, especially in the North, were not developed for the purposes of a war. However, they made a huge difference to the Civil War (1861-5), tactically, operationally, strategically, and economically. Such a difference was in evidence at the very outset, when the

Union (Northern) forces rushing to Washington in order to prevent a possible Confederate takeover were obstructed in and near Baltimore, in part by the destruction of the railway track. Nevertheless, they got through. Operationally, the railways created links along which troops could move. In 1862, the Confederate (Southern) commander Braxton Bragg was able to move his troops 776 miles by rail from Mississippi to Chattanooga, and thus create an opportunity for an invasion of Kentucky. Such a potential was totally different to the situation during the previous wars in North America, for example that of 1812-15 with the British in Canada, and, if the term revolutionary is helpful, then the capacity to plan for rapid movement was a significant development.

As a result, rail junctions, such as Atlanta, Chattanooga, Corinth, Manassas and Nashville, or river ports where steamship services and railways were linked, for example Memphis, became operationally highly significant and the object, or at least focus, of much of the campaigning; although that might have happened anyway as they were principal settlements. Corinth, indeed, was founded in 1853 as Cross City because it was the junction of the Memphis and Charleston Railroad, en route to the Mississippi River, with the Mobile and Ohio Railroad. Control over the junction proved significant to the campaigning in northern Alabama.

From the outset, Union advances aimed at such junctions, which the Confederates struggled to protect or regain, while also being mindful of Union junctions when they advanced north, particularly in 1862 and 1863. Plans were discussed in these terms. Richard, Lord Lyons, the British envoy, reported in February 1862 on Union moves and options west of the Appalachians:

The fall of Fort Donelson and Fort Henry has given the Federals the command of the Cumberland and Tennessee Rivers – They to be thus enabled to occupy the Western part of Tennessee, to obtain possession of Nashville and the railroads which united at that point, and in this way to interrupt the communication between Virginia and the South through Tennessee.

Indeed, west of the Appalachians, the Union forces planned to gain control of the Mississippi River and to advance into the Confederacy along the railways running southeast through Tennessee and Georgia. This goal helped make Chattanooga a key point of contention.

In 1862, in the campaign east of the Appalachians that led to the Battle of Second Manassas or Bull Run, the Confederate General 'Stonewall' Jackson hit the Union supply route along the Orange and Alexandria Railroad, destroying the supply depot at Manassas Junction. Later that year, the Union commander Ambrose Burnside planned to move south toward the Confederate capital, Richmond, along the Richmond, Fredericksburg and Potomac Railway after he had captured the railway river crossing point of Fredericksburg, which, in the event, he failed to do.

In 1864, the Union failure to cut the Richmond and Petersburg Railroad meant that the Confederate Army of Northern Virginia under Robert E. Lee retained its major supply line, for there was no substitute for rail. In contrast, the remorseless success of the Union forces under William Tecumseh Sherman in cutting rail links that year led the Confederates to abandon Atlanta. This victory helped ensure Abraham Lincoln's re-election, which had looked less probable earlier in 1864. Meanwhile, at the tactical level, man-made landscape features created for railways, such as embankments, repeatedly played a part in battles.

At the strategic level, rail technology, use and potential combined in the Civil War to ensure organisational attention and advantage. Building on the already strong relationship between the army and civil engineering, notably the railways, the Union created the US Military Railroad (USMRR) as a branch of the War Department. This was part of the process of wartime mobilisation, the scope of which expanded as a result of the organisational demands stemming from new capacity and needs. US Military Railroad's remit included the building and repair of track and bridges. This capability provided a quick-response system to such requirements for transport links as the exigencies of the war required. As with the purchasing networks and naval dockyards established by European powers in the early-modern period to sustain warships, this system was necessary in order to harness the new technology, as well as earlier systems operating at the same time and in concert, notably wagon-based logistics. The Union side benefited from effective direction of the railway system combined with impressive engineering capability. The contrast was clear, for example, in the conflict around Chattanooga, with Confederate movements from Virginia less prompt and effective than comparable Union ones. Given the significance in battles and campaigns of feeding in fresh troops, this was an important capability.

Alongside the weaknesses of the Confederacy's railway infrastructure, it is important to put the use of the railway in the Civil War in context. Railheads were very significant to campaigning, but the rail network did not necessarily determine where the campaigns were fought. Rivers, not least because of the valleys and thus corridors they create through mountain ranges, probably had a greater effect on where operations were mounted. Moreover, the technological aspects of railway warfare were limited. There were no major developments in the specifications of locomotives during the war. Rail design and fabrication methods, as well as railway construction systems, were crucial to the speed of laying of new track, in addition to the safety of trains on it, and the speed at which they could travel and thus move supplies. Changes in these factors were not driven forward by the Civil War; and economic developments after the conflict, rather than the war itself, were responsible for the growth of a large-volume rail system. At the same time, as a strategically significant factor, the wartime breakdown of its railways greatly hit the Confederacy's economy and military effort. This breakdown owed much to the weakness of the local manufacturing base (which made repairs difficult) combined with the Union blockade and very poor Confederate railway management.

The years after the Civil War saw rapid redirection of investment from the war economy to new opportunities, a process eased by speedy demobilisation, despite possibilities of war over Canada with Britain and – more probably – over Mexico with France. The Civil War had encouraged a reliance on rail in the North and the expansion of metallurgy. From 1850 to 1870, America tripled the production of iron, having already done the same in 1830-50. The availability of Western bullion and of demand from the American industrial belt helped underwrite the financing of new railways, as did rampant speculation. The legal and political contexts, the two linked, were favourable to rail. The standardisation of common law and the development of a system of universal duties, such as that 'to get out of the way', provided an opportunity to clarify the issue of liability on such issues as people and animals killed or injured by trains. The pro-big business stance of successive Republican administrations after the Civil War served the needs of railway companies, not least in ensuring that early anti-trust pressure was not driven home, a situation that did not significantly change until the 1900s.

Railways helped open up resources across the country, as in Piedmont (western) South Carolina, where the major expansion of textile mills from the 1880s to the 1910s was linked to access to them. Indeed, although the South was not an area of rail investment, pre- or postwar, comparable to the North-East and the Mid-West, even so, and as evidence of the major significance of rail across the country, railways were important to its postwar economic role of providing raw materials for Northern industries. A major one, tragically, was cotton, and the rail system thus served to maintain the socio-political order in the South, with African Americans no longer slaves but restricted after the failure of postwar Reconstruction by disfranchisement and sharecropping. So also with the very disproportionate use (still to this day) of African Americans as leased out convict labour, some of which was employed by rail companies.

Rail linked the South into networks looking north, with development essentially being postwar. In Arkansas, for example, railway companies were chartered from 1853 and the first line opened in 1858, but most construction did not take place until after the Civil War, when subsidies and land grants helped, leading to 822 miles of track by 1880 and 3,167 by 1900, construction peaking in the early 1930s. Short-line railways were used to tie in local needs to trunk lines, and the expansion of the railways made possible a major growth in logging.

Across America, as more generally, railways also made farm specialisation and cash crops easier. A major element that tends to be overlooked is the movement of fertiliser by rail to farms. This was very important to raising production in areas of both good and poor soils and reduced the need to rely on local animal and human waste.

In *American Progress* (page 11), his powerful and much reproduced allegorical painting of 1872 about American expansion, John Gast has, following the wagons of the pioneers, three trains steaming across the prairies. There was a sense of mission: 'The building of railroads toward the setting sun' was to be proclaimed in 1927 by Robert McElroy as part of America's 'epic of glory'. Building a transcontinental railway was the key goal. It had been advocated with energy from the early 1850s but was delayed by the bitter sectionalism that led to the Civil War. The rebellion by the Confederacy in fact encouraged the Union to press ahead, in part as a geostrategic measure to anchor the West, in terms both of support and of moving troops to suppress any opposition. Founded in 1862 under the Pacific Railroad Act, the Union Pacific Rail Road began laying rails in Omaha in 1865 and joined the Central Pacific, constructed eastward from Sacramento, California, at Promontory Summit, Utah, in 1869. This was the first transcontinental railroad. The Union Pacific advertised to customers that it provided a 'short, quick, and safe line to all points west' in what it described as 'The Central Short Line', one that 'saves time, money, distance, and changes of cars'.

The *Sacramento Daily Union* of 18 June 1866 noted: 'Almost the entire work of digging is done by Chinamen… They are found to be equally as good as white men, and less inclined to quarrels and strikes. They are paid $30 per month and boarded, and a cook is allowed for every twelve men.'

The reality was far grimmer. The Chinese who cleared the route, levelled the railbed, and lay the track were subject to terrible conditions, notably as they blasted fifteen tunnels through the Sierra Nevada. There were no real safety provisions. Many times, they were given a bundle of dynamite and after setting it among the rocks, were told simply to swing away from the blast as they dangled from a rope. Sometimes, someone would pull them to safety. Many died in these dangerous working conditions, while there was scant care for those who were injured. The Chinese also worked in tunnels under the snow and sometimes these caved in, and no one made any attempts to rescue them. If their bodies were recovered, it was often in the spring. In addition, the Chinese were paid less than the white workers, which encouraged their use. Something approaching 20,000 Chinese were hired.

Around the world, rail construction involved very heavy labour, and if many workers, particularly locomotive drivers, were skilled and relatively expensive, large numbers of low-paid workers were essential for construction and maintenance, for example, cleaning. In part, this employment was made possible by the major growth in the world population, from about one billion in 1800 to about 1.8 billion by 1918. As with greater capital availability, this was a crucial contextual enabler that can be too easily forgotten due to the standard emphasis on technology. It was not only an aggregate increase in population, much of it perforce young and active, but also its availability due to more liberal attitudes toward migration than is the case today. In particular, there were large movements of Chinese across the Pacific world, including to North and South America and to Australia, and of Indians, including to East and South Africa. In contrast, the operation of railways was more commonly handled in these areas by workers of European origin. Thus, in southern Africa, in the British colony of Natal, where railway construction started in 1876, the railway department became the biggest single employer of Indian labour in the 1880s and 1890s. The contract of 1875 for the first section of the line had stipulated that two-thirds of the labourers needed for building the line were to be recruited from outside the colony, a measure stipulated to prevent local labour rates from rising and thus an attempt to prevent rail from disrupting the local situation, and notably the relationships between employers and workers. Many of the Indians were recruited in Mauritius. There were also African labourers recruited from Mozambique.

Four more transcontinental lines were to follow in America by 1900, by when there were about 215,000 miles of track compared to 45,000 in 1870. Although delayed by Native American resistance, notably by the Sioux, the railroad was an important part of the American policy of securing the West through economic integration, investment, migration, urbanisation, public relief and law enforcement. Reservations were intended to clear threatening Natives from the rail routes, notably from those along the Platte and Kansas valleys, the routes for the Union Pacific and Kansas Pacific lines. These railroads helped settlers to move into claimed and conquered areas, consolidating the American presence, a process also seen elsewhere, for example in Argentina. Further north, the Northern Pacific and Great Pacific Railways made Montana and the Dakotas more accessible and profitable for settlers, enabling them to outnumber the Native American population. More generally, areas that lacked access to river trade, or all-year-round river trade, were opened up by rail, or, if they had access, it was made easier and more predictable. Grain elevators and stockyards, which were located by stations, were a dramatic demonstration of the importance of rail and constructions that recentred settlements.

Railways were constructed across often inhospitable terrain, with this frequently involving losses of life and heavy expenditure. The routes chosen could even influence territorial boundaries, as with the Gadsden Purchase of 1853. Named after James Gadsden, American envoy in Mexico, a railway promoter who had himself appointed to that post in order to further his transportation plans, the purchase from Mexico for $10 million of 45,535 square miles of land south of the Gila River provided a route to the Pacific as sought by Southern businessmen and politicians, and others wanting rail links and landholdings that would serve their interests and provide an alternative to northern links focused on Chicago or St Louis.

Criticism was widened by the extent to which railway companies were associated with fraud and/or the use of rate structures to gain profit at the expense of communities and farmers. This led to populist criticism across the West, as in novels such as Frank Norris's *The Octopus: A Story of California* (1901), which focused on the rivalry between ranchers and a railway and influenced Theodore Roosevelt (president 1901-9), who was critical of rail companies, in pressing for the control of freight rates. This novel drew on the Mussel Slough Tragedy of 1880, a clash between the Southern Pacific Railroad and squatting settlers in the San Joaquin Valley in California that led to seven killings. The railway company won the subsequent legal battle. The clash had already led to anti-railway novels including W.C. Morrow's *Blood-Money* (1882), Charles Cyril Post's *Driven from Sea to Sea* (1884) and Josiah Royce's *The Feud of Oakfield Creek* (1887). The Southern Pacific Railroad was depicted as an octopus and as corruptly linked with the state Railroad Commission.

Railways, notably but not only in America, became known for those referred to as 'robber barons', and many individuals, companies and communities were harmed by the ruthless competition of these proprietors, who extended their reach to include railway construction in other countries, such as the swashbuckling and ruthless Vanderbilt interest in Costa Rica in the 1850s. There were repeated scandals about railway financing. In 1876, the alleged fraudulent sale to the Union Pacific of essentially worthless bonds in the Little Rock and Fort Smith Railroad in Arkansas helped to sink the campaign for Republican nomination of James G. Blaine who, earlier, had been the favourite.

On the pattern already seen with wagon road grants from the 1820s, land in the public domain was given to railway companies from the Illinois Central in 1850 on. These grants were much greater in the West, such as for the Northern Pacific Railroad in 1864, and larger in the federal Territories than in the area already allocated to states. There was a major element of speculation involved in the railways, as the Panic of 1873 demonstrated, and in the related land speculation. Jay Cooke and Company, a major bank based in Philadelphia, overextended in railways, becoming the key financier and shareowner in the Northern Pacific Railway, which could not pay the bank what it owed. This led to a run on the bank, which failed in 1873, with the cost of construction underestimated. In the resulting 'Panic', a major financial crisis, there were other bank runs and failures. By the first anniversary of the crisis, about 115 railway companies had gone bankrupt, and it became difficult to raise fresh finance. As a result, the construction of new lines in America fell from 7,500 miles in 1872 to 1,600 in 1875, while wage cuts led to a major railway strike in 1877, a strike that caused much violence. That year, President Hayes used the army to overcome the strike. Federal troops were deployed in Illinois, Maryland, Missouri, and Pennsylvania, after National Guard units and *ad hoc* militias had failed to restore order. The worst violence was in Baltimore, Albany, Philadelphia, Reading, Chicago, East St Louis, and Pittsburgh, with the Pennsylvania Railroad and Union Depot burned, and 104 locomotives and 1,245 freight and passenger cars destroyed. There were also crises for railway finance elsewhere, notably in France and Germany.

Railways gained much land; for example, the Oregon Central in 1870 obtained valuable forest land. Trees could be logged and easily moved by rail. In 1884, the map publisher Rand McNally produced a map for the Democratic Party showing the wide tranches that had been granted to railway corporations, with an accompanying text that stated, 'We believe that the public lands ought ... to be kept as homesteads for actual settlement.' There was scant concern about the indigenous population in the discussion of land grants and settlement.

Topography as much as technology was to the fore, and railways were generally depicted in terms of the former, as in Albert Hart's *American History Atlas* (1918):

> The close relationship between the lines of the railroads and the old trails and roads should be noted. They testify to the fundamental influence of topography in fixing the lines of communication, which in turn influence the establishment of cities and towns as commercial, industrial, or cultural centers.

Settlements owed their origins or their growth to the train. Founded by a trapper in 1846, Ogden in Utah became a major passenger and freight railway junction as it was where major east-west and north-south routes crossed. Westbound passengers changed there from Union Pacific to Southern Pacific services. As with other rail towns, the city, which was less dominated by Mormons than other Utah settlements, was known for brothels and bars. On a recent visit, I bought a t-shirt proclaiming 'I've tried Polygamy in Utah,' Polygamy being a beer brewed in Ogden. Las Vegas was established in 1905 by the San Pedro, Los Angeles and Salt Lake Railroad as a division point to house train crew.

Politics was integral to the processes involved in the building and operation of railways, processes from routes to organisation, ownership to taxation, finance to labour relations. Although railways and their arrangements were frequently presented as an immutable consequence of human progress and economic necessity, in practice this was not the case at all and never has been. For example, there was segregation in train carriages between whites and blacks. This was an example of the general role of rail in replicating and thus affirming ethnic, class, gender and age differences. The class differences were dramatically seen in the rolling stock, notably in the contrasts between private cars (carriages) and accommodation on trains for the less well-off, who had lower charges and also benefited from reduced-price group fares. There were also contrasts in railway waiting rooms.

More positively, America saw many improvements in railway methods, not least the invention in 1869 by George Westinghouse and his patenting in 1873 of the railway air (pneumatic) brake, a system employing compressed air and a single compressed air pipe along the length of the train that allowed the braking of all carriages simultaneously. This capability was important to rapid stopping and thus safety, as hitherto brakemen had had to apply the brakes manually on each carriage. Westinghouse also improved railway signals.

Aside from technology, services for passengers got better, most notably for the wealthy, although not only for them. An advertisement of 1869 for the New York Central Railroad claimed:

> This popular route is unsurpassed for speed, safety and comfort, having double track from New York to Buffalo, and all other modern improvements, and travellers are not subjected to the numerous changes and vexatious delays incident to other lines. Elegant Drawing Room Cars on day trains, and luxurious and thoroughly ventilated sleeping cars on night trains.

In the same year, an advertisement for the Chicago Alton and St Louis Rail Road noted: 'The old and familiar cry "20 minutes for refreshments" abolished. Trains on the Chicago and Alton

RR do not stop for meals – dining luxuriously at the same time making 30 miles an hour – can provide 48 passengers with a meal.' This addressed a major issue for passengers, that they all arrived at stops at the same moment, with consequent pressure on refreshment and lavatory facilities.

For Canada, there was an overt political dimension, not only the immediate point of British Columbia joining the Confederation of Canada, but also the wish to block American expansion and in particular any focus by the Canadian West on American rail links and hubs, especially Chicago. Launched in 1852 to build a railway line between Montréal and Toronto, and with corporate headquarters in London, the Grand Trunk Railway had leased the Atlantic and St Lawrence Railroad in 1853, which gave it an extension to the harbour at Portland in Maine; but this increased a sense of Canadian vulnerability to American pressure. In addition, in 1859, the Grand Trunk established a ferry service across the St Clair River to what is now Port Huron in Michigan.

In 1862, at a time of serious tensions with the Union over Britain's stance in the American Civil War and the possibility therefore of a Union invasion of Canada, the British government had offered to underwrite the Halifax-Québec railway, for geopolitical and geo-military reasons. This line reduced reliance on the St Lawrence waterway and on railways via America. Military plans in North America had increasingly depended on using or threatening rail links. In 1861, Captain William Noble of the Royal Engineers had produced a report on the defence of Canada arguing that the American presence on the St Lawrence waterway was a threat to British communications, as the only railway west from Montréal went along the north bank of the river. As a result, Noble pressed for Britain taking the initiative if war broke out with America and pushing the enemy away.

Subsequently, in peacetime, Sir Frederick Bruce, the British envoy in Washington, saw the railway as crucial to the future of Canada, writing in 1867 to the Foreign Secretary:

As population and industrial development increase in Minnesota, Montana, and other North Western states which adjoin the British frontier, it is not difficult to foresee that the demand will arise for communication by the line of the Saskatchewan River which is said to offer the greatest facilities for reaching the Pacific. And if the Provinces aided by Great Britain are unable to meet it when it becomes necessary and show themselves incapable of providing greater facilities for the transit of produce from the Lake region through the St Lawrence to the Atlantic, the desire of the United States to drive their British rivals off the continent will be powerfully reinforced by the material interests of the North West which will be enlisted in favour of conquest or annexation. Whether the policy adopted by Great Britain in the Northern part of this continent contemplates provincial connection with the mother country as a permanent relation, or looks to it merely as a step towards provincial independence in the future, its success will materially depend upon our ability to deal in a sufficiently liberal and comprehensive manner with the transit question.

Thus, the economic imperative was to the fore, but as part of geostrategy, which is a pattern that for many states has lasted to the present. The British North America Act of 1867, a key element of the Canadian constitution, included a provision for an intercolonial railway. In 1871, it proved necessary for the Canadian government to pressure the British to guarantee a loan for the transcontinental railway that was pledged when British Columbia entered the Confederation that year. That America had such a railway was regarded as a comparative disadvantage for

Canada, and therefore the British empire, as well as a model that required emulation. There was a concern that without such a rail link, British Columbia would enter the ambit of America's Pacific coast, not least after the American purchase of Alaska from Russia in 1867, which put America both north and south of British Columbia. In 1844, James Polk had successfully campaigned for President in part on the pledge to gain the entire Oregon County including British Columbia for America, a claim clarified as '54°40' or Fight'; and many Americans thought that goal still appropriate.

The Canadian transcontinental railway scheme was delayed by a political funding scandal in 1873, the Pacific Scandal, which contributed to the fall of the government: many railway financial schemes and scandals had political dimensions. Nevertheless, the plan was reconceptualised and a new contract agreed with the government in 1880, leading the following year to the formal incorporation of the Canadian Pacific Railway Company. It was to receive $25 million in credit from the government, a grant of 25 million acres of land, and tax exemption for twenty years. The railway began at Bonfield Ontario, where the Canadian Central Railway system ended. Granville, a township with a natural harbour, was incorporated as a city and renamed Vancouver in 1886 when the first transcontinental railway arrived. It was the terminus. This was a factor in the success of many Pacific cities.

As in America, the transcontinental railway also led to the establishment and growth of many interior towns. Sudbury in Ontario was developed by the Canadian Pacific Railway in 1883, and the rail construction was also accompanied by the discovery of nearby nickel-copper ore. Sudbury was an instance of the 'division points' established by the Canadian companies every 130 miles, where the engines would take on coal and water and the crews were changed. The mineral discoveries gave Sudbury a raison d'être other than the railways, although the railway yards strongly marked the city's geography for years to come, and were critical to mining, refining, and shipping to distant markets. The 'division points' created towns like this in both America and Canada, which was a contrast with Europe where towns largely came first. Other divisional points included Calgary, Edmonton, Jasper, and Winnipeg.

Faced by the rebellion of the *Métis* (mixed-blood population) in Manitoba and Saskatchewan in 1885, the Canadian government sent more than 4,000 troops and their supplies west over the Canadian Pacific Railway, achieving an overwhelming superiority that helped bring rapid victory. This display of rail-based capability was followed by a new increase in government subsidy for the transcontinental railway that enabled its completion that year, although trains did not run until 1886. This railway represented a formidable engineering achievement. Steel rails helped give durability, a key issue in the climate. Much of the labour was provided by 17,000 Chinese workers, although they did not feature in the Last Spike photograph. At least 600 of these workers died, many as a result of landslides or of the unsafe use of explosives. As in other countries, the Chinese were paid less than the other workers.

Elsewhere in the British empire, rail also developed rapidly, as in New Zealand where there was great interest in the expansion of the railways, with the Public Works Department, formed in 1870, playing a major role. 1881 was an important year, as the Railways Construction and Land Act allowed joint-stock companies to construct and operate private railways as long as they were connected with the government railway lines and built to its standard gauge. This synergy helped ensure further development, including the authorisation of the Wellington-Manawatu Line on North Island, and from 1885 the building of the central section of the North Island Main Trunk. The 1867 railway tunnel to Lyttelton was the first in the world to pierce an extinct volcano and, at the time was the longest in the British empire. On South Island, construction was easier on the Canterbury plains and rolling downland of the east coast, but there were wide-braided riverbeds to cross, and these were major obstacles for a while. The Rakaia River Bridge opened in 1873 and the Waitaki Bridge in 1877, taking the line south to the port of Oamaru in North Otago.

The New Zealand railways owed much to British norms, technology, expertise, engineers, and finance. As in Britain, Canada and elsewhere, a detailed look at development shows the significance of politics in that different ministries backed particular plans, and there could be major changes. Sir George Grey had supported the plan for a line from Foxton to Wellington on the North Island, but the fall of Grey in 1879 as the government, hit by economic problems, lost electoral support, was followed by a new ministry under Sir John Hall, a South Island politician who sought to cut expenditure and accordingly ended both the Foxton line and that between Wellington and Manawatu. In turn, Wellington businessmen formed a company that, aided by government land grants, built the latter, albeit with a shorter route to Napier and Auckland that did not connect to the port at Foxton. The Wellington-Manawatu Line was completed in 1886.

The first Australian railway, opened in 1831, was a short gravitational railway designed to service a coal mine in Newcastle, New South Wales. The first Australian steam-powered railway, from Melbourne to Port Melbourne, opened in 1854; that from Sydney to Granville following in 1855. Dealing on a scale different to New Zealand and operating in a contrasting governmental environment, the early systems were based not on Australia but on the particular colonies, later states. Their circumstances owed much to financial considerations. Whereas in the colony of South Australia, a colony with a strong corporatist identity, railways were publicly owned from the start, this happened in New South Wales and Victoria only because the private companies proved financially weak. Thus, the Sydney Railway Company became the New South Wales Government Railways.

Despite British advice for a standard gauge, New South Wales and Victoria, neighbouring colonies, built to different gauges. This reflected the absence of a central government to provide control and the degree to which individual states had a very strong sense of identity. As between independent countries, for example Spain and France, this made transhipment at break-of-gauge points a major issue. This occurred at Albury on the Main Southern Railway from Sydney. The Main North Line built in 1857-88 was the original main line between Sydney and Brisbane, the capital of Queensland, with a change of gauge at Wallangarra.

More positively, Australia played a key role in the development of the articulated steam locomotive referred to as a Garratt or a Beyer Garratt. A British mechanical engineer, Herbert William Garratt (1864-1913) had worked in Britain, Argentina, Cuba, Nigeria and Peru, not an unusual career, before becoming the inspector of British-made locomotives for New South Wales Government Railways. He was granted a patent in 1908 and his locomotives proved highly effective on narrow gauge lines with low load-bearing capacity such as those in Australasia and Africa. Aside from well-distributed weight (they had extra unpowered bogies), they were good at going round curves (a key requirement in adapting to the terrain) and had a high capacity to generate steam, which increased their power output, cutting costs. Early clients included the governments of Tasmania, Western Australia and Victoria, and, in total, over a thousand were built by the British manufacturers. Britain no longer sets the standard in this fashion.

That imperial presence and expansion were accompanied by rail construction was particularly the case in India. There, the first railway was built from Bombay (Mumbai) to nearby Thane in 1853. The opening 21-mile journey required three locomotives for the fourteen carriages, and the departure of the train, the first passenger railway journey in Asia, was marked by a twenty-one-gun salute from Fort George. From Mumbai, railways were to be built north to Surat and north-east to the Ganges valley. Howrah, on the bank of the Hooghly River opposite Calcutta (Kolkata), became the terminus of the first railway in eastern India in 1854, with a station on the Calcutta side built at Sealdah in 1862. Railways spread to reach other cities, Lahore in 1862, and came to cover the country.

A key role was taken by private companies whose shareholders were, under legislation and contracts of 1849, guaranteed an annual return of five per cent by the East India Company, the governing British body, until 1858. The first operational years of the key companies were 1853 for the Great Indian Peninsula, 1854 for the East Indian, 1856 for the Madras (Chennai) and 1860 for the Bombay, Baroda, and Central India. The effect of the coming of rail in India is neatly exemplified by David Donaldson in his study, *Railroads of the Raj*:

The railroad network designed and built by the British government in India (then known to many as 'the Raj') brought dramatic change to the technology of trading on the subcontinent. Prior to the railroad age, bullocks carried most of India's commodity trade on their backs, travelling no more than 30km per day along India's sparse network of dirt roads. By contrast, railroads could transport these same commodities 600km in a day, and at much lower per unit distance freight rates.

James, 1st Marquess of Dalhousie, the Governor-General from 1848 to 1856, was a keen supporter of rail, as he had been as President of the Board of Trade in Britain in 1845-6. Dalhousie emphasised in 1853 that railways would enable Britain 'to bring the main bulk of its military strength to bear upon any given point in as many days as it would now require months, and to an extent which at present is physically impossible'. He also stressed the economic and social advantages from the expansion of railways. Dalhousie, who had unsuccessfully supported a degree of government direction in the development of a system of British rail routes, pressed in India for a system of major trunk lines, notably to provide lines between Bombay, Calcutta, Lahore, Delhi and Madras. The plans were ambitious, but also reflected an awareness of current technological operating factors; Dalhousie wanted an average gradient for trunk line of no more than 1 in 2,000. Dalhousie also saw the potential of future developments. Thus, even when single track was installed, the bridges were to be strong and wide enough for eventual double-tracking. Dalhousie's plan was to be followed, with the lines built from the major administrative centres – Bombay, Calcutta and Madras – all ports. A utilitarian moderniser, Dalhousie also backed uniform postage and the telegraph for India, where he greatly extended British territorial power.

Large amounts of capital and labour were deployed, and many Indians died in the construction of railways. The last point may be seen as an instance of contemporary racism, and that could then be amplified by reference to the deaths of Chinese rail workers in construction elsewhere. At the same time, death rates in rail construction were generally high, indeed very high, by modern standards, and that included European labour.

The Indian Forest Service was set up in part due to concern about deforestation for railways. Hugh Cleghorn, the Conservator of Forests for the Madras Presidency Forest Department established in 1856, estimated that a mile of railway required 1760 sleepers (not a particularly complex mathematical procedure), which had a lifespan of only eight years. In addition, the need for wood in place of the coal used in Britain for powering the locomotives was also a pressure on timber stocks.

From the late 1860s, there was a switch in policy in India, away from the original uniform 5'6" gauge to some lines being 3'3", which was adopted as less expensive to construct and operate. This of course meant frequent breaks of gauge. Indian Railways was to adopt a uni-gauge policy in 1992.

As it was for India, the raising of capital in London for railways elsewhere was a major activity in the nineteenth century, and not only in the empire. This was very much the case in Latin America, which became a major field for investment from independence in the 1810s, notably, but not only, in Argentina. The British were not alone. Launched in Paris in 1852 and Vienna in 1855 respectively, the *Crédit Mobilier* and the *Creditanstalt für Handel und Gwerbe* were major suppliers of finance for railways. Foreign investment reflected capital availability, the practice of such investment in a liberal global order, and a willingness to take risk, in large part to support the export of goods to European and North American markets. In contrast, the delayed and often uncertain return on railway investments, and the often poorly developed nature of local capital markets and liquidity, deterred many outside Europe and North America, for example most Latin American investors, although not in Chile.

A prime example was the Central Uruguay Railway. This was established in London in 1876, to take over the railway of the same name founded in Uruguay to work a concession granted by the government in 1866, under which construction had begun in 1867. The new company operated from 1878. In Brazil, the

Dom Pedro-Segundo railway of 1855 and the Santos to Sao Paulo line of 1860 were significant early lines. Rail links were also important to the sugar monoculture in western Cuba, where the area thus cultivated and the number of slaves had greatly increased in the first half of the century. The first steam railway line in Latin America was opened in 1837, covering 27.5 kilometres (17 miles) from Havana to Bejucal. It was swiftly expanded.

Growth in Uruguay, Argentina, Brazil, Chile, and Cuba contrasted with the situation across most of Latin America. In part, there were factors of opportunity, with the exports of those five countries encouraging and funding investment and operation. There was also, as with all other systems, whether state, private or partnerships, the question of management and sound finance. Thus, in the 1860s and 1870s, Peru sought to link its coastline to the interior, but excessive expenditure and expensive debt hit these plans hard. The gradients posed by the successive ranges of the Andes limited the speed of trains and posed major maintenance issues. From Lima on the coast, the railway went up to 4783 metres at the tunnel of Galera on the *Ferracarril Central Andino* line from Lima to Huancayo, a line finished in 1908. The Peruvian railway played a role in the Tintin story *Le Temple du Soleil* (*Prisoners of the Sun*), 1946-8.

In Mexico, the more widespread problems arising from political instability proved especially disruptive. Although a line from the capital, Mexico City, to the leading port, Veracruz, received a concession in 1837, work did not begin until 1864 and then because it served the political interests of Emperor Maximilian who was using French troops, supplied through Veracruz, to support his war with republican opponents. The Imperial Mexican Railway was incorporated in 1864, but the overthrow of Maximilian led to it being renamed the Mexican Railway in 1867. The line was opened in 1873.

At a very different level, there were bold plans for a Pan-American railway, notably as a result of advocacy by Hinton Rowan Helper (1829-1909), a Southern opponent of slavery who also wanted an exclusively white America, American Consul in Buenos Aires from 1861 to 1869, proposed the 'Three Americas Railway', the title of a book he published in 1881, and his ideas were taken up by politicians, in part as a way to limit British influence, notably James Blaine, Secretary of State in 1881 and from 1889 to 1892, and an advocate of American commitment to Latin America, and Presidents Benjamin Harrison (1889-93) and Theodore Roosevelt (1901-9). The scheme was pushed in the First International Conference of American States (1890). The Pan-American railway was part of the American wish for a customs union, while Helper saw it as a means to help ensure a white hemisphere. In *The Three Americas Railway*, Helper declared:

> That surpassing railway, once well constructed and in operation, will indeed make America the New World; a world so conspicuously new and superior in its natural riches, that its attractions to the peoples of the Old World will be absolutely overwhelming.

In practice, there was considerable opposition, notably in Argentina, to what was regarded as an aspect of American imperialism, and the Pan-American Railroad was never built. Instead, the major American effort was in the shape of rail links with neighbouring Mexico, the first of which occurred in 1882 with Nogales and Sonora linked to north and south: the *Compañia Limitada del Ferrocarril de Sonora* was owned by the Atchison, Topeka and Santa Fe Railroad. Incorporated in

Massachusetts in 1880, the Mexican Central Railroad followed in 1884, with a line from Mexico City to Ciudad Juárez in Texas across the Rio Grande in 1884. By the 1920s, Pan-Americanists emphasised road construction rather than rail.

More modestly in scale, there was continuing development in Europe, and the results could be highly impressive. There were the headline achievements, notably lines under the Alps where the Mont Cenis tunnel between France and Italy was completed in 1871 and the Gotthard in Switzerland in 1882. Switzerland posed many problems for the development and operation of a rail system. The most obvious was the terrain. This had caused major problems for road construction in Switzerland and more generally, but roads could take gradients that were impossible for railways. Railways could attempt to hug the valley bottoms, but they were still difficult, not least due to rivers being in spate when the snow melted, while many valley bottoms were narrow, rocky, and already in use. Tunnelling was an alternative, one that was to be made much easier by high explosive in place of gunpowder, but it was still very expensive and dangerous, with many workers killed. Moreover, the volume of rock that had to be moved increased as a result of the use of high explosive.

Aside from construction problems, those of maintenance were far more serious in Switzerland than in warmer climates. Ice and freeze-thawing affected the rails, and snowmelt flooded the railbed, while snow was a major issue in running the trains. There were also the major cost implications in Switzerland of a shortage of coal.

The year 1847 saw both the short *Sonderbund* civil war, in which about 100 troops died, and the first internal Swiss rail line, from Zurich to Baden, ten miles (16 kilometres) away. The aftermath of the civil war created a potential for national planning that was enshrined in the 1848 constitution and in 1850 the Swiss Federal Council commissioned plans from British engineers for a national network. However, in the event, the Railway Act of 1852 transferred responsibility for regulation to the cantons, while the lines themselves were built by private companies, with contributions as appropriate from cantons and towns. This use of the British model created rival companies but provided a way to tap the liquidity necessary for investment, and particularly so given the terrain. By the end of 1860, the relatively populous and more easily crossable northern and western Switzerland to the north of the main mountain chain was covered. In turn, in the 1860s, there was a measure of consolidation among the operating companies and of foreign, principally French, investment.

The situation was called into question by delays in Swiss mobilisation during the crisis caused by the Franco-Prussian War of 1870-1, a mobilisation designed to protect the territorial integrity of neutral Switzerland against the risk of troops being moved through its territory. This led, under the 1872 Railway Act, to a transfer of oversight from the cantons to the federal government. Separately, with the cities all linked, the focus on new lines switched to the building of branch lines and also of lines designed to cross the Alps, with the Gotthard line opened in 1882.

There was expansion of rail in areas where it had hitherto been limited, such as in Scandinavia. There, rail became most developed in Denmark and Sweden, and less so in Norway, which was in a union with Sweden from 1814 until 1905. It had a smaller population, less wealth and political significance, and more difficult terrain in the shape of mountains, steeply indented valleys, limited flat land, and rivers greatly swollen by spring and summer snow melt. After initial Swedish attempts from 1845 ran out of funds, the state took over the trunk line projects in 1854, and the first steam railway there opened in 1855. The line from Stockholm to the North Sea port of Gothenburg was completed in 1862, and on to Malmö in 1864. There was a determination to avoid reliance on the Baltic coast, which had been successfully attacked by Russian warships in recent wars, most recently in 1808-9. Sweden had the largest network in all of Scandinavia by the late 1850s. In part, this reflected the greater size of Sweden and in part the availability of funds. Denmark was smaller and Norway had less money than Sweden and a more difficult terrain. For Sweden, it was important to link to the North Sea coast, both to avoid the winter icing in the Baltic and to ensure that the major cities were all in close contact. Gothenburg provided maritime links with the British Isles and America, and Malmö did so with Copenhagen from which rail links were available to Germany. Mineral exploitation was also an aim. In 1888, a line was opened from the iron ore mines at Gällivare to the Swedish port of Luleå on the Gulf of Bothnia. A line extended to the new iron ore workings at Kiruna in 1899 and to the ice-free Norwegian port of Narvik in 1903. This line provided the opportunity to move iron ore that led to British naval and later amphibious intervention in Narvik against German takeover in 1940.

Denmark's first railways opened between Altona and Schleswig in 1844 and Copenhagen and Roskilde in 1847, and were operated by private companies, although the government took an increasing role from 1867. After initial horse-drawn railways from 1805, Norway used steam engines from 1854, first with the Kristiana (Oslo)-Eidsvold railway line which was designed to move timber to sawmills, timber being Norway's leading export, largely to Britain. British expertise and capital were significant in rail construction and operation. The governmental role increased from 1857.

Finland's first railway, the Helsinki-Hämeenlinna line, taking goods to the coast, opened in 1862. As part of the Russian empire from 1809 to 1918, and thus prefiguring the situation with Eastern Europe in 1945-89, Russian military considerations were significant in the opening of the line from Finland to St Petersburg in 1870; but so also was the export of paper. In Finland, as elsewhere, railways replaced earlier interest in canals, which were less flexible, slower and froze in the winter. The Scandinavian figures in kilometres are:

	1850	1860	1870	1880
Denmark	30	109	770	1584
Norway	-	68	359	1057
Sweden	-	527	1727	5876

Although the Scandinavian systems were modest, they contributed to a marked expansion in the total length of European tracks (in kilometres):

1860	51,900
1870	104,900
1880	169,000
1890	224,000
1900	283,000

Most were in Western and Central Europe, but other areas, notably South-Eastern Europe, were playing a role. In 1869, Baron Moritz von Hirsch (1831-96) guaranteed to build a network of 2,500 kilometres of railway in the Ottoman Balkans. This was part of the Ottoman effort at modernization. In 1871, Hirsch's first train steamed out of Constantinople (Istanbul) and, in the face of many difficulties, notably instability in the Balkans, he was responsible for the Constantinople-Vienna main line which opened in 1888. This was the start of what became the Berlin to Baghdad rail story, for Hirsch sold his interests to what became the German concern.

The navigation of the European system was facilitated for the well-heeled by the Belgian company *Compagnie Internationale des Wagons-Lits*, founded in 1874 on the example of the American Pullman night trains. It was the sole group providing luxury international travel, and its trains included the Paris-St Petersburg *Nord Express*, established in 1896, and the Paris-Lisbon *Sud Express* launched in 1887 and extended to London in 1888. The latter provided important competition to ocean liner services between London and Lisbon. Established in 1883, the Orient Express initially went via Bucharest, the capital of Romania, to the Danube river port of Giurgiu, after which ferry, train and boat took passengers via the port of Varna in Bulgaria to Constantinople. In contrast, the first direct train to Constantinople left Paris in 1889. The opening of the Simplon Tunnel in 1919 ensured that the Simplon Orient Express via Venice also became possible. The novels *Stamboul Train* (1932) by Graham Greene and *Murder on the Orient Express* (1934) by Agatha Christie were two of many works set on the train or on similar services.

This was a Europe linked for the élite, but also many others, as never before. Most rail travel remained within states, and most travellers did not journey in luxury. It is always important to consider rail by the typical rather than the uncommon; and that is a matter for future projection as well as the assessment of the past and the consideration of the present. There were of course always national boundaries, in part due to related rail parameters. Thus, although it was easy to get from Prague to either Berlin or Vienna by rail, it was not easy to get to Frankfurt, Munich or Salzburg: imperial and national borders remained significant, as did the friction of expensive terrain that it was expensive to build and operate across.

The impact of national and international considerations was seen in conflicts and war-planning. Thus, in the Austro-French war in Italy in 1859, both sides employed railways in the mobilisation and deployment of their forces, Austria using the newly completed line from Vienna to Verona. In the opening stage of the conflict, despite problems with only single-track lines and insufficient locomotives on the part of their ally, Piedmont, the French moved

130,000 troops to Italy by rail in a matter of weeks, thereby deploying force so as to be able to gain the initiative. This number included those transported within France by train to the ports of Marseille and Toulon for subsequent movement by sea to Genoa.

More generally, the relationship between sea and land transport, the two motive aspects of steam power, continued to be important. This relationship came much to the fore with the transcontinental railway across America completed in 1867: this line opened a new passage to the Pacific, and thus for onward voyages to East Asia where America was developing interests, and it apparently brought into prospect more such railways across other continents and subcontinental areas. In practice, the difficulties of such construction were greatly underestimated. In one light, that was just as well because so, also, were the difficulties of maintaining such lines that were considered, let alone of making money from them. Continuing costs ate into revenues, a lesson still valid today.

These points also serve as a reminder of the extent to which rail involved hustlers, the hustlers of political projection, those of its economic counterpart, and the would-be commercial implementers. This hustle was present from the outset, as prospects of profit and benefit attracted interest and investment, not least from the possibilities offered of benefiting from control of other assets and gaining possession over land. The ready availability of finance for plans, both plausible and less so, was important, as was the extent to which there appeared certainties of profit and political advantage from a new technology and in the face of limited regulation of fares and a governmental oversight that was subject to influence. The nature of the hustle and the context of the projecting varied, but it was ever present, and this remains the case.

4

THE STRATEGIES OF RAIL

Sergei Witte (1849-1915) the Russian statesman who served as the first prime minister of the Russian Empire, replacing the emperor as head of the government. He expanded the Russian rail system and made it a state monopoly. At the same time, he made it highly profitable – and this extremely rare sequence of events must surely make him one of the greatest railwaymen of all time.

The sheer drama and ambition of rail was on display in 1904-5 with the construction over the River Zambezi near Victoria Falls of a bridge that opened the way for a direct service from Cape Town to what is now Zambia. Prefabricated from steel at Darlington in England, the bridge was shipped to Beira in Mozambique and then transported by rail to the site where it was constructed. It still provides the sole rail link between Zimbabwe and Zambia. In Africa, however, as elsewhere, for example across the Brahmaputra in India, many rivers remained unbridged, which meant reliance on ferry.

Meanwhile, electric-powered, armoured trains firing cannon and machine-guns were depicted by Albert Robida, a French illustrator and futurist, in the 27 October 1883 issue of the French magazine *La Caricature* a vision of future warfare that he further developed in his book *La Guerre au Vingtième Siècle* (1887). The idea of conflict was hardwired into the peacetime assessment of rail. This was so from early days, because rail was seen as a way to enhance and/or fulfil capability. This was particularly necessary because there was otherwise no clear capability gap between armies. In America, Brigadier-General Edmund Gaines, a critic of investment in coastal fortifications, pressed, instead, from 1826, for a rail and canal system financed by the federal government, able to move militia from the hinterland to the coasts to oppose any British invasion (there had been war between the two powers as recently as 1815), as well as for the construction of large warships.

For Gaines and others, railways fundamentally altered the relationship between amphibious attack and land defence, providing a great strength for the latter. Many of influence had these views. In 1854, Sir James Graham, the First Lord of the British Admiralty, wrote to Fitzroy, Lord Raglan, the Master-General of the Ordnance, about the defence of England's east coast: 'I quite concur in the opinion that the permanent presence of a large military force at Hull is not requisite: that inland concentration, with rapid means of distribution by rail road is the right system.' This defence would have been against Russian attack from the Baltic, as the Crimean War continued.

The importance of trains in the American Civil War (1861-5) and the Austro-Prussian War (1866) encouraged renewed interest in their military possibilities. After their heavy defeat, the Austrians understood the advantages of rail, and Archduke Albrecht, who became Inspector-General of the Austrian army in 1869, a post he held till 1895, sought – although a conservative – to follow Prussia in improving rail transport. It was the only rapid way to move troops and supplies on land, or, in combination with steamships, to and from ports.

In the late nineteenth century, such ideas, planning and provision sat alongside the peacetime emphasis on economic benefit. Rail as power, economic, political and military, was central to construction across the world, for power meant true profit. In conception or reality, railways spanned continents and sub-continents, such as India. Railways also focused on the ports that were imperial nodes. Thus, Singapore had a long railway history, with two main factors playing a role: serving the docks and helping move people in a crowded environment. The first saw the use of trains to help transport goods and the people in and from the docks, beginning with a shunting railway on the wharfs opened in 1877. Far more significantly, a railway to serve the New Harbour began operation in 1903, with an extension in 1907. The Singapore-Kranji Railway used British built locomotives, with trains reaching a top speed of 17 miles per hour (29 kilometres). Electric tramways, which were first commercially operated in Germany in 1881, also developed in Singapore, with services begun in 1905, the year in which a power station was built. In 1923, the opening of the Causeway meant that there was a continuous rail link between Singapore and Penang, with the ferries required to cross the Straits of Johor no longer necessary from 1909, when the railheads had reached both sides.

Technological enhancement around the world created a sense that there would be more such enhancement. As an important aspect of the improved capacity and effectiveness of rail, not least greater durability, steel rails, first used in Derby station in 1857, were widely introduced from the 1880s. The invention of the Bessemer process in 1856 had greatly reduced the cost of making steel, and in 1865 the first American steel mill to employ the process was built. Steel rails were far more durable than iron, and America, which rapidly became the major producer of steel, was best placed to use them in bulk. Moreover, as an aspect of more general synergy, the movement of coal and iron to steel mills became a major task for railways.

At the transcontinental dimension, the task confronting rail construction was greater in Russia than America. In part, that was because although America bought Alaska from Russia in 1867, it was of scant interest to American rail companies. Indeed, only 72 miles were built in Alaska by 1914. In Russia, in contrast, Siberia was seen as a key sphere for rail construction. It was far less marginal to Russian geopolitics than Alaska was to the US. The desire, notably on the part of Sergei Witte, Transport Minister (1892), Minister of Finance (1892-1903), Chairman of the Council of Ministers (1903-5) and Prime Minister (1905-6), to open up markets for Russian goods was important. Nevertheless, the prime driver for the Trans-Siberian Railway was strategic, in the shape of competition with Japan and a related concern to increase Russia's ability to play a role in the future of China and thus thwart European rivals as well as Japan. The Russian capacity to be a Far Eastern power was seen to rest not only on the establishment of the port of Vladivostok in 1860, but also on the ability to link it, and the related naval base, to the centres of Russian power. Poor road links in Siberia and the rivers there that flowed south-north and were affected by winter freezing and spring floods, were of scant help. Initial plans for trans-Siberian rail links were advanced from the 1850s, but construction began in 1891, only finishing in 1916. The World Exhibition in Paris in 1900 provided a major public show for Russia's transcontinental rail project. A carriage from the line proved an attraction, not least because a diorama of over 100 metres depicting the journey was drawn past the window.

Witte (1849-1915) had made his career in the railways, beginning on the Odessa Railways and attracting attention by using double-shift operations in order to speed rail use in the war with Turkey in 1877-8, one in which the ultimately successful Russian advance south of the Danube was thereby supported. In 1889, he became Director of State Affairs within the Finance Ministry, and as such sought to extend the system as well as make it a state monopoly. Witte was a keen supporter of the Trans-Siberian Railway and a reminder in the history of rail of the importance of particular individuals and the interest, connections and expertise they offered. More generally, the significance of engineering knowledge in the upper reaches of many governments was important in this period, and contrasts clearly with the situation today.

'Trans-continental railways are now transmuting the conditions of land power.' In 1904, Halford Mackinder, the leading British geopolitician, argued in a lecture to the Royal Geographical Society in London that the railway had moved the balance from sea power to land power. He particularly justified the argument in terms of the Russian construction of the Trans-Siberian Railway on the pattern of transcontinental lines in North America, but which was, he argued, because of the Eurasian context, of greater geostrategic significance. Already, in his book *Britain and the British Seas* (1902), Mackinder had forcefully argued that the development of rail technology and systems had altered the paradigm of economic potential away from maritime power. This view seemed borne out by American and German economic growth, both of which benefited greatly from the impact of rail. In 1904, Mackinder argued that the Trans-Siberian Railway made possible the movement of forces rapidly around a Eurasian 'Heartland' and 'Pivot,' such that Russia could threaten its opponents, whether Japan in the Far East, or British interests in India, or European rivals. That thesis was unrealistic; but Mackinder, like so many interested in rail and indeed geopolitics, was apt to underplay the frictions of distance and issues of scale in terms of usage. As Robert, 3rd Marquess of Salisbury, then Secretary of State for India and later Prime Minister, had pointed out in Parliament in 1877, the habit of looking at maps that misleadingly suggested proximity was a serious problem.

> I cannot help thinking that in discussions of this kind, a great deal of misapprehension arises from the popular use of maps on a small scale. As with such maps you are able to put a thumb on India and a finger on Russia, some persons at once think that the political situation is alarming and that India must be looked to. If the noble Lord would use a larger map – say one on the scale of the Ordnance Map of England – he would find that the distance between Russia and British India is not to be measured by the finger and thumb, but by a rule.

No such map was available, but similar caveats could be offered about many rail plans.

Territorial expansion and interest, nevertheless, were generally helped by rail, which served the interests both of maritime states, such as Britain and France, looking to develop overseas influence from port-positions, and continental states, such as Russia, seeking to exploit possibilities. Thus, from 1879, Russia constructed the Trans-Caspian Railway from Uzun-Ada (later Krasnovodsk) on the eastern shore of the Caspian Sea, to Merv in 1886, Samarkand in 1888, and Tashkent in 1898, with a permanent bridge over the Oxus (Amu-Darya) in 1901. This line was seen as consolidating Russia's recently established position in Central Asia and greatly worried the British in India. In 1900-6, this line was linked to the Russian system by the Tashkent or Trans-Aral Railway, from Kinel to Tashkent. This could move troops to Central Asia and cotton from there to mills in Moscow.

Further east, in 1896, by the Li-Lobanov Treaty, the Russians obliged China to grant a concession for a Russian-gauge railway to Vladivostok across Manchuria, which was a more direct route than one restricted to Russian territory. Witte was instrumental in the negotiations, which included Russia having the right to station troops in order to protect the railway. This was an important application of the idea that railways established an interest that then had to be protected, a protection, in turn, dependent on the railway and its ability to move troops. This argument was more easily employed by states, and on behalf of them, rather than private companies; but governments could intervene on behalf of companies, as the American one was apt to do.

In accordance with the treaty, the Chinese Eastern Railway was constructed in 1897-1904. In 1898, China granted a southern extension from Harbin to the port of Dalian (Port Arthur). When the Russians advanced against the Chinese in Manchuria in 1900, part of the crisis affecting China at the time of the Boxer Rising, the railway served as an axis of movement. This Chinese Eastern

Railway proved a key means and projection of Russian power until it was purchased by Japan in 1934 and used instead by the Japanese. What was also called the Southern Manchurian Railway Company, whose concession Japan gained from Russia as a result of the Russo-Japanese War, had an attached right to administer the land alongside the railway. As a result, the company's work far exceeded the normal management of a railway.

The scope of the Russian rail system became an issue during war with Japan in 1904-5, in this case with the need to reinforce and sustain across the vast distance of Siberia the strategically significant position in the Russian Far East and Manchuria against Japanese attack. Although in 1904 the Trans-Siberian Railway, itself only single track, was incomplete at Lake Baikal (ferries were used for a four-hour crossing, until the Circum-Baikal railway was completed in 1905), the Russians transported 370,000 troops along it to the east. Lake Baikal, the world's seventh largest lake by surface area, has a maximum length of 395 miles and maximum width of 49 miles. The Russian ability to use the railways as an integrated element of strategy-making has been queried: capacity did not feed through into a predicted movement of troops for deployment-based operational planning. In the event, the Amur River Line north of the Chinese border was not completed until 1916, thus providing a direct service to Vladivostok through Russian territory. Although the cost was high, this route was seen as strategically worthwhile. Revolution in China in 1911 had contributed to that end. Passing Lake Baikal by rail symbolised the power of rail to overcome geography and impose a new geometry of human creation.

The competing British system was very different in context and control. The railway route mileage of British India (which included what is now Pakistan and Myanmar) rose, thanks to private railway contractors, from 5,400 in 1872 to 25,511 in

1901 and 42,528 in 1931. The comparable figures for British-ruled Ceylon (Sri Lanka) were 70 in 1872, 297 in 1901 and 951 in 1931. The track mileage was second only to America. Economic advantage was a key element, as in the concentration of railways on the Bengal coalfield, a pattern seen across the world. Usage developed rapidly, both for freight and for passengers, but the carriage arrangements and fare structure in terms of classes very much benefited wealthier travellers, who tended to be British. The grandeur of imperial railway stations was at its most imposing in the Victoria Railway Terminus in Bombay, completed in 1929. With a massive dome, this multi-towered building borrowed from many styles including Classical, Gothic, Byzantine, Moorish, and what was seen as Indian.

In Burma (Myanmar), the first line was opened in 1877, from the port of Rangoon to Prome. This was seen as important to the export of rice from the Irrawaddy valley to India. A second line, from Rangoon to Toungoo, followed in 1884, following the valley of the Sittang. The British annexation of Upper Burma after the Third Anglo-Burmese War of 1885-6 led to the extension of the latter line to Mandalay in 1889, in turn extended to Mytikyina in 1898. Two years earlier, the rail companies in Burma were combined into the Burma Railway Company. In Ceylon (Sri Lanka), coffee, a major export crop produced in the interior near Kandy, took 10-12 days to be moved to the port of Colombo, a distance of 73 miles, by bullock carts. Begun in 1858 and taken over by the government in 1861, the line to Kandy, the historic capital in the interior, was completed in 1867.

The railways the British built in India helped ensure that troops and their supplies could be moved to areas of unrest, as in 1897 when they were sent to the North-West Frontier (of modern Pakistan) to assist in overcoming resistance among the Waziris. With railway expansion significant in the 1880s and 1890s, railheads, notably Peshawar, Quetta and Chaman, played a key part in British planning both on that frontier and with regard to power projection into neighbouring Afghanistan. In turn, these railheads and the routes from them had to be protected; while an anxious eye was kept on the development of the rival Russian rail network into Central Asia.

> You will be glad, I feel sure, to hear that at last the Railway through the 75 miles of country from Pungwe River is settled, and the contract placed firm at £2300 per mile, ie. £172,000 of which the contractors take £40,000 in Bonds. The money required has been privately subscribed so that the success of the Railway does not depend on the circular we [British South Africa Company, BSAC] are about to issue to our shareholders inviting subscriptions.

Writing to Robert, 3rd Marquess of Salisbury, the Prime Minister, in 1892, Horace Farquhar, the Chairman of the Exploration Company and a member of the board of the BSAC, was keen to show that the prospect of extending British power in southern Africa was feasible, as well as to argue that there was gold in Mashonaland (now part of Southern Rhodesia). The railway in question was part of the Beira to Umtali (now Mutare) line, linking the Portuguese Indian Ocean port of Beira in the colony of Mozambique to what is now Zimbabwe, but was to be named, after Rhodes, Southern Rhodesia. The same year, Cecil Rhodes, the central figure of the BSAC and a keen protagonist of imperial infrastructure, offered to extend the telegraph from Fort Salisbury [now Harare] to Uganda at his own expense.

Rail schemes in Africa were linked to imperial expansion and consolidation, and also advanced in a competitive context. Compared to the terrain and disease factors affecting the construction of railways in eastern and West Africa, the situation was slightly less hazardous for rail construction in some other parts of the continent. This was true both for Sudan and for southern Africa. The railway company used by the British in Egypt in 1882 when they invaded was an improvised unit, as the British army lacked a railway department, unlike its Indian counterpart. However, in 1896, the Anglo-Egyptian army invading Sudan from Egypt built a railway straight across the desert from Wadi Halfa to Abu Hamed. The 383-mile-long Sudan Military Railway, constructed across the bend of the Nile, was pushed onto Atbara in 1898 and Khartoum in 1899. This railway played a major role in the supply of the British forces, and thus in operational effectiveness. Rail offered an important complement to the use of steamships on the Nile. This railway building entailed the harsh use of forced labour. There were numerous accidents in its operation. As so often, it is unclear where to place the emphasis.

In Southern Africa, there were more terrain issues, notably rivers and mountains to cross, than in the northern Sudan, although the construction of railways could be easier and less expensive than across much of Africa. However, the railways in Southern Africa could also be very difficult to construct. George Pauling who was the main contractor on the Beira-Umtali line, later recorded:

I fervently wished that I had never heard of the Beira Railway. At one time practically every white employee on the job was suffering from malaria. In one fortnight we lost six white men, including my bookkeeper and in one year sixty per cent of the men died.

There was malaria, blackwater fever, tsetse fly and lions. Once the mosquito-infected forested swamps were cleared, it was necessary to climb two escarpments. The railway reached Umtali in 1898.

The opportunities offered by gold and diamond discoveries in the interior of Southern Africa unsurprisingly proved particularly attractive, Cape Town and Durban competing to establish profitable rail links, but British competition with the Boer states of the Transvaal and Orange Free State led to the First Boer War in 1881. Similarly, Transvaal sought an alternative outlet to the sea via the Portuguese colony of Mozambique, opening a line to Delagoa Bay in 1895; with the Boers soon after, in the Drifts Crisis, challenging the reliance on the Cape Line. Delagoa Bay won about two-fifths of Transvaal's transit trade, which encouraged British interest in the future of Mozambique.

As the result of a loan in 1891, the Orange Free State proved more willing than Transvaal to co-operate with Cape Town on rail links until 1894, accepting and operating lines to Johannesburg accordingly. The resulting railway receipts were important to the finances of the Cape and Natal colonies, and an example of the way in which rail established shared interests and moderated them. In the competition between lines to Cape Town and Durban, there was a parallel to the earlier one between railways to ports on America's Atlantic coast. In addition, the British sought to open a line to Bechuanaland (now Botswana), an area where they were competing with the Boers.

Competing interests and overconfidence in violent confrontation led to the Second Boer War (1899-1902). In this, the railways that ran inland from the South African ports, notably Durban and Cape Town, facilitated the deployment of British military resources; first, against Boer advances and, subsequently, in 1900, in the successful conquest of the Orange Free State and the Transvaal. This deployment was very important as the British needed a considerable superiority in manpower in order to defeat the guerrilla warfare of the Boers, and this superiority had very serious logistical implications. Most of the supplies could not be obtained in the zone of hostilities.

The Sudan and the South African wars, each of which were in the shadow of earlier British failures, were different to most earlier colonial conflicts both in scale and in duration. This had major consequences for communications, justifying, indeed requiring, the investment in the fixed infrastructure of rail. That infrastructure, as well as the locomotives and rolling stock, had to be brought to the area of operations. This entailed major expenditure in steamships and in unloading facilities, which were under great pressure.

East Africa was not a key sphere for British imperialism like Sudan and, even more, South Africa. The British moved into the interior of East Africa with only limited thought about its value to them and in part simply to match the expansion of the other European imperial powers, notably Germany in what is now Tanzania. Rail links were seen as a way to develop and consolidate links, with the British government undertaking, from 1896, what it called the Uganda Railway, a route from the port of Mombasa, the key position on the coast, to a terminus on the eastern shore of Lake Victoria, reached in 1901. The route thereafter was by steamship across the lake to Entebbe in Uganda. Such rail-ship linkage was commonplace.

This railway was intended to facilitate settlement, exports and hunting, and was highly disruptive for both the local population and wildlife. It was also very costly in terms of the lives of many of the local and Indian workers, notably due to disease. George Nathaniel, Lord Curzon, Viceroy of India, observed in 1904 in a speech at the Guildhall in London: 'If you want to build a railway to Uganda or in the Soudan [Sudan], you apply Indian labour.' This was the British equivalent to the use of Chinese labour around the Pacific, especially in California and Queensland.

Denounced by the radical MP Henry Labouchere as 'a lunatic line,' the Uganda Railway was far more expensive than had been envisaged. The taxpayer put in £5.5 million for a line with little economic or strategic value, but it was difficult to oppose it. The cost of construction was not only a short-term problem but a major burden for the colony. The development of export freight income was the standard attempt to alleviate this burden and was accompanied by a search for fare income. In this case, the attempt was linked to the settlement of British estate owners in what became known as the 'White Highlands,' a process that involved the dispossession of native people.

Settlement was not comparably the goal with the French railway north from the port of Abidjan (now in the Ivory Coast). However, as with the British line in East Africa, this was boldly intended to consolidate the newly expanded French presence in West Africa, not least by linking to a line from the port of Dakar to Bamako. In the event, begun in 1903, the forest proved very difficult, not only because of the often waterlogged terrain and the trees that had to be cleared, but also due to disease. By 1906 the railway had only been built to Agneby (82 kilometres), moving on by 1910 to Dimbokro (181), when the line was cut and works destroyed in a rebellion. However, once into the savanna, progress was very rapid and Bouaké (315) was reached in 1912. In 1894-1917 (construction work started in 1897), France also built the 780-kilometre Djibouti-Addis Ababa railway in order to challenge Italian influence in north-east Africa. This line gave Ethiopia access to the sea in French Somaliland. The promoters, Alfred Ilg and Leon Chefneux, were Europeans close to Emperor Menelik II. The company failed in 1906 with the line unfinished. In 1908 a new firm was organised and construction began again in 1909.

In the German colony of Cameroon, the railways in 1914 both ran from the port of Douala: one to Bare and the other to Yaoundé. There was no linkage to the neighbouring British and French colonies. So also in German East Africa (later Tanganyika) where a line from the port of Tanga to Moshi was completed in 1911 and one into the interior from the port of Dar es Salaam in 1914.

Meanwhile, the French protagonists of trans-Saharan railways between the colony in Algeria and the French colonies of West Africa were fertile in ideas. There were bold plans from an early stage for far-reaching railways in Africa, indeed plans for areas not yet under imperial control. Thus, with France developing its imperial presence southwards from Algiers and eastward from Senegal, there was a plan in 1879 for a line from Algiers via Timbuktu, where the French did not gain control until 1893, to St Louis in Senegal. Georges Rolland, an engineer attached to the office of Charles de Freycinet, Minister of Public Works, was one of the key individuals as he linked different episodes and periods of bold conceptions. In 1879, Freycinet ordered three expeditions to investigate possible routes south, from Oran, Algiers and Constantine respectively. The last was stopped by the Tuaregs in 1879. When launched again in 1880, most members of the expedition were killed and the plans abandoned.

Rolland, who had been on the central expedition, maintained his interest, and, in 1890, under the aegis of the Minister of War, pushed the scheme anew. Rolland played a key role in trying to establish a company but that did not gain traction, in part because there was a lack of agreement in Algeria over the terminus. The railway from Biskra south of Constantine to Ouargla was authorized but not built, and the Dakar-Niger railway completed in 1904 only reached Koulikoro (Bambara) on the Niger River. Upstream of Koulikoro the river is blocked by the Sotuba Rapids, while downstream, transport is not possible in the dry season.

The scheme was revived more than once in the early twentieth century, including by *La Société d'Études du Chemin de fer Transafricain* which was established in 1912 and organised expeditions prior to the First World War. The society proposed a line across Chad, which had been conquered by the French in 1900 by an expedition sent from Senegal to Zembo on the border of the Belgian Congo and then two lines on, one via Nyangue to link with the line to Cape Town and secondly to Mombasa, providing a route to the Indian Ocean. This line was never even begun. It was fantastical, like much of the planning of the period.

Nevertheless, the political and economic arguments for a Trans-Saharan railway continued to be advanced, for example in the 1920s. It was seen as a way to derive profit from empire, notably by moving cotton, and, in wartime, troops, from the Niger valley to Algeria for transport on to France. This was the proposed alternative to transport to the ports of Senegal, notably Dakar, and then on the longer ocean route to France. As Senegal was also a French colony, this was strictly a debate about alternative transport routes. Time and cost factors played a role, costing being a matter of construction, equipment, operation and maintenance. The frequency with which over-optimistic assessments were offered is noticeable.

Rail was far less prone to mishap and disruption than river and sea routes. This was true across the world, for example with the high rate of sinkings on the Great Lakes in North America and on the major waterways, such as the Missouri. In part, this high rate was the result of poor boiler design, use and maintenance, but there were also issues arising from the often inaccurately charted nature of waterways. Previous sinkings could become new dangers. Railways had fewer issues.

Many imperial careers came to involve railways, as with Percy Girouard (1867-1932). Born in Montreal, he graduated from the Royal Military College of Canada, worked for two years on the Canadian Pacific Railway in London (1886-8), was commissioned in the Royal Engineers (1888), and was in charge of the Woolwich Arsenal Railway (1890-5). He built the railway across the Sudan desert from Wadi Halfa (1896-7), was President of the Egyptian Railways (1898-9), became Director of Imperial Military Railways in South Africa (1899-1904), High Commissioner of Northern Nigeria (1908-11), and Commissioner of Kenya (1909-12). He briefly played a role in Belgium in Allied rail administration during the First World War.

The railway strengthened the relationship between colonial ports and their hinterlands, for example for the French Djibouti, a settlement they had founded in 1888, and the independent state of Ethiopia, and in British West Africa, the port of Freetown, the capital of Sierra Leone, and the interior. From 1872, there had been proposals for a railway in Sierra Leone, but they had not been pursued. Instead, in 1893, one financed by the Liverpool Chamber of Commerce was adopted. Colonel Sir Frederic Cardew, Governor of Sierra Leone in 1894, reported that year to George, 1st Marquess of Ripon, the Secretary of State for the Colonies, who as Viceroy of India had overseen the rail system there: 'Obviously the best way of developing the products of the country is to facilitate communication between the different districts of the interior by opening up routes and laying down railways,' the products being specified as rubber, kola nuts and oil palms. Cardew had particular views on the route:

In any project for a railway it should start from Freetown ... feasible to the valley of the Sulima River ... the line might be extended along its course without meeting with severe gradients as far as Kanre Lahun (Kailahun) .... trade would be opened up with the hinterland of Liberia ... the products of the interior alone if properly developed would make such an increase in the volume of trade as to largely swell the revenue.

Cardew did not want the line to go instead to the mouth of the Bum Kittam River, as he feared that it would divert trade from Freetown, where colonial interests were centred. Nor did he want a line to Bumpan, as such an extension would be difficult because of the hilly terrain. Such surviving correspondence is not available for most railways, and this record is therefore generally valuable as showing the factors more widely considered. Construction began in 1896, with Bo reached in 1903. Although an extension had been envisaged to the Liberian frontier, there was no economic or political incentive to that end. Instead, the line reached Pendembu, near the frontier, in 1907.

Two branch lines were built, one in 1903 of 5.5 miles from Freetown to Hill Station, at 748 feet (229 metres). This, the Sierra Leone Mountain Railway, was intended to ease the access of Europeans to the healthier hill area south-west of Freetown. The other branch did not follow until 1914, and went to Makeni, the largest city in the Northern Province of Sierra Leone, which is to the north of the Rokel river. The locomotives were supplied, from 1897, by the Hunslet Engine Company in England, and were appropriate for the narrow gauge railway, which could not take a heavy axle load. The line was closed in stages from 1968 to 1974.

The report on the railways was drawn up by Frederic Shelford, the consulting engineer to the Crown Agents for the West African Railways, a group under the authority of the Colonial Office used by the colonies for their economic planning. On 10 June 1904, Shelford was criticised by name and at length in the House of Lords by Newton, 6th Earl of Portsmouth, an opposition peer, with suggestions of incompetence at least, and corruption at worse. Portsmouth complained about the cost per mile of the

Gold Coast (Ghana) Railway. Shelford's father-in-law, Montago Frederick Ommanney, however, the Senior Agent of the Crown Agents, had become Permanent Under-Secretary at the Colonial Office in 1901-7. In 1893, he had written of the Lagos Railway that he supported 'a real survey; made by competent engineers under the supervision of a Consultant Engineer, not a red line on a plan, intended to grade a Syndicate's Prospectus for the railway investor'. Suspicious of the railway sector, Ommanney backed the Crown Agents' system of construction, but most of their lines exceeded the estimated cost and few carried enough freight to cover loan and debt charges. Indeed, in 1894, Ommanney wrote to the Colonial Office about Sierra Leone: 'The traffic of the light line [narrow gauge] would require to be trebled before it could cover its working expenses and pay interest and sinking fund on the loan raised for its construction.'

In 1895, forwarding Shelford's report on a railway for the Gold Coast (Ghana) to the Colonial Office, Ommanney noted:

> The line appears to hold out a better prospect of success than that at Sierra Leone. The existing traffic is much more considerable, the country greatly more populous and, apparently, possessed of more abundant and varied natural resources.

Railway construction encouraged interest in the activities of other powers which, in the case of Britain, was not only Russia in Asia and France in Djibouti. There was also growing anxiety about Germany as it developed a *Weltpolitik*. In part, this was a matter of challenging Britain at sea in a 'Naval Race', but there was also a German commitment to rail-based geopolitics. This involved the development of colonies, notably in Africa, with rail serving as a way to support advances into the interior and the resulting economic exploitation. There was also a desire to use rail to enable Germany to breach any geographical attempt to limit it on land to Europe. Breaking out entailed rail links from Germany via its leading ally, Austria, into the Balkans, and thence the use of rail to benefit from the geopolitical possibilities offered by the far-flung Turkish empire. This became more significant once Germany failed to beat Britain in the 'Naval Race', a failure that was apparent by 1909. In this sense, the Mackinder approach of a focus on Continental rail links appeared to have greater salience.

In 1888, the first train from Austria reached Constantinople (modern Istanbul), the capital of the Turkish empire. This led to interest in moving further east, the Germans finishing a line from the eastern side of the Bosporus across western Anatolia to Ankara in 1892. The British, in turn, having themselves dropped the idea, sought to thwart plans to develop a rail route through the Turkish empire to the Persian Gulf, not least by persuading Kuwait not to be a terminus: in 1897, when the Shaikh of Kuwait was assassinated by his half-brother, Mubarak, the latter won British naval support against his Turkish overlords. As a result, in 1899, Mubarak agreed not to receive foreign agents or cede land without British permission. However, instead, in 1899 a German company was granted a Turkish concession to build a line to the Turkish-ruled port of Basra on the Persian Gulf.

Having travelled along the Asian route of the projected Berlin to Baghdad Railway in 1908, David Fraser, a special correspondent for the *Times*, was in no doubt in his book *The Short Cut to India* (1909) that, although very expensive for both Germany and Turkey, the railway represented a threat to Britain: '...a great rival is penetrating into our commercial preserves [and menacing] a possession which all the world envies us,' a reference to India. Fraser saw the motivation as strategic, not economic: 'our trade [to the Gulf] is unlikely to be affected by an enterprise from which economic results are not expected.' He argued, however, that the project would hit British prestige and influence, and added that it would be worrying if the railway fell to Germany or a hostile Russia:

> We might very well wake one morning to find that Russia has bought the Baghdad Railway and intended linking it up with her Trans-Caucasian system. A remote contingency, no doubt, but one which not so very long ago was regarded as worth discussion in political circles in Europe. The very thought of it smells of war.

A German military mission arrived in Turkey in 1913 and German influence grew, such that in August 1914, the two negotiated an alliance. Nevertheless, that June, Germany was willing to agree with Britain not to extend the line south of Baghdad. In practice, war intervened, but the strategic importance of the Berlin-Baghdad railway had been greatly exaggerated by both sides.

The Turkish empire was not only subject to the rail plans of others, but also a player in its own right, and more so than China. The Hejaz Railway was long-projected, with army support, as a means to strengthen the position of the empire in its distant Arabian dominions and with a planned extension from Medina to the Yemeni centres of Hodeida, Sana and Tais. Turkish suzerainty had been recently re-established in Yemen, with Sana captured in 1872. However, a rebellion in 1876 was only suppressed with difficulty, and there was an even more serious one in 1904-11. A railway would permit the deployment of forces without needing to rely on Red Sea routes, which were under effective British control after the establishment of British control in Egypt in 1882 and the consequent British dominance of the Suez Canal and naval base at Alexandria. From 1839, there was also a British base at Aden. The establishment of Italy in Eritrea, with a naval base at

Massawa from 1885, underlined this issue and in 1911, during the Italian-Turkish war, the Italians attacked Red Sea ports in Arabia, following in 1912 with completely destroying the Turkish Red Sea squadron in the battle of Kunfuda Bay on the Arabian coast.

Separately, the Italians constructed a railway from Massawa to the main inland city of Asmara, but begun in 1887, that was opened only in 1911, being extended to Keren in 1922 and Bishia in 1932. It was similar to the standard coast to interior pattern of railways in Africa.

The Hejaz railway was seen in part as a way to help pilgrims to Mecca, and thus to demonstrate the religious credentials of the ruling dynasty. A postcard map of the railway shows the different mediums used for providing images and details of railways. Postcards were employed to solicit donations for the project, which was presented as one to be funded, built and managed by the Ottomans; although, in practice, most of the construction engineers were Europeans.

Manual labour was in short supply, as was water (a problem for the Djibouti to Ethiopia line), food and fuel, while local Arab tribes, which saw their autonomy and their interests threatened, were hostile. This helped ensure that the railway terminated at Medina and not, as originally intended, Mecca; a change was a classic instance of the gap between plans and achievements so that, to take the example of the Eritrean Railway, it never connected with the Sudan Railway as had been hoped Stopping at Medina could be seen as affecting the Turks' ability to consolidate their position in Yemen and to threaten the British colony in Aden to the south, but it was a rational response to the difficulties facing the project. Begun in 1900, the 1,320-kilometre (820-mile) narrow gauge railway, which also had a branch from Syria via Haifa to the port of Acre, was opened in 1908, and in 1912 ten Swiss locomotives were built for it.

Attacked and damaged during the First World War, most famously in 1916 by T. E. Lawrence (Lawrence of Arabia) as the adviser of British-backed Arab insurgents, the conflict saw insufficient maintenance of the track. This was a particular problem in the heat of the region, and again was seen in the Djibouti to Ethiopia line from the 1980s to 2000s. A victim also of the postwar division of the Turkish empire among a number of states, including British control in Jordan and Palestine (later Israel), and French in Syria and Lebanon, much of the Hejaz line was disused by 1922, with the section in modern Saudi Arabia not used from 1920.

Although Chinese labourers played a major role in building railways elsewhere, notably in America and Canada, the government of China, which was suspicious of foreign intervention and models, was reluctant to see railways built and had the first two dismantled in 1865 and 1877. The first railway to last was built in 1881 by a British engineer to move coal from T'angshan to the port of Tianjin, which was opened to foreign trade and extended by 1894 to Beijing. Railways were also built in Taiwan in 1887-93 as part of a modernisation strategy under Liu Mingchuan, Governor from 1884 to 1891. A 29-kilometre railway connected Keelung and Taipei from 1888 with nine imported locomotives. British and German engineers played a key role and Liu celebrated the completion with a couplet ending 'human power triumphs over God's work.' Less positively, many deaths and accidents arose from the construction, notably of the first Taiwanese railway tunnel.

The defeat of China by Japan in 1894-5, a defeat that resulted in the annexation of Taiwan, led other foreign powers, including Russia, to demand concessions for railway construction in China. Although only 292 miles had been built by 1900, another 4,000 were being planned. Having undertaken a tour of China at the behest of the British Chamber of Commerce, Lord Charles Beresford produced in his *The Break-Up of China* (1899), a map showing railways built and projected. The role of rail as an enabler of Western power and modernisation helped to ensure that track and trains became strategic targets for their opponents. In China, in 1900, the destruction by the Boxers, an anti-foreigner movement, of part of the track between Tainjin and Beijing forced the abandonment of the initial attempt to relieve the foreign legations in the capital.

Yet, formal railway control was less significant than financial concessions in which loan agreements provided aspects of foreign control, notably by Britain, which formally controlled only a modest mileage. British-financed railways were a product of financial strength. By 1914, about 6,000 miles of railway had been laid including the 614-mile Anglo-German railway from Tianjin to Pukou (on the Yangtze north of Nanjing) built in 1908-12. To go on to Nanjing, it was necessary until 1968 to use a ferry. France controlled the Yunnan Railway between the port of Haiphong in French-ruled Vietnam and Kumming, which was a detached line, not part of any system within China. Haiphong became the port for that part of China. This was an aspect of the threat to China apparently posed by Western rail interests.

Only about ten per cent of the rail system was under full Chinese control. This meant that the republican era that began in 1912 was to see a major assault on the foreign ownership and control of railways, one that was to be continued in the subsequent Chinese accounts of railway and general history. The context in China was different to that in areas of colonial rule such as India, in part because there was not secure control in China, in part because of competition between the imperial powers, which was very much not the case in colonies, and in part due to the limited time in which the system existed prior to the 1911-12 revolution.

There were only limited internal waterway routes in Japan, whereas China had well-developed routes and also far larger rivers that were difficult to bridge. The terrain of Japan is very mountainous, about seventy per cent being mountain. The potential for canal development is limited to a few areas of plain. Thus, there was no real rivalry with canals. Instead, rail competed with the very developed coastal traffic.

Before the start of Japanese modernisation, the political system was a highly decentralised semi-feudal one, with the political units often divided by steep mountains. From the government point of view, the development of railways, together with the spread of school systems, was a powerful means to promote centralisation, breaking the mountain barriers between the political units. As a result, tunnels and bridges were very important.

From the regional point of view, the railways and schools were the most important agents of modernisation. This desire of the regions to have railways as the agents of civilisation has survived and is present in their political campaigns for new high-speed routes. The political context of railway history was amply demonstrated by the contrast behind early Chinese reluctance and a Japanese commitment to railways. Interest in rail was apparent prior to the Meiji Restoration in 1868, a restoration of the power of the Emperor that led to a powerful stress on regeneration. There had been Japanese discussion about a possible railway from Edo (Tokyo), the shogunal capital, to Kyoto, the imperial capital, when a British locomotive had been demonstrated. Subsequently, British expertise and finance were important in the construction and operation of the first Japanese railway in 1872, from Tokyo to the nearby port of Yokohama. Other railways followed rapidly, and on all the major islands. In contrast, roads were not seen as of great significance prior to the car.

Leading cities, such as Osaka, became railway hubs and more ambitious lines were introduced. By 1894, Japan, as part of its process of economic modernisation, had over 2,000 miles of track in operation, a reflection of strong central government lacking in China as well as of the financial and business infrastructure, domestic and international, necessary for such rail construction. The railway network depended upon both government funding and the role of private companies. The former was encouraged by the interest of the army, which was more marked from 1887. The German example was important as the Japanese army looked to German models from the mid-1880s. Major-General Katsura Tarō, who became Vice-Minister of War in 1886, had been military attaché in Berlin.

On Honshu, the main island, the network stretched nearly the entire length of the island and included two lines from the Pacific coast to the Sea of Japan. Thus, the San'yō Main Line from Kobe had reached Mitajiri, but did not reach Shimonoseki until 1901. Shimonoseki was to provide a ferry connection to Moji on the island of Kyushu, and the Kyushu Railway Company then took services on. The Railway Construction Act had stipulated priority routes, with 3,700 kilometres of track split into two phases planned. Despite support for nationalisation, four-fifths of the network was privately owned by 1905. This was unwelcome to the government, but it benefited from a considerable degree of control over the private system, as well as from a strong basic cohesion in the Japanese élite.

The limited funds available to the Meiji government had forced it to switch to rail development by private companies. However, because of security concerns led by the army about foreign investment in rail, as well as experience of the cyclical volatility of company management, the political camp arguing for the nationalisation of the trunk railways won the debate in 1906. Another factor was the government's need to have sufficient valuable assets to use as collateral for the foreign war loans for the Russo-Japanese War.

The trunk railway network was built in parallel with the existing and new major roads, but the definition and choice of what was major and necessary was politically decided. This factor was linked to overinvestment in the construction of uneconomic routes and the overextension of the life of such routes, both of which were made possible by the nationalisation.

Japan spread its commitment to railways to its foreign conquests, notably Korea, where the Japanese built the Seoul-Busan line in 1901-4 and in 1906 created the Railway Management Bureau. Korea was to be part of a Japanese-run system extending to Manchuria that was more integrated than the rival Russian system, which provided only a tenuous link across Siberia. Japanese activity was also shown in major improvements to existing lines in Taiwan, in part made necessary by neglect under Liu's successor and also due to sabotage by withdrawing Chinese troops. Military purpose was to the fore in the restoration in 1895, as Japan wanted to use the railway to move supplies to help troops in the suppression of local opposition. There were also new lines. In 1908, a 429-mile (691 km) line from Kaohsiung (Takao) in the south to Keelung in the north was finished. Given the mountainous terrain, this was a formidable achievement, albeit one aided by cheap local labour. The Japanese chief engineer, Hasegawa Kinsuke, played the key role. He had started his railway career in 1877 and arrived in 1899. A statue commemorated his role at Kaohsiung station from 1910 but was removed with the end of Japanese rule in 1945. This line accorded with broader Japanese planning as Keelung, the port closest to Japan, became a major harbour. A formidable amount of Japanese government money was spent on this line, not least with investment in new rolling stock.

Alongside imperial expansion, lesser powers also benefited from rail in extending their power. Thus, the building of a railway across the rebel area in 1900 helped to end longstanding Mayan resistance to the Mexicans in Yucatán. Moreover, in addition to development in the economic core of industrialisation, there was also the introduction and expansion of rail provision and services elsewhere. This included the poorest area of Europe, the Balkans. There, integration vied with competition. Thus, whereas Serbia was an Austrian client state in the 1880s, relations subsequently deteriorated and the Austrians tried to circumvent Serbia by means of a narrow gauge railway via Novi Pazar in 1908. When the Hungarians built the railway system in their part of the Austro-Hungarian empire, they made sure all the lines went to Budapest, not Vienna.

The economic significance of national rail systems included hitherto unprecedented rapid commuting into major centres. Freight movements, however, were of particular importance. Railways played a central role in industrialisation, capitalism (domestic and international), urbanisation and governmental expansion, while also being difficult to disentangle in causative terms from these very forces. In many countries, railways therefore served as a lightning rod for political, economic, social and cultural tensions. In some, such as Argentina and China, these were fuelled by anger at the influence supposedly represented by foreign investment.

In America, there were strongly expressed grievances, notably in the West, about the power of Eastern-dominated railways, which was seen as manipulation of the terms of economic life and social organisation, and criticised as wielding local or even regional monopolies. There was strong hostility to what was seen as the callous nature of expropriatory capitalism. The term 'robber barons' was used to describe figures such as Cornelius Vanderbilt, Charles Crocker, Jay Gould, E. H. Harriman, James J. Mill, and Collis Potter Huntington, and to affirm that rail broke the bounds of societal norms.

Manipulation was more easily accepted in the adoption by the American railways of a Standard Time System in 1883, in order to provide a system that permitted accurate timetabling and lessened the risk of missed connections and also of crashes. The risk of the latter was increased by greater usage and by the shared running on track by different train companies. Crashes became more deadly as train speeds increased.

As a very different hazard, the people who lived in railway towns had shorter average life spans than those in non-railway towns, in part because the railways brought new people and therefore new germs. And of course, railway towns were generally more industrial and such work posed serious health problems. There was no real effort to remove particulates from the engine smoke before it was pumped into the atmosphere. As a result, railway towns that were not exposed to persistent wind often sat in a pall of smoke, with air quality and therefore health greatly affected.

Yet, the railway also brought activity, jobs, and a measure of prosperity, all necessary in a world in which competition for work was fuelled by population growth. This was readily apparent in rail towns such as Crewe and Swindon, and in the rail districts of towns. In America, aside from the role of rail in the older established centres with lines integrated into the urban framework, all the major new cities were reached by rail and those in the Mid-West were more or less all railway cities, as with Kansas City. Opened in 1869, the first bridge across the

Missouri River was important to the development of the city, ensuring that it was the key local node, rather than Leavenworth. In 1886, a tornado hit hard and the bridge had to be rebuilt. A centralised rail terminal was provided by the Union Depot opened in 1878, designed in Gothic Revival style and prone to flooding. Expansion continued, the Kansas City Suburban Belt Railway beginning operation in 1890, and eventually becoming the Kansas City Southern Railway.

Further south, Fort Worth, Texas, also served as an intermediary between a grazing hinterland and the processing to meet urban demand to the east. The city had a railway by 1876 and a stockyards by 1887, and became a key centre for the Armour and Swift meat packing companies from 1902, with the companies owning the relevant linked railway. Railways delivered live cattle and refrigerated carcasses, with the Swift Refrigerator Line established in 1880 owning 7,000 ice-cold rail cars by 1920. Hell's Half Acre, the red light district of Fort Worth, developed between the railway station and the central business district.

Chicago's first railway, the Galena and Chicago Union, was chartered in 1836 to build a connection to the lead mines at Galena. The first tracks, however, were not laid until 1848 and then to Oak Ridge. Many railways followed, including the Chicago, Rock Island and Pacific Railroad, which began operation in 1852 and, despite its title, only reached Joliet then; Rock Island (on the Mississippi) following in 1854. The Chicago, Danville and Vincennes Railroad was chartered in 1865, its main line being completed in 1872. Moran's Map of Chicago and Suburbs, 1892, listed 22 'railroads entering Chicago,' in the sense of distinct companies; there were 38 district lines into the city, ensuring a degree of congestion, though less than in the more difficult sites of Boston and New York.

Commuter railways, streetcars, elevated railways, and underground lines and platforms were well developed in American cities, for example Philadelphia, helping commuting and therefore both the strength of the central city and suburbanisation. Railways, like skyscrapers, contributed to the importance of 'downtown', the central district in which activity was concentrated. Seen as disruptive, elevated railways were unpopular and uncommon, but underground lines were very expensive. The 1890s saw major new stations, such as Broad Street Station, Philadelphia: in 1890, the Philadelphia and Reading Railroad Company consolidated its four Philadelphia terminals to build one large terminal in downtown Philadelphia. The Company purchased a parcel of land which included the Butchers' and Farmers' Market and the Franklin Market. The new train shed, built in 1892-3, had the largest single span of any station roof in the world: 306 feet (91 metres).

New York City confronted two major railway problems: serving a major urban area, one on a difficult site with waters that were expensive to bridge or tunnel, and secondly, that of operating as a major national hub, in competition with other Atlantic port cities. Moreover, there was a requirement for interaction between the inter-urban and inner-urban networks. Like Boston, Buenos Aires, Rio de Janeiro, Montevideo, Dakar, Cape Town and Halifax, New York was one of the cities that developed as major ports serving the Atlantic trading system. All these cities had a major, if not central, role for rail, as did the comparable oceanic cities that were built on the Pacific, such as Auckland and Vancouver, and those on the Indian Ocean, such as Bombay (Mumbai) and Mombasa.

Rather than treating rail as a distinctive travel system, it is necessary to underline the central role of interoperability with other transport means, a situation that remains to this day. At the same time, it is important to accept that the terms of the latter changed with technological developments, economic circumstances, political requirements and social norms.

The larger iron, and later steel, ships that were used in the nineteenth century required deeper anchorages, more sophisticated, purpose-built facilities for particular goods, and strong linkages with the rail system. The last, in turn, brought exports from the hinterland, for example the wheat and flour for Britain that provided about half of all Canadian exports by value in 1891-1915. So, also, with timber. In contrast, goods with a high rate of perishability were not generally moved such distances, for example fruit, vegetables, and milk.

New York benefited greatly from access to a bigger and more prosperous hinterland than Boston or the Southern Atlantic ports, notably Charleston and Savannah, although Baltimore remained a rival. From New York, the Hudson Valley provided an effective route to upstate New York, while there were also good links into New Jersey and Pennsylvania. These benefited greatly from clear access corridors that were relatively long-established, compared to those being driven through in the American West at the expense of other interested parties, such as ranchers and Native Americans.

As more generally with improved communications, but more so, the railway helped ensure a massive lowering in price differentials: whereas, for wheat, they had varied as much as 69 per cent between New York and the wheat producing state of Iowa in 1870, this had fallen to 19 per cent by 1910. As such, rail was crucial to the liberal economic order. The ports were central to immigration as well as to trade, Halifax and New York being the major points of entry for immigrants to America and Canada respectively. They then moved on into the interior by rail. A greater percentage stayed in New York than Halifax, as the former offered far more opportunities. There was no concern at this point in New York about vulnerability to naval attack, although Halifax, in contrast, was well-fortified as a naval dockyard by Britain.

Aside from passenger and freight routes into its continental hinterland, New York, like London but more so due to more prominent waterways, posed the challenge of travel within a very crowded city, with Manhattan overloaded with streetcars and omnibuses. This led to a series of attempts to provide urban rail solutions. In 1868, the city's first elevated train began service from the Battery at the south of Manhattan, to Cortlandt Street, which was a classic instance of a port-to-centre route. In 1870, employing the technology used by the Royal Mail under London, a 95-foot-long pneumatic steam railway tunnel was opened as a show to attract investment, only for the project to be blocked by political opposition linked to the omnibus companies. Whatever the ownership structure, forms of transport are generally rivals if not in active opposition. Whereas elevated railways were available in New York from 1868, the crash of 1873 ended all underground (subway) schemes for a while, when the city's population was growing rapidly. It was not until 1904 that the city's first subway line, the Interborough Rapid Transit, opened, going from City Hall via Broadway to 145th Street and using motors powered by an electrified rail on the tracks. This line was extended to 157th Street in 1904 and 221st in 1906.

In the 1900s, during the presidencies of Theodore Roosevelt, the fiscal environment in America moved against rail companies, with the federal and some state (including New York) governments placing legal restrictions on institutional holdings, in part in order to pursue 'trust busting'. Moreover, from 1907, despite wage and price inflation, rail companies found rate increases banned. As with other cases, including British rail companies from 1945 and India in the 2010s, this led to low profits and dividends, which caused limited creditworthiness and investment and pressure on solvency, not least in the 1910s when industrial stocks and war finance provided other investment opportunities.

The financial situation had already caused a crisis for British rail prior to the outbreak of the First World War in 1914 and therefore prior to the major expansion in car, bus and lorry use in the 1920s and 1930s. The fragmentation of the railway industry meant that companies often lacked the necessary capital base and liquidity to provide investment or to attract it from elsewhere. In part because the time horizons were inappropriate, the regulation of fares and freight rates exacerbated this problem and made it harder to cover running costs. These were a matter not only of maintenance and the purchase of coal, but also of the wages demanded by workers, wages that the industry could not manage. The 1911 railway strike led to intimidation and violence and the deployment of troops. Supporting the government and worried about radicalism, George V referred to 'what was fast becoming a terrible calamity'. The low rate of return on capital hitting share prices and investor returns would not have been of interest to the workers, but it was a crucial issue.

In the face of the more general difficulties of rail, there was talk of nationalisation and certainly of consolidation. The latter was backed by David Lloyd George as President of the Board of Trade (1905-8). A radical moderniser, he argued that consolidation would enhance profitability and efficiency. However, the measure lacked political traction at this point. There was in economic and financial terms an over-provision of services and spare capacity in Britain, which contrasted with the situation in Germany where provision was more efficient. On the other hand, not that this was the intention, this spare capacity enabled Britain during the First

World War to maintain existing services while also adding new ones. Germany lacked comparable flexibility then, not least due to pressures on resources, including coal supplies.

In peacetime, new rail lines shaped, as well as responded to, opportunities, for example in encouraging commuting. Thus, the building of a direct route from London to Southend via Upminster, avoiding the Tilbury detour, opened in 1888, cut the express journey time from 95 to 50 minutes and was followed by an alternative route via Shenfield, which opened in 1889. As a result, commuting from Southend into London rose rapidly, as did the population of Southend, from 7,979 in 1881 to 62,713 by 1911. The same happened when rail commuting began from the North Sea coast to Newcastle. Rail helped direct population changes.

Meanwhile, the capital of empire, London, had been given added transport flexibility, as well as distinctiveness, by an underground railway system. No other British city had an underground until Glasgow opened one in 1896, providing the third oldest in Europe after London and Budapest, where the first line, an electrified one, was opened in 1896. Istanbul had an underground funicular railway, built in 1875. The Glasgow underground was powered by a steam-driven clutch-and-cable system until converted to electricity in 1935; the fifteen stations had island platforms. In a lunch party in Guy de Maupassant's novel *Bel-Ami* (1885), the men

> ... were discussing the big project of the Paris underground railway. The topic was not exhausted until they reached the dessert, because everyone had a great deal to say about the slowness of communications in the city, the disadvantages of the trams, the inconvenience of the buses and the boorishness of cab-drivers.

London was in a different league at this point; Paris did not follow until 1914.

Train services, both over and under ground, were crucial to London's character and sense of identity. The great success of the Central Line between Shepherd's Bush and the Bank, opened in 1900, encouraged the building of other underground lines, the Bakerloo, Piccadilly, and Hampstead to Charing Cross (part of the Northern Line) lines, the key figure being Charles Tyson Yerkes, an American financier of dubious practices (in fact an ex-convict) but boundless energy who had been responsible for the Loop in Chicago. Opened in 1906, the Piccadilly initially ran from Hammersmith to Finsbury Park, making it the longest line that fed commuters and shoppers from West London into the West End. Sensing the possibilities of expanding London, Yerkes planned an extension for the Hampstead Line to Golders Green, which opened in 1907. There was no large-scale expansion of the system into less prosperous Dockland, although, in part, that was catered to by overground services. The 'tube' meant that London had the largest underground railway system in the world and it came to affect the imagining of the city.

The tube caused less destruction than the establishment of main line rail services. Massive demolition resulted from the construction of London's stations, culminating with the building of Marylebone in 1893-9, the last of the termini, which led to the destruction of Blandford Square and the eviction of over 4,000 mostly working-class people. Earlier, there were battles between English and Irish workmen at London Bridge where expenditure on the line itself meant that, although services began in 1836, the station buildings came later. Railways were by their nature really or potentially interim, as lines as well as stations could be extended or added.

Whether by tube or by other means, commuting was scarcely value-free, and this was notably so in terms of provision and costings. In London, the Cheap Trains Act of 1883, passed against the wishes of the railway companies, obliged them to operate more cheap trains, and by 1914 had ensured that 1,000 cut-price trains were taking workers into London daily. The parliamentary debate on a Cheap Trains Bill in 1900 indicated the different views at play. Charles Stuart-Wortley, MP for Sheffield Hallam, who opposed the extension of such measures, emphasized the need to treat railway companies 'in a reasonable manner, so as to induce the investing public to come forward when their money is required'. Lieutenant-Colonel Amelius Lockwood, MP for Epping and a Director of the LNWR, also spoke in favour of the shareholders:

> It would appear that when some enterprising individual wants to enter upon private legislation, the railway companies are to be his favourite hunting ground ... a Cheap Trains Bill ... secures a certain amount of popularity in the constituencies... The railway companies having large capitals are looked upon as fair game for any attacks made upon them. When the representatives of the railways attempt in the constituencies or in the House of Commons to defend the companies from these continual attacks they are called bloated capitalists or the railway ring... The two largest items which have affected the net revenue of the companies are the increased wages, curtailed hours of labour, and increase of local taxation.

As was invariably the case, the British rail system included much that was less impressive than Marylebone. Arthur Conan Doyle in his non-Sherlock Holmes short story 'The Brazilian Cat' (1898), has a character travelling to the fictional Clipton-on-the-Marsh in Suffolk: 'After changing at Ipswich, a little local train deposited me at a small deserted station.' Such unmanned stops became more common as the network expanded.

In countries poorly provided with trains it could be worse. They could speed tourists to Monaco, which the train reached in 1868 as part of the development of the Riviera. Specific routes for tourists around the Mediterranean developed, including combined train and steamship tickets, as for the sailings between Marseille, Tunis and Palermo by the French company Touache in 1905. However, around much of the Mediterranean, the spread of train routes had to cope with difficult terrain, especially with mountains running down to the coast. The poor shape of the local economy also limited the appeal to investors. Thus, per square mile, there were far fewer railways in the Balkans, southern Italy or Spain, than in Germany, the Low Countries, or England. Nevertheless, each line that was built made a difference, and potentially a major one.

Rail provided plentiful opportunities for the imagination to range. In *Bel-Ami* (1885), Georges Duroy is 'aroused from his dream by the shrill whistle of a locomotive which came out of the tunnel on its own, like a large rabbit bolting out of its hole, and then puffed full speed ahead towards the shunting-shed where it would be able to relax.' Rail was the means for the overland sections planned by Phineas Fogg in his travel round the world described by Jules Verne in the novel *Le tour du monde en quatre-vingts jours* (1873). The original plan was for rail to Brindisi, from Bombay to Calcutta, San Francisco to New York City, Queenstown (Cobh) to Dublin, and Liverpool to London. However, the travellers discover that 50 miles of the Indian railway from Kholby to Allahabad had not yet been built and have to use an elephant. Crossing America, they confront bison crossing the tracks, a falling suspension bridge, and a Sioux attack on the train.

Station architecture was the most powerful visual impact of rail, as many saw stations, whether or not they travelled by train.

Their sites and sheer size made this was most particularly true of central stations. John Ruskin in *The Seven Lamps of Architecture* (1849) foolishly declaimed that expenditure on station aesthetics was mistaken as those 'in a hurry and therefore miserable' would be heedless, but that was not the view of most of the corporate or governmental patrons of termini, fortunately. The buildings had of course to adapt to their sites and were driven by their purpose, covering from the elements the long platforms from which passengers boarded. As a result, large train sheds were the central feature. These were supplemented, generally fronted, by service facilities including booking halls and waiting rooms, and their facades provided opportunities to display architectural style. The changing styles reflected a variety of artistic factors and can be differently explained. The Neo-Gothic, as in London's St Pancras station, has been presented as a way to respond to change, reimagining the culture of the past for the needs of the day.

The impact of rail on the collective imagination can be seen across the arts, from paintings to games. Nineteenth-century painters were fascinated by rail, in part because it was an important new world that could be depicted and in part due to the interest in showing features such as speed and steam. In probably the most famous example, J. M. W. Turner's *Rain, Steam and Speed – The Great Western Railway* (1844), the recently completed Maidenhead Railway Bridge provides steam, mist and rain in a blur given energy by the rapidly moving train. Claude Monet's series of twelve paintings on the Parisian station at Saint-Lazare (1877) were suffused with smoke. In Henry Tanner's *Low Tide, Cannon, Street Bridge* (c.1901-3), smoke from the trains crossing the Thames merges with the hazy clouds above. Trains crossing bridges were frequently depicted, although the setting could be calm, as in Monet's *Railway Bridge, Argenteuil* (1873), in which the train crosses a river on a bridge that is supported by massive columns, or Camille Pissarro's *The Railway Bridge at Pontoise* (1873). Trains could also be shown as peaceful additions to the landscape, as in Pissarro's *Railway to Dieppe* (1886), in which the real centre of attention is the fertile landscape.

There can be an idea of places, routes, times and vehicles that orders experience, or, indeed, takes precedence over them. The recording of space in memory, correspondence, the arts, and other forms, is therefore part of the geography. This process from the outset had affected the response to the new technology of rail, turning rail into experience. The public also rapidly became knowledgeable about the new railway geography, as with 'Oh, Mr. Porter' (1892), a British song popularised in the music halls by Marie Lloyd:

'Oh! Mr Porter, what shall I do?
I want to go to Birmingham
And they're taking me on to Crewe'

Crewe was also the crossing point for theatrical repertory companies each Sunday night as they swapped theatres and relied on trains to move them.

Meanwhile, the economic difference made by rail was seen across the world. Fought for in the War of the Pacific (1879-83) and won by Chile from Peru, the nitrate-rich area of Tarapacá was served by rail from 1870, when the first line was opened. Railways linked the works to the ports of Pisagua and Iquique and were financed by the profits from an export that was required for high explosives and fertiliser, and of which Chilean production had risen to about three quarters of world supply by 1900, from nothing in 1870. In Chile, the railway replaced slower and less reliable transport by mule carts, which in any case could not cope with the scale of expansion in the nitrate industry; there was also insufficient forage and water for a large number of mules. Coal, forage for the locomotives, was much more efficient in calorific terms. Water supply for the locomotives, however, was a problem, as in crossing the coastal range the gradients reached the highest point on the railway at 3,812 feet. This was a difficulty faced by all the states where the Andes Mountains were present.

As an instance of the extent to which British investment was a catalyst across much of the world, British capital was crucial to the development of both the Chilean nitrate mines and the Nitrate Railways Company, which was launched in London in 1882, and had a near monopoly in the export until 1929. The company's role caused controversy, in part due to the foreign influence it represented. In 1889-90, the Chilean government developed a rival railway between nitrate works around Agua Santa and the port of Caleta Buena, with the nitrate moved in part using wagons on rails on inclined planes to overcome the gradient.

By 1900, Chile had about 3,000 miles of railway in operation, which was considerably fewer than in Argentina or Brazil, although central and northern Chile was fairly well covered. Northern Chile in particular, although still difficult, was easier for railway construction than Peru where the problems of terrain pushed up costs and the total mileage in operation was less than that in Chile. Across the world, fertilisers were dependent on rail, as their supply to farmers was generally by train. And the high explosives produced from nitrates helped in rail construction.

In Brazil, the coffee planters expanded west into the province of São Paulo, using the railway to create new links and opportunities. By 1904, there were 10,000 miles in operation in Brazil, compared to 6,000 in 1889. However, outside the wealthy state of Sao Paulo, development was patchy and there was less British investment in Brazil than in Argentina.

The significance of openness to foreign, notably British, investment was seen not only in Argentina, Chile and Uruguay, but also in Mexico, which, as a result, saw major growth in railway mileage from the late 1870s as well as an expansion of mining, notably of copper. Mileage rose from 398 in 1876 to 15,360 in 1910. In a boom in the early years of the twentieth century, American companies built 12,000 miles of track, largely in order to move ore to smelters in America. In contrast, there was far less rail mileage in Central America and northern South America.

In the Caribbean, as with the Chilean nitrate railways, there was a contrast between the development of commodity-linked freight lines that were privately run, and general-purpose public lines. In the Dominican Republic, where 700 miles of track were used on sugar plantations, there was far less of an achievement in the shape of public lines. In 1880, the government agreed a contract with the firm of A.A. Baird and Co. of Glasgow for the construction and operation of a line from Santiago in the interior to the port of Samaná, in part in order to develop the Samaná peninsula. The line was only partially completed, and then only in 1909. The contrast between these two types of line can be seen to the present, notably in Africa, but not only there. Indeed, this contrast is in evidence in mineral lines more generally, for example in Australia.

Across the world, railways, with their large and often unionised workforce, could be a major source of difficulties for railway operations and one that affected profitability. In 1911, the first general rail strike in Britain, a strike that arose from anger with the Conciliation Board established in 1907, led to the deployment of troops who killed two people at Llanelli where the Great Western Railway line had been blocked. This was followed by riots that included the vandalization of the station.

This strike was an aspect of the political role of rail; another was the significance of trains for electioneering. Just as Queen

Victoria was able to travel around Britain in a way her predecessors could not, politicians such as William E. Gladstone employed the train to reach out to the electorate in a fashion that had not been possible hitherto. In America, whirlwind train tours were used by politicians such as William Jennings Bryan, Theodore Roosevelt, and later, Harry Truman and Dwight Eisenhower in order to greet the voters, often with speeches from the back of the train. Train hustings faded away with John F. Kennedy, who had little interest in rail.

Significantly, no railways were built in Afghanistan, a country not brought under Western control. In 1928, there was talk in the international press of a line from the capital, Kabul, to Jalalabad, about 80 miles (130 kilometres) east and close to the Khyber Pass to British India. That this was never constructed, and its non-appearance was linked to the civil war of 1928-9, which led to the fall of Amanullah Khan, a moderniser who sought economic development. Jalalabad had been a family stronghold for him. Earlier in the decade, the British had built a 52-kilometre line from Fort Jamrud close to the Afghan frontier, and any Afghan railway from Kabul thither would have been part of a potential alignment of British India with Afghanistan.

Further west, by 1888 the Russian Trans-Caspian railway from Krasnovodsk had been brought to within 100 miles of Herat in western Afghanistan, a city over which control had been in longstanding dispute between Persia (Iran) and Afghanistan. Moreover, the previous year, the Shah of Persia agreed to consult Russia before granting any foreign companies concessions to build railways. There was no effective steam-powered railway in Persia by the time of the Great War. The international context was always important for rail, in terms of comparisons, competition, investment and pressure.

5

THE FIRST WORLD WAR

GWR steam locomotive Rod 5322 (class 43xx) was built at Swindon in 1917 and served in France during the Great War. Rescued in the late 1960s from a Barry scrapyard it has been on display at Didcot in khaki since 1973. (Tony Hisgett)

The deadlock of trench warfare of 1915-1918 was a revolution which changed the character of war. But the prime cause of that change was only partly weapons, it was still more numbers; and the reason why armies of millions could be maintained in the field was, I think, first the development of railways, roads, and mechanised transport of all kinds, which enabled supplies to be brought to the front in almost unlimited quantities.

Major-General Sir Frederick Maurice, 1927.

War *as a result of* rail, indeed by timetable, appeared a possible factor. But despite the frequently repeated later claim of A. J. P. Taylor that the war was 'imposed on the statesmen of Europe by railway timetables … an unexpected climax to the railway age', was rail really *the* cause of this deadly conflict or, indeed, a cause at all? National rail systems had been developed earlier in part for the mobilisation of troops. France financed the building of railways in the Russian-ruled part of Poland in order to help speed up the mobilisation of its ally against Germany, and thus, by distracting German attention, providing indirect protection for France. Conversely, the German aim was for a knockout blow against France before turning against Russia. Unlike Moscow, Paris appeared to be within reach of German forces. This strategy, however, depended on the key rail-linked capability gap between rapid German mobilisation and its slower Russian counterpart. This gap, however, had uncertain operational results and strategic consequences.

As a result, there was concern in Germany about Russian preparedness. Count Helmuth von Moltke (Moltke the Younger), Chief of the German General Staff from 1906, pressed in 1913-14 for war. He feared that Germany would increasingly not be able to win later (a verdict endorsed in very different circumstances by the Second World War). By 1916, he thought, Russia with its larger population would be in a position to start attacking effectively before the Germans had had an opportunity to defeat France. In Moltke's view, Germany's existing plans for an attack first on France could not operate after 1916.

If this was war as initiated by concern over rail, it was not justified. Although the Russians had built up an army superior to that of Austria, against whom they repeatedly did well in 1914-16, and had quickly recovered from defeat by Japan in 1904-5, the Russian attack on Germany was to be defeated easily and rapidly, and by only a small section of the German army, in 1914; and much of Russian Poland was conquered by the Germans in 1915, even though Germany was then fighting on two fronts.

Both sides suffered from rail-related strategic overreach in 1914: the Germans in France and the Russians in East Prussia advanced too far from their railheads, and in doing so pushed their opponents closer to theirs. Railways also made offensives far more predictable: they had to happen not far from where the railways were. The issues of rail capacity help to explain why the Germans were unimpressed by the plans of their ally Austria in the Balkans or later against Italy from Tyrol: with so few railways, there was relatively little that could be done.

It is going too far, as has been argued for Germany, to say that the war plans of 1914 with their dynamic interaction of mobilisation and deployment made 'war by timetable' (a reference to the railway timetables that guided and registered the pace of mobilisation) difficult to stop once a crisis occurred. Such an argument exaggerates the role of one particular factor – which is always a mistake – and underplays the extent to which rulers, generals and politicians were not trapped by circumstances. In fact, as was understood, their own roles, preferences and choices were important. An underplaying of the importance of choice reflects an anachronistic, later sense that no one could have *chosen* to begin the war; but, in fact, in 1914, decision-makers believed that war was necessary and could lead to a quick victory. Such an underplaying also permits the convenient blaming of 'the system,' as opposed to individuals who were foolish, over-confident, unremittingly bellicose, or weak. Linked to this, the war was not so much a failure of statecraft, as some have argued, but instead a breakdown of deterrence accompanied by a willingness of key figures to turn to war. These, combined with a strategic confusion at the heart of decision-making, made that combination deadly. Alongside this came the extent to which the dynamic of the crisis meant that constructive ambiguity was no longer credible. It is also unhelpful to assume that there were system-appropriate policies, as this approach underestimates the major policy divisions within decision-making élites. Thus, an account of the causes of the war can be written without once mentioning rail. The French railways were able to move French and British troops to the front rapidly, but that scarcely explained French and British policy.

In addition to using rail for military operations, there was also planning to cope with the disruption of rail in wartime. In 1910, the British Committee of Imperial Defence expressed concern that war with Germany would affect the movement of supplies, notably from the ports on the North Sea. A sub-committee took evidence from the general managers of the leading railway companies and in 1911 concluded that the closure of these ports would create grave problems for feeding Londoners. These managers pressed for a central body to respond in wartime, not least by coordinating government requirements from rail. In the event, in the face of German submarine attack, notably, but not only, on the vulnerable North Sea coastal shipping that was additionally exposed by the German seizure of Belgian ports, and the possibility of attack by surface warships, the war created problems for British coastal trade which forced more goods onto the trains. This concern led in 1912 to the establishment of the Railway Executive Committee (REC) and in 1914, with the outbreak of war, to the railways coming under government control, an Irish REC following in 1917. In practice, that meant control by a committee of prominent railway managers and its range of sub-committees.

Rail density varied considerably between the fronts, being affected by prior provision, wartime construction and damage. The last was a particular problem for the Hejaz Railway in Arabia. The situation was best on the Western Front, and it was there that trench railways were most extensively constructed. Once war began, construction companies of troops were recruited from rail workers at home, 45 for the British alone. The British trench railway system also benefited from the skills developed in narrow gauge industrial and, particularly, mine railways. The British formed a Railway Operating Division in April 1915 and by the end of the war it had over 20,000 men and was responsible for over 800 miles of track. These were generally 600 mm narrow gauge and were often prefabricated. Small locomotives and light rolling stock were built and used, but the smoke produced made these trains vulnerable to artillery in daylight.

Damage led to rapid rebuilding, as by the Germans in Eastern Europe and the Balkans and the insertion of their own locomotives and rolling stock, as well as the conversion of broad gauge tracks to standard track. For example, having captured Belgrade in 1915, the Germans first replaced the broken railway bridge with a pontoon and then repaired the main bridge. Once Serbia was overrun, the rail-strategic position in the Balkans was transformed. As described in John Buchan's novel *Greenmantle* (1916), the German supplies to the Turks were moved down the Danube in 1915-16 to Rustchuk and then transferred to the Bulgarian railway using steam cranes. The Germans also constructed many light railways.

The Russians were not the only power on the Eastern Front with inadequate rail systems for the purposes of war. Austria suffered from the lack of good rail support for Austrian Poland, which was attacked by the Russians in 1914. There were poor connections between Romania, which entered the war in 1916, and its ally Russia. Where lines existed, they could face many problems of capacity. This was particularly so on the Eastern Front in Russia, Hungary and Romania.

The railways were crucial on the home fronts, not least with regard to the high levels of industrial production necessary to support the war effort. This entailed the movement of labour to new war factories, for example at Gretna, such that commuting patterns changed. Unprecedented demand for wartime workers on the railways introduced inexperienced labour, as men of military age volunteered or were conscripted: 184,475 out of the pre-war workforce of about 600,000. In response, the number of female employees on the British railways rose from 13,046 to nearly 69,000, with 36,000 in occupations that had been hitherto restricted to men, such as station mistress. Their wages and bonuses were lower, which was more generally true of female war work. After the war, there was to be a rapid return to the dominance of men in the rail labour force.

In Britain, in order to focus on the war effort and to save on coal and locomotives, 601 of which were sent abroad, there was a reduction of services deemed unnecessary, such as dining cars, express speeds, and provision to many stations, all also seen in the Second World War. The Bideford, Westward Ho! and Appledore Railway was pulled up for transfer to the Western Front, only to be sunk by a German submarine. The majority of locomotives remained in Britain, but there was not the usual pattern of replenishment, and the huge amount of work contributed to worn-out engines. This created major operational problems for the postwar railways.

The war could both encourage demand for rail, but also hit it hard, as for the neutral Netherlands. The profitability of Dutch railways suffered, in large part due to a British blockade aimed at stopping German trade via the Netherlands. The Dutch, moreover, were affected by a shortage of coal, the price of which also rose during the war.

In contrast to Alfred Robida's caricature mentioned at the beginning of the last chapter, there was relatively little use of armoured trains in First World War, although they did play a role. Such trains provided a vivid image, as in *Armoured Train in Action* (1915), a painting by Futurist Gino Severini, depicting men and cannon firing from a train. States deploying armoured trains included Austria, Italy, and Russia, as well as Britain in Belgium and Iraq. The British also deployed two armoured trains on the east coast as a preparation against German amphibious attack, but they were not required for action.

In contrast, on the pattern of the Crimean War, the American Civil War, the Franco-Austrian and Franco-Prussian wars, the Zulu War, and Boer War – but on a far greater scale – there were ambulance trains. These trains were often long because, aside from carrying the wounded, who despite triple bunks took up more space than troops who were not casualties, it was also often necessary to pull operating rooms, pharmacies, staff accommodation and kitchens. By 1918, 51 had been built in Britain, 20 for use in Britain and 31 for the Continent. The trains operated with hospital ships to move casualties across the English Channel. There were also hospital trains for other militaries, including the French, German and the American, although alongside the specialised, new-build hospital trains, there were also those comprising essentially converted rolling stock.

The geopolitics of rail predicted prior to the war were not to the fore during the conflict. For example, the Berlin-Baghdad line was both incomplete and not able to determine strategy or operations, although it was important in helping in the movement of Turkish troops and supplies. This was particularly so as Turkey had scant road transport. Rather than transcontinental lines, it was domestic systems that were of greatest significance, as they made it possible to mobilise the economic potential of the combatants. Rail also underlined the significance of Germany's position, for the conquest of Serbia in 1915, most of Romania in 1916, and of much of western Russia in 1915-18 by Germany and its allies, Austria and Bulgaria, produced a rail-linked bloc of territory. The movement west of resources, notably food, from these new conquests gave Germany great potential, not least to offset the highly damaging British-organised blockade. Yet, in the event, the oceanic transport systems that provided both articulation for the British formal and informal empires and the means to deploy American resources to Europe proved more significant to eventual Allied victory.

6

POLITICS TO THE FORE, 1919–38

From Kartaly to Magnitogorsk, we played soccer along the tracks, then we ran to catch up with the train, which had gone only a little way.

American passenger, 1930, on a new rail line that was crucial to Soviet industrial plans.

This is the night mail crossing the Border ....
Pulling up Beattock, a steady climb:
The gradient's against her, but she's on time....
Letters of thanks, letters from banks....
News circumstantial, news financial.

W.H. Auden's poem for the 1936 British documentary *Night Mail* memorably captured the rhythms of the train. (Few British school children from 1950-70 would not have heard the clackety-clack, either in the documentary or from an oratorically enthusiastic teacher.) On the London to Glasgow run that he celebrates, there were 34 points at which post was picked up or dropped off. In contrast, Boris III of Bulgaria (r. 1918-43) is scarcely a household name among rail enthusiasts, but he should be. He enjoyed

French engineer André Chapelon (1892-1978) brought a scientific rigour to the design of steam locomotives that had been lacking, with most designers working hitherto by trial and error. This is a design for a 2-10-4 'Selkirk', which could have squeezed 6000hp from a fire grate area of just 65 sq ft. Chapelon's designs were so efficient that French rail mandarins were worried his engines were better than the new electric ones they were championing. This limited the number of his designs actually entering into production.

travelling on the footplate as well as driving the locomotive himself. In 1937, he drove the first train over a new line. Boris also drove his car himself.

Images of modernity changed abruptly in the early twentieth century. The train, that potent symbol and bearer of the new and powerful in the previous century, was replaced by cars and aircraft, and rapidly so, as befitted an emphasis on the new. Both presented speed, style and streamlining, and, while the train did the same, it did not offer the shock of the new. In his detective novel *The Black Spectacles* (1939), John Dickson Carr, an American writer who had settled in Britain, referred to Bath as a 'noble town, where the tall eighteenth-century houses look like tall eighteenth-century dowagers, and turn blind eyes to trains or motor-cars,' but this was an instance of nostalgia as obsolescence, not least in seeing cars as equivalent to trains.

A major aspect of the history of rail in this period emerged from the differing approaches taken by particular governments, and therefore societies, to both rail and the potential of particular transport systems, and especially the extent to which these approaches were taken up in times of ideological coalescence, propaganda and policy. Thus, the Nazis, who took power in Germany in 1933, were particularly associated with aircraft and cars, and far less so with rail. Indeed, the unionised nature of the latter made it suspect for some regimes. Although Hitler frequently met foreign leaders at railway stations, for example Francisco Franco, the Spanish dictator, in a railway lounge car at Hendaye near the Franco-Spanish border in 1940, airmindedness was very important to Nazi propaganda. They also devoted great attention to the building of *autobahns* (motorways) and encouraged the idea of the people's car, the *Volkswagen*. Mussolini opened the first Italian *autostrada* in 1924 and built airports. That was very different to the ideologies and imagery offered in the Soviet Union which, in contrast, was far more focused on rail.

More generally, and in so far as there could be separation from politics in its widest respects, the challenge from the rapid development of freight and passenger traffic by road after the First World War did not automatically cause a crisis for rail. Instead, aside from simple competition, which was important, there was also a measure of synergy as there had been between rail and existing horse and carriage provision in the nineteenth century. Both types of road traffic, freight and passenger, could be linked to the rail system. Thus, railways provided goods for the depots used for lorries. In addition, bus services focused on rail stations, and on the pattern also seen with steamships and aircraft, some of these services were owned by rail lines, or were in partnership with them. A rail-bus partnership remains significant today. Rail stations are frequently centres for bus services, for example in France, Germany, Japan and Switzerland, with stopping places and timetables arranged accordingly.

The expansion of cities greatly helped rail as well as road. Suburbanisation, which was particularly significant in the 1920s, saw demand for both increase. Thus, taking advantage of the ease of building surface lines across farmland in a liberal regulatory environment, the Northern Line overground extension of the Underground to Edgware in 1923-4 was followed to the north of London by other extensions.

Road competition was not the sole element of change in the railway world. In particular, the role of coal, although it remained the principal fuel, was diminished by the growing use of electricity as a power source, for example on Britain's Southern Railway and in Italy and the Soviet Union. Electricity was seen as more modern. It was cleaner and easier to control and required less labour than the use of coal: the engine did not need to be stoked, and this was important given the rising real wages of railway workers. There was not the same need for maintenance, either. In 1922, the French electrified the line from Pau to Tarbes, the *Times* noting on 9 November:

There is no longer doubt as to the advantages of electrification in safety, convenience of working, and freedom from smoke. But the deciding factor is cost. When local coal is abundant a steam engine is still the most economical. When the mines are far from the railways, the respective merits of transporting the coal and of generating electricity at the pithead for distribution by cable are still in dispute. But when there is a choice between importing coal from a foreign country and using a permanent natural resource such as water-power, prudence can give only one answer. Electrification must be undertaken as quickly as the water-power can be harnessed.

French rail services saw further electrification. They benefited from hydro-electric power generated from the rivers flowing from the Pyrenees.

Meanwhile, aside from road vehicles, the establishment of air services led to competition for rail, for example on the London-Paris route. This began in 1919, from Hounslow Heath Aerodrome to Le Bourget in Paris. From 1920, Cricklewood Aerodrome, where the Golders Green Estate was to be built, was also a base for Paris services, as was Croydon Airport, which opened in 1920 on the site of Beddington and Waddon aerodromes and became Britain's leading airport. By 1921, six companies operated a London to Paris service and the Croydon-Le Bourget route became the busiest in the world. There were also flights from London to Amsterdam and Rotterdam from 1920, and to Berlin from 1923. The airport was greatly expanded in 1926-8.

However, the London-Paris example of successful operation in part was a matter of competition with the ferries. In contrast, overland rapid train services benefited from their city centre to city centre character, and from the small carrying-capacity of aircraft, which were also vulnerable to weather conditions, far more so than trains. Air services were of course more expensive than trains and had a higher accident rate. Airships appeared to offer potential for longer-range services, but spectacular accidents helped ensure failure.

Railway companies tried to benefit from the growth of air services. In Britain, in 1933, the GWR Air Service began a twice-daily service between Plymouth and Cardiff via Haldon airfield near Exeter, a service later extended that summer to Birmingham. In 1934, the Big Four railway companies and Imperial Airways formed formed Railway Air Services, a domestic airline which linked at Croydon, the main base, to international air routes. This company continued until nationalised in 1947. The major route, between London and Glasgow, had intermediate stops, including for Birmingham and Manchester.

In part in response to air and road competition, there were improvements in aspects of rail service, with new speed records part of the headline nature of national passenger services, trumpeted in rail posters. In Britain, the streamlined *Mallard* set the world steam record of 126 mph (203 km/h) in 1938 south of Grantham. This record has not been surpassed. Other examples of prestige services included the Slovak Arrow, an express introduced in 1936 to cover the route between Prague and Bratislava, the leading cities of Czechoslovakia, at a maximum speed of 130 km/h and with unique motor units. Express trains included the *Nord Express* which, by the 1920s, ran from Riga via Warsaw, Berlin and Paris to Calais daily, the last providing a link to

London. After the Communist Revolution in Russia, this service no longer ran from St Petersburg.

Bold, ambitious expansion in the nineteenth century and a lack of investment, as well as heavy use in the First World War, had left the railway industry across the world in a very difficult position. The difficulties were greatly exacerbated by interwar economic problems. The context was easier in the 1920s than the 1930s, as the former were more prosperous, and credit, both domestic and international, easier to obtain. Not least owing to deflationary policies, investment, notably international, was far harder to secure in the 1930s. Nevertheless, a focus on the Depression can obscure the many earlier difficulties in the interwar period, some of which dated from prior to the Great War. Indeed, the Depression hit hard in part due to this highly problematic legacy, and the problems of the 1920s repay consideration, especially as many were to recur after the Second World War. Problems were seen in the areas where rail was already well-established and also in areas of recent and current expansion. Thus, in 1917, when the line from Djibouti reached Addis Ababa, it stopped, whereas it had been planned earlier to extend the railway to the Didessa River near Jimma in order to allow the railway to move coffee from the major producing areas.

In areas where rail was well-established, under-investment, over-capacity, and a massive wages bill were major interwar issues, requiring short- and longer-term solutions. So also with economic transformation: the newer consumer industries tended to have lower freight needs, many of which were met by road transport. Whereas access to rail needed special facilities – passenger stations, freight sidings, marshalling yards – road transport was different. One can access a road at any point. The vehicles were far less expensive to purchase and maintain, the majority were owned by individuals, and they did not require comparable training in their use.

Owing to regulations, rail companies were frequently, as in Britain, not allowed to become road hauliers other than at their railheads. Inexpensive lorries and petrol, and no need to pay for road construction or maintenance, provided the road hauliers with major advantages. They could set their own prices and wages, and were not obliged to be common carriers, which could entail unprofitable loads for rail companies. Separately, lorries could readily move materials from warehouses, which proved more efficient than marshalling yards many of which had legacy problems including cramped sites and unionised workforces. Road freight warehousing required less space. Buses offered a flexibility that trains generally lacked, not least with special services and the resulting ability to tap potential demand. As a result, the trains had to share excursion business.

In Britain, the war had seen national wage bargaining for rail workers rather than at the level of individual employers. This situation continued postwar, as did the implications of a rise in union membership from 43 to 60 per cent of railway employees. The wartime situation was consolidated as a result of the 1919 national rail strike in response to the government attempt to cut pay rates, which had risen greatly during the war. Finding himself cut off in Balmoral in Scotland from all London letters and newspapers, George V felt his royal office drifting out of control, and he returned to the capital by car.

The strike, and the subsequent Railways Act of 1921, led to full union recognition, a new wages board, and an eight-hour day. Helped by the strength of the National Union of Railwaymen founded in 1913 and the wartime acceleration of the development of railway trade unionism, the railwaymen had done better than the miners would when faced with significant wage cuts in 1921. On the other hand, fares rose, while in 1919, without resorting to repression, the government showed an ability to cope with the strike. Emerging road transport ensured food deliveries, and aircraft, both military and civil, provided capacity, while volunteers from the public helped keep transport moving. However, there was still a need to face immediate problems as Sir Eric Geddes, the Minister of Transport, pointed out in a Cabinet memorandum of March 1921:

> The Coal Strike, the disturbances in Ireland, and more recently the sudden and sharp depression in trade have exercised a disastrous effect on Railway Revenue and the hopes of financial equilibrium have not been realised... In order to secure the permanent financial stability of Railway Companies, a consolidation of railway interests is essential.

In 1918, there had been government consideration of nationalisation, and although that did not happen, the Railway Act of 1921 ensured large-scale reorganisation, such that in 1923, when the railways were returned to their private owners, they were grouped into four large companies, a radical change from the pre-war situation. Originally, there had been proposals for five or six companies for England and Wales and one, later two, for Scotland; but there was opposition in Parliament to a separate system for Scotland. Geddes had supported this separation as he did not see why Scottish railways should be cross-subsidised by English customers. The four companies competed.

In place of a range of earlier regulations, a Rates Tribunal established a target return on capital in what was now a highly regulated industry, which took away flexibility and made it very difficult to stem the speedy loss of freight to the road. As a result, railway companies pressed for the revision of the regulatory framework.

In Agatha Christie's *The Secret Adversary* (1922), a meeting of agitators reveals links with the unions, notably the miners and the railwaymen. The General Strike of 1926 saw the railways again a centre of union opposition, whereas road freight was more flexible. Moreover, despite cuts in services, the reorganisation of 1923 had not produced massive cost savings, nor the necessary investment, for example in large railway wagons able to carry 20 tons of coal. Yet, there was significant change, especially mechanised marshalling yards, such as Whitemoor near March. Opened in 1929 on the site of an old yard, this had Frohlich hydraulic brakes, the first time they had been used in Britain. Whereas the previous yard had 24 sidings and could take 1,265 wagons at any one moment, such that about 3,000 could be handled daily, the replacement had 43 sidings and room for 4,000 wagons at once, and by 1939, 8,000 wagons were sorted each day. The down yard, added in 1933, was closed in 1972. After 1982, there was scant use of Whitemoor.

An attempt was made in the interwar period to assert modernity in Britain as elsewhere. London and North Eastern Railway from 1929, for all its publicity, used Gill Sans lettering, which was created by Eric Gill in 1926 and released in 1928. Much building on the rail network used modern architectural techniques, for example Surbiton station and Southern Region 'glasshouse'-style signal boxes. Originally built in 1838, Surbiton station was totally rebuilt in 1937 in art deco style by James Robb Scott, the Chief Architect of the Southern Railway. Earlier, he had played a major role in the reconstruction of Waterloo Station between 1909 and 1903, not least of the main entrance and war memorial referred to as the Victory Arch. Other stations Scott was responsible for included Ramsgate, Exmouth,

Wimbledon, Hastings, Richmond, Horsham, and Chessington North. At Hastings, as at Surbiton, Scott used new island platforms. The station was in a neo-Georgian style that was replaced in 2004. Opened in 1939, Chessington North, Scott's last work, was built, in contrast, in an art deco style.

There was a lot of streamlining in train design in the interwar period, which reflected both functional criteria and also stylistic demand. Streamlining involved international co-operation and emulation, both always significant in train design. Thus, three French 'Atlantics' were purchased for the Great Western, while Nigel Gresley of the LNER learned internal streamlining from the French engineer, André Chapelon, a master of scientific method, proponent of efficiency, and a key figure of what was to be called modern steam. Gresley drew for the wedge-shaped front of the streamlined A4 locomotives on the designs of his friend, the Italian racing-car builder, Ettore Bugatti.

Stylistic demand involved a modernist rejection of the legacy of rail, which was often, at this point, Gothic in character or suggestive of it, sometimes exhibiting the flamboyance of Gothic castellation, pinnacles, and other features. Streamlining was particularly important to the new aesthetic, but it had practical applications. Functionalism was a central requirement. So, also, with the skilful advertising campaigns of the period and their use of brilliant posters highlighting the railways as the gateway to gorgeous holiday destinations.

Across the world, domestic politics were intertwined with rail. The contest between rail and road, coal and oil, was one that was significant for trade unions, which were far stronger in the former, and also significant for the nature of the economy. The contest featured in struggles by, and within, the political Left, as in France. There, in 1920, against the background of large-scale strikes, notably in the railways, the Socialist Party divided, part becoming a Communist Party. In 1937, the left-wing Popular Front government nationalised the railways. They have not subsequently been privatised in France, though in 2020 the SNCF became a private company with public capital and was obliged to open the rail market to other companies. De-nationalisation was a relatively rare occurrence, although it has been seen, notably in Britain in 1993-7. There has also been privatisation to some degree in Australia, Canada, Greece, Japan, New Zealand and Sweden, and there have been moves elsewhere, including in Egypt and India. In Argentina, privatisation was reversed in 2015. EU competition policies have led to pressure for the end of national monopolies over services.

The strategic sensitivity of rail was shown in America in War Plan White, a plan drawn up in 1919-20 by the War Plans Division of the War Department General Staff to deal with an insurrection. Focused on a supposed Communist threat, the planners focussed on control of the railways, which was seen as central to any insurrection. There was anxiety about the risk that they would be seized or sabotaged. This encouraged planning to move emergency supplies.

In Italy, where road usage was less significant than in America or Britain, the system was nationalised in 1905-6. Rail played a major role in the disorder and instability of 1919-22. In 1920, the year of a major rail strike, there was specific action to prevent troops from intervening against insurgents in Ancona, while in 1921-3 there was frequent firing on, and from, trains. In November 1921, Fascists fired at rail workers in the San Lorenzo neighbourhood in Rome, which was close to the main railway station and where many rail workers lived. An engine driver was killed, leading to strikes. There was more violence there in 1922. That year, Benito Mussolini 'marched' on Rome to seize power, in fact taking the night sleeper from Milan. Cheering

Fascist blackshirts applauded Mussolini at the stations he passed through. Many of the 'marchers' also took trains there and back, including one commandeered at Bologna.

One of the more famous achievements claimed by and for Mussolini, the Fascist dictator of Italy from 1922 to 1943, involved electrification, in which, encouraged by only limited coal availability for steam trains, Italy was far advanced: it was the first by mileage in Europe and the second in the world after America, which provided Italy with both technical and financial assistance. Lenin was also a supporter of electricity. By the early 1930s, after two decades of work, most of the trains in northern Italy were electric-powered. Prior to that, the Italians, who lacked coal, were dependent on imports which largely came by sea, a route dominated by Britain. Mussolini's achievement bruited so memorably by Miss Jean Brodie was in part a matter of claiming credit for a rail improvement programme that was already in progress, with the building of dramatic new central stations, and it was also due to breaking the relevant unions. Police were put on trains and the railway workers' union was abolished. In practice, the big Italian expresses tended to run on time, but local trains and the low-cost weekend excursion trains designed to keep the working class happy were not so punctual. This is more generally true of rail services, and reflects prioritisation in investment, equipment, maintenance, signalling, and timetables.

Under Mussolini, the development of Milan as a railway hub was completed, and there were new lines between Rome and Naples and between Bologna and Florence. After eleven years, the latter opened in 1934 and included the 18.5-kilometre Apennine Base Tunnel. Ninety-seven workers died during the construction of the line. The route was cut from 131 to 97 kilometres, with a lesser gradient and a new maximum speed of 180 kilometres per hour compared to the previous 75. Trains speeds of over 200 kilometres an hour were achieved.

The new state of Yugoslavia brought together the kingdom of Serbia, Montenegro and the State of Slovenes, Croats and Serbs, the southernmost part of the Austro-Hungarian empire, and the National Railways of the Kingdom of the Serbs, Croats and Slovenes was the result. It was renamed Yugoslav State Railways in 1929. It was damaged and divided by the Axis conquest of Yugoslavia in 1941 with a partition that included an independent Croatia and zones controlled by Germany, Italy, Hungary and Bulgaria, although the Italian zone was taken over by Germany in 1943.

Czechoslovakia, Lithuania, Latvia and Estonia were other new states after the First World War, with new state railways accordingly, such as Czechoslovak State Railways founded in 1918. Austria and Hungary were separated, and lost territory. Thus, whereas Trieste had been the major Adriatic port for Austria and was served accordingly by rail, it was part of Italy after the war. Similarly, Romania had gained Transylvania from Hungary. Lithuania, which became independent from Russia, took Klaipéda (Memel) in 1923 from the semi-autonomous status it had held since detached from Germany in 1920. Its railway system was then linked to Klaipéda, the most northerly of the ice-free ports on the eastern shore of the Baltic. Separately, Lithuania saw the development of its network, particularly in the rural areas that backed the authoritarian, conservative, pro-Catholic regime of Antanas Smetona, who governed from 1926 until 1940.

Poland's modern railways were only fixed in 1945, as part of the postwar settlement. When previously independent in 1918-39, having emerged from the defeated Austrian, German and Russian empires, Poland had sought to adapt to its new identity (earlier independence had ended with partition in 1795) and to new borders. These were not designed with the logistics of transportation under consideration. The managerial difficulties were acute. In 1918-19, Poland inherited three different rail systems and the inclusion of part of what had been Russia meant two different gauges. That helped the *Wehrmacht*: in 1939, they seized Polish wide gauge rolling stock that proved useful during their invasion of the Soviet Union in 1941.

In Poland, as with many countries, notably in Eastern Europe and after 1945 in areas previously ruled by empires, the legacy that had been dictated by earlier powers had to be adapted for new needs, although, in each case, it would be mistaken to think that decisions were uniformly agreed and free from contention. Indeed, a post-imperial railway 'new age' of clear requirements involved a measure of rhetoric. In the case of Poland, there were new boundaries and different economic priorities. Thus, for the German Empire, the railways in Silesia were designed to help the economic development of this industrial region. This continued to be a priority during the twentieth century, including when Silesia became part of Poland from 1945. However, the context fundamentally altered as Silesian economic activity was then directed within Poland. Postwar, nearly all of the 4.5 million Silesians of German descent fled or were interned in camps and expelled.

The Poles had adapted from 1918 with new lines and locomotives that from 1923 were made in Poland. From 1927, there was also some electrification, and in 1936 the first electric line was completed. As with railways elsewhere, the Depression of the 1930s hit profits and investment, and in Poland the railways remained in serious difficulties until 1937. Whereas the 1920s had seen some new lines, there was far less new construction in the 1930s.

Politics of course dominated all rail decisions in wartime. Thus, in the Mexican Revolution of 1910-17, the Carranza faction came to a commanding position in 1916 in large part thanks to the control of the cities and the rail system. Damage and neglect hit the railways hard, and they were nationalised from 1929 (partially then), with a workers' administration put in charge in 1938. This involved a particular political position, notably bringing to fruition the partial government control seen earlier, especially under Porfirio Díaz, President for most of the period from 1876 to 1911, and the strengthening of opposition to foreign ownership. Article 27 of the 1917 constitution decreed the need to address social utility and national benefit when considering the use of private property. There was more general socialism in Mexico in the 1920s, not least pressure on the oil companies and on major landowners. Such policies were pushed even more firmly from 1934 when Lázaro Cárdenas became President, allying with the unions. Rail and oil nationalisation, both in 1938, were pressed hard alongside land reform, with British interests suffering from both types of nationalisation. Such nationalisation was increasingly common in the early twentieth century and adversely affected the opportunity to secure private investment.

In the Russian Civil War (1917-21), the difficulty of sustaining military operations, not least due to the logistical pressures if units remained static, had encouraged the emphasis on advances and hence the significance of the railways. Key junction cities, such as Moscow and, in Russian Central Asia, Tashkent, provided interior lines and the ability to move troops to areas of opportunity and need. The industrial centres, where Bolshevik Communist support was greatest, were also the hubs of the transport system. A British General Staff report of 1919 saw the Bolsheviks as able in a very fluid conflict 'to concentrate at will' against individual opposing armies. For example, the White advance under Nikolai Iudenich on Petrograd (St Petersburg) was thwarted in large part because the failure to cut the railway from Moscow enabled the Bolsheviks to bring up large numbers of troops – as well as Leon Trotsky, who proved an effective commander. At the tactical level, armed trains were a form of mobile artillery, notably so for Russia and its opponent Estonia. These trains combined firepower with the rapid movement of troops, thus offering a form of manoeuvre warfare and potential at the tactical and operational levels.

In China, the 1911 revolution owed much of its origins to opposition to the nationalisation for sale to foreign creditors of locally controlled railways. Local investors organised the Railway Protection League in Sichuan in June, and the government's attempts to suppress protests in September led to violence in the city of Chengdu. The situation escalated with an uprising in Wuhan in October and the rapid fall of the government, with the Chinese Republic established in January 1912. Sun Yat-Sen, the republican leader, argued in *Jianguo Fanglue*, his work on nation-building, for 100,000 miles of railway. Earlier, as General Manager of the China Railway Corporation from 1912, the totally inexperienced Sun supported the development of railways, proposing 78,000 miles of new lines. Little was achieved during the warlord era of the early 1920s however, and nothing by Sun, but even had the country been peaceful, there were no funds or revenues for this purpose and Sun's ideas of raising foreign capital, to which end he visited Japan, were unrealistic.

The role of the railways in China was enhanced by the scarcity of oil for vehicles. In the 1920s, although very limited in mileage, a partial national rail system existed as a result of expansion in the late 1920s and 1930s: 3,600 kilometres (2,237 miles) in 1928-37, and 900 (559) in the autonomous region of Manchuria from 1928 until 1931. Radical disruption stemmed from the outbreak of full-scale war with Japan in 1937. This conflict affected the rail plans of the Chinese government, notably the construction of lines from Shanghai to Hangzhou and Ningbo, and that from Chongqing to Chengdu. The financing of these lines was by the Shanghai-based China Development Finance Corporation established in 1934, and the British and Chinese Corporation, which was a British company. In the war, as earlier in Manchuria in 1931-2, Japanese forces advanced along rail links. An abrupt demonstration of the impact of war was the destruction in November 1937 of the Qiantang River Bridge at Hangzhou, which had only been finished two months earlier, the work of the British company Dorman Long which was also responsible for Sydney Harbour Bridge.

Conversely, there were grave difficulties for operations when railways were not present, a British officer reporting in 1933 from the Bolivian side of its Chaco War of 1932-5 with Paraguay, noted: 'Bolivia suffers a separation of 1,000 miles between her forces and her main base at the capital, of which only 500 miles are covered by rail. Over the remaining distance runs a narrow and broken road ... thick with dust in the winter and often washed away in summer.'

Where railways were present, they were vulnerable. Trains as well as track could be sabotaged far more effectively than comparable road capacity. There was extensive damage to the Irish rail system during the insurrectionary campaign of 1919-21 against union with Britain. A general strike by railwaymen refusing to carry British soldiers complicated life for the Irish rail companies Subsequently, damage continued during the civil war in newly independent Ireland. In December 1922, the government of the new Irish Free State executed four railway workers and three labourers who were part of an anti-Treaty IRA column attacking trains in County Kildare, derailing engines by obstructing the line and looting goods trains. These methods were to be important to insurgencies, because of what could be specifically achieved but also in order to create an impression that the government was not in control.

Yet, despite the disruptions of conflict, as well as competition from road vehicles, including the expansion of freight travel by truck, rail remained very important for passenger travel and freight in many countries, and in most where it was already established. It was especially significant for the bulk movement of goods. Thus, oil exploitation in the Soviet Union and America saw the expansion of railways, for example in north-west Texas, although ironically, that oil greatly helped the competition provided by road travel in the US.

Air freight could not yet compete. The fascination with road and, even more, air of these years can lead to a tendency to underplay the extent to which rail remained crucial as a mature industry that represented a considerable capital investment in the form of loans, pensions, property portfolios, and skill sets. The capital investment was a matter not only of locomotives, rolling stock, track, bridges, tunnels and stations, and human capital in the shape of expertise, training and pensions, but also of the organisation of relevant urban infrastructure such as street patterns. Accumulated economic integration was more the case for rail than with other freight systems.

However, in many countries, a lack of investment meant ageing locomotives, rolling stock and track, a poor basis for competition with road traffic that offered increased relative speed, frequency and efficiency. Rail remained important in the sugar plantations of the Dominican Republic, for example, but the government lacked a commensurate commitment.

An approach to rail in the interwar period centred on the competition between rail, road and air is in danger of providing a technologically driven account of change through development at the expense of other factors. In practice, politics came first, both domestically, as with regulation, and internationally. The broader politics of rail varied greatly by country, in part as a consequence of the commitments bound up in existing infrastructure, economic interests and trade union power. All of these interacted with ownership, liquidity, and profitability. These factors and pressures were aspects of the rail industry from the outset, but in the interwar period, the advantages of road affected them all profoundly. The 1930s, in general, proved difficult. In Spain, there was growth and modernisation in the 1920s, but in the 1930s recession, insolvency, and a lack of new construction and locomotives. The competition of road freight was therefore even stronger: by 1933, Madrid received 64 per cent of its fish by lorry, compared to 4.5 per cent for Paris. Now the fish arrives by air. In 1936-9, the situation was transformed with the railways hit hard by civil war.

The Glenn Miller big band number *Chattanooga Choo Choo* (1941) did not provide much of a clue to the myriad difficulties of American rail. In contrast, written ten years earlier, there was 'Brother, can you spare a dime?'

> Once I built a railroad, I made it run
> Made it race against time
> Once I built a railroad, now it's done
> Brother can you spare a dime?

The lament was written by lyricist E. Y. 'Yip' Harburg and part of the 1932 musical *New Americana*, which was number 1 in popularity that year.

The railway expansion of the late nineteenth century in America had proved difficult to sustain in the face of an upsurge in anti-trust pressure and federal intervention from the 1900s.

The latter began with railway charges but extended to labour conditions. In 1916, the Adamson Act, the first federal law regulating the hours of workers in private companies, was passed in order to avoid a nationwide strike. It established an eight-hour day for interstate railway workers with overtime pay for more work. In 1917, the Supreme Court upheld the constitutionality of the Act.

In December 1917, under the Army Appropriations Act of 1916, the railways were nationalised as a wartime measure and placed under the United States Railroad Administration, which retained control until March 1920. The railways were organised into three divisions (East, West and South), duplicate passenger services were reduced, priority given to freight, and standardised locomotives ordered. After the return to peacetime conditions, by the Transportation Act of 1920, a greater degree of control of railways survived in the shape of the Interstate Commerce Commission. Government and law had moved from serving the interests of railways to regulating them, but not really in the interests of workers.

A higher cut in wages paid to maintenance and repair workers provoked the Great Railroad Strike of 1922, a nationwide strike launched by many (but not all) of the railway labour organisations, in total about 400,000 workers. In response, the companies hired strike-breakers, replacement workers who were protected by private guards. Opening fire on strikers led to deaths, and there was also violence and sabotage by strikers. US Marshals and National Guard units helped the companies who rejected compromise and they were backed by the courts, leading to the end of the strike.

At the same time, there were the other classic inequities of American society. African American railway workers were poorly treated, given the low-paying jobs, excluded from unions, and expected to behave with servility. In the 1920s, while white stewards working in Pullman cars had sleeping berths, African American dining-car men were expected to sleep on dining car tables. Like the porters, they at least were partly visible, unlike the African Americans who put in hard work in building and maintaining the system.

State regulation was presented as a way to ensure that a public service acted accordingly, in the interests of the public, even though privately owned. The central problem with this approach was that of ensuring sufficient investment. The period had seen the culmination of earlier plans, including finishing in 1919 a rail link from San Diego to the east to connect with the transcontinental lines of the Southern Pacific. Construction of the 146-mile line had begun in 1907, but had been delayed by disorder in Mexico, construction problems, and the impact of the First World War, which increased the cost of railway construction in part owing to the shortage of material. Whereas the estimated cost was $6 million, the San Diego and Arizona Railway cost $18 million. Once complete, the line was hit by landslides in 1932, rainstorms in 1926, 1927 and 1929, fires in 1932, and disputes with Mexico, across 44 miles of which the line ran. In 1932, the founder's heirs sold their share to the Southern Pacific. Yet again, system extension did not equate with profitability – but there was still expansion to meet particular opportunities.

Freight movements ensured that American (and non-American) rail companies generally did well in the 1910s and 1920s, only to be hit hard by the Depression of the 1930s. The importance of rail for passengers was shown by the spread of the 1918 flu epidemic along rail links. Technological innovations included in 1925 the first commercially successful diesel-electric locomotive to enter service, as well as the first modern 'Super Power' steam locomotive. A key organisational innovation in 1927 was the American Centralized Traffic Control System, which helped ensure safe running. It was installed on a forty-mile stretch of the New York Central Railroad and enabled the train dispatcher to control train movements directly rather than relying on local operators.

The Depression hit railway companies not only with greatly reduced freight and passenger business, but also because of the scarce availability and high cost of credit. Smaller companies found it difficult to manage their debt, which meant that they could be taken over. Railway income fell from a profit of $977 million in 1929 to a loss of $122 million in 1932. There were deficits anew in 1933, 1934 and 1938. This fall led to a major decline in maintenance, railway employment (by 42 per cent), and locomotive sales, the last therefore driving up the unit costs of new purchases and ensuring the obsolescence of existing locomotives as the older ones were not replaced. The manufacturing base was hit hard. There was an attempt to cope by pushing up freight charges in 1931, but this resulted in business moving to road.

As a result of the highly leveraged nature of most companies, by 1938 about a third of all railway mileage was in bankruptcy. In 1915, the Missouri Pacific had declared bankruptcy, and it did so again in 1933, entering into a trusteeship that lasted until 1956. The larger companies had more access to outside finance and financially sound companies continued maintenance, whereas those in difficulty saw their system decline. This encouraged the consolidation of the industry with larger companies taking over the smaller.

The Depression brought earlier issues to a head, notably the spread of car use in America. In 1929, the railways provided far fewer passenger miles than cars did, although the situation was less bleak for freight. With one in five American households having cars, it was not surprising that a number of prominent companies, such as the Rock Island (1933), Chicago and North Western (1935), Milwaukee Road (1935), New York, New Haven and Hartford (1935), and Erie (1938), all went bankrupt. Whereas, in 1916, the American rail industry had handled a billion passenger journeys, there was only 700 million by 1930, and that would fall another 36 per cent in the 1930s.

Yet, there was also improvement in the 1930s, notably significant initiatives in existing services. In 1931, mechanical systems of air-conditioning were first applied to an entire train, on the New York-Washington service. Elsewhere, forced ventilation systems were generally found adequate.

Shot welding was developed in the 1930s to join stainless steel. Shot welding replaced the use of riveting and greatly speeded up production. This was an application to railways of the use of all-steel automobile bodies, developed by the Philadelphia-based Budd Company. The company's stainless steel streamlined rolling stock were known as silverliners, and began with the diesel-powered *Pioneer Zephyr* of 1934, built for the Chicago, Burlington and Quincy Railroad. The *Pioneer Zephyr* set a speed record for travel between Denver and Chicago and was the inspiration for the film *The Silver Streak* (1934), which used the original train for the external shots. A heroic emergency journey sees the train rush seven iron lungs to the Boulder Dam where there is an outbreak of polio. The drama includes a fugitive wanted for attempted murder. This was one of the more dramatic train films of the interwar period.

The *General Pershing Zephyr*, constructed in 1939, was the first passenger train to have fitted disc brakes. This was an application of car technology. Streamlined trains suggested modernity, and there was an attempt to provide more appeal for long-distance passengers, not least with the introduction of truly impressive streamliner services. New Deal loans led to the electrification of the Pennsylvania Railway's track between New York City and Washington, as private funds proved unavailable.

The mileage of American railways that were owned (not all were operated) fell from 249,052 in 1930 to 234,398 in 1940, a fall considerably greater (5 per cent) than in the 1920s (1 per cent). At the same time, there was flexibility: as an enticement to marry in Las Vegas, there was a license bureau in the train station. Rail continued to be an important part of America's image of itself. 'Portrait of America 1939', a double-page illustration in the 'America's Future' issue of *Life* magazine on 5 June, pictured a train headed west. Alongside cars and aircraft, trains continue to play a major role in interwar American films, not least those of Buster Keaton, such as *One Week* (1920), in which his newly built house, stuck on a train crossing, is destroyed by a train, and *The General* (1926), in which he saves a train hurtling toward destruction.

The developments in America were impressive but could not fundamentally change the economics of rail. They improved following the recovery from the Depression and because of the demands of the war, which America joined in 1941 but began to mobilise for in 1940. Engines became more powerful, with the Union Pacific 9000 Class, built between 1926 and 1930, followed by the introduction in 1941-4 of the Union Pacific Big Boy, which weighed more than 600 US tons and was able to produce 5,500-6,290 horsepower. These engines could pull loads over the mountains from the key junction of Ogden to Wyoming.

The density of American railways was not matched in other large countries, but there was a degree of 'catch-up', as in Canada, where engineering, investment and more powerful locomotives were all enablers for entrepreneurial ambitions. The emphasis on transcontinental railways did not capture the economic centre of gravity for many Canadian customers, both passenger and freight, a centre of gravity that focused on eastern Canada and the routes to the US.

As in America, earlier, often speculative development had been brought to a crisis due to wartime controls and postwar financial issues, which led to the establishment by the government in 1919 of Canadian National Railways, a catch-all for companies in difficulties. This became the major competition for the Canadian Pacific Railway but suffered from the difficulty of cutting uneconomic services due to its public ownership and the resulting public service commitment, a point more generally valid across the world. Despite these difficulties, there was significant progress in the interwar period in Canadian railways, improvement of the existing system and its extension.

The Australian economy was badly hit by the Depression of the 1930s. Crises elsewhere meant a fall in demand for Australian exports, a process accentuated by a rise in global protectionism. As a result, the profitability of Australian rail declined. Though there was no abandonment of rail freight, not least because there was no significant domestic production of oil, and Australia had coal for steam trains. Despite the issues posed by different gauges, the rail system was seen as an economic necessity and a strategic reserve.

The same was true of India, where the very large and impressive Indian Railway Staff College inaugurated at Dehradun in 1930 might seem an appropriate episode for this chapter. However, the choice of examples has to be handled with care, as retrenchment led to its closure in 1931. In India, the combination of the Depression with road competition led to the increasing lack of profitability and creditworthiness of the railways. The state-owned Burma Railways became Burma's largest debt item. Plans for a line from Rangoon in Burma to Yunnan in China could not be pursued, although such a plan was not viable in any case.

Similarly, although the French pressed on with the line in Vietnam from the Chinese border via Hanoi to Saigon, approved in 1897 and finished in 1936, the lines in French Indochina (Laos, Cambodia, Vietnam) that were described at the time as projected, were far from being realized. These included lines to link a planned Cambodian railway to Saigon and to Thailand, as well as a line parallel to the coastal one but further inland, from Saigon northwards in Vietnam and Cambodia. With the exception of the 4.3-mile portage railway built in 1893 to deal with rapids on the Mekong River, there were no lines in the French colony of Laos, although after 1945 there was briefly a project for lines to its capital, Vientiane. In 1954, independence from France meant separate networks in Indochina. In the event, Vientiane only gained a rail link in 2021, and then on the Laos section of the Kunming-Singapore railway.

This discussion reminds us that America and Europe did not define the experience of rail. While that point is self-evident, a focus on states with a leading system does reveal the significance of differing systems of governmental control and regulation and of contrasting public ideologies. Politics was to the fore in the determination of governments to develop rail systems, and notably so with authoritarian systems where there was not a comparable emphasis on road transport. This was the case with the Soviet Union and its Communist ethos of heavy industry, which was intended to contribute to the dictatorship of the proletariat, among whom the rail workers were regarded as a key element. In June 1918, Lenin, who had arrived in St Petersburg from exile in 1917 by train, wrote a draft decision for the Council of People's Commissars on the need to rehabilitate rail transport and keep the industry Soviet. Rail was to be used by the Communists to spread the message by means of special propaganda trains.

The Russian Civil War greatly diminished rail use, but by 1926 usage had passed the level of 1913. The length of the network rose from 81,000 km in 1917 to 106,100 in 1940 and in that period the amount of freight allegedly increased fourfold, although all Soviet figures are open to debate as there was a tendency to exaggerate achievements. There were certainly aspirations, including classes of powerful locomotives – the *Joseph Stalin*, manufactured from 1932 to 1942, of which 649 were built, and the *Felix Dzerzhinsky*, built from 1931 (mass production from 1932), of which 3,213 were built – as well as stronger track thanks to heavier rails and better ballast, heavy rolling stock, automatic brakes and coupling, and better signalling. The importance of rail was shown by Stalin's close associate Lazar Kaganovich being People's Commissar for Transport in 1935-7 and 1938-42. So with his predecessor Andrey Andreyev, who having earlier been important in the political departments of the railway, held the post in 1931-5. The AA20 was a one-off locomotive named after him. In true Soviet style, it set out for superlatives, having the largest number of coupled axles on a locomotive (14), and being the longest rigid frame locomotive in Europe. It proved, however, to be too heavy, too large for turntables and subject to derailments. As a result, it was withdrawn from service. Alexey Bakulin, who held the post in 1937-8, was executed in 1939, as was Moisey Rukhimovich the year before, the holder of the post in 1930-1.

In 1926, construction began on a line linking the 'Magnetic Mountain,' the iron-ore mountain that was to become the gigantic steel city of Magnitogorsk, to the rail system through a junction of Kartaly, 145 kilometres away. Steel production there depended on movement of coking coal nearly 2,000 kilometres from the Kuznetsk basin of western Siberia. The two were linked as the Ural-Kuznetsk Combine. Only 40 kilometres of track were constructed by the end of 1928. In 1929, the work was renewed and completed with military assistance, but the track was put down without ballast and due to repeated accidents a speed limit of 10 km/h was imposed. As a result of the poor state of the line, there were major problems with capacity. Rail transport on the site faced significant difficulties, with the resulting bottlenecks hitting production. Much of the rolling stock there in the mid-1930s was inoperative, there was a severe shortage of rails and ties, recently repaired locomotives required repairs almost immediately, and in 1936 it could take as long as two weeks for freight to pass from one shop to another. Quantity claimed proved no guidance to quality of output. Yet, however wasteful, there was output.

A major new line, planned under the old order but built largely between 1927 and 1930, was the Turkestan-Siberia railway, linking Central Asia to the Trans-Siberian Railway and bringing to fruition an idea expressed from the late 1880s onward.

Force played a major role in the development of the Soviet rail system. Felix Dzerzhinsky ran the brutal secret police from 1917 and also, from 1923, was the founding Chairman of the Transport Commissariat. A major class of steam locomotive, built from 1931 to 1942, was named after him. Peasants were moved to perform forced labour. *Gulags* proved a major source of manpower. This was especially the case with the useless Salekhard-Igarka Railway that was worked on from 1947 until 1953 as part of Stalin's plan for a line across northern Siberia.

The general tendency across the world in the 1930s was for increased state control. The impact of the Depression on the private sector was significant in this, besides political ideology. For example, the Dutch General Staff sought in the nineteenth and early twentieth centuries to influence the construction of railways, which it considered of military importance, but with scant result. Rail nationalism as a phenomenon relating to military matters did not really exist in the Netherlands. At most, there was fear about German rail construction that seemed aimed at facilitating attacks on Dutch territory. The recent example of nationalisation in France was an encouragement. On 1 January 1938, 99 years after the first Dutch rail company was founded, the two rail companies that still existed merged into NS (*Nederlandse Spoorwegen*, Dutch railways). All stocks were state-owned. This decision for unification and more state control was made as a result of experiences during the First World War, when mobilisation had made it clear that a more centralised structure would have been much more efficient. In the case for more efficiency, Germany was an important example.

There was of course a major contrast between the Soviet Union, with its focus on rail, and the United States, where state regulation without financial support contrasted markedly with the public subsidies provided to roads and airports. The common element, however, was the extent to which the rail industry was affected by the political context, rather than being able to define the future in terms of technology and investing accordingly. In America and Europe, the ability of rail to provide a comprehensive service for freight and passengers had gone, never to return. In certain countries, the resulting financial problems for companies then appeared to bolster the case for nationalisation. Meanwhile, prior to the Second World War, there was not the detailed planning with railway timetables that featured before 1914. In Britain, there were talks between the government and the railway companies before 1939 about the finances of the companies in wartime, but there were no significant attempts to direct rail operations or capacity in the pre-war rearmament period. Yet the new world war was to place great pressure on rail systems, to hit the profitability, then and later, of companies, and to make state control more normative.

7

THE SECOND WORLD WAR

C56 31 was the first locomotive to run on the Thai-Burma Railway, the Death Railway. After the war it was brought back to Japan and restored. It is now displayed in the museum attached to the Shinto Yasukuni Shrine in Tokyo, dedicated to those who died in the service of Japan.

In its issue of 13 February 1942, the *Philadelphia Inquirer* included a train in its picture of an America fully committed to war production; and rightly so. Trains served America and other combatants in moving troops and equipment, and also in facilitating unprecedented rates of industrial production. Moreover, devastating German submarine attacks on American coastal shipping in 1942 further encouraged a reliance on rail, as they had already done for Britain. Rail dominated the land-choice of transport, although pipelines, river and canal barges, and road transport all played a significant role.

The development of air power posed a major threat to rail services during the war. There was a massive focus on air attacks on railways, bridges, stations, and rolling stock, with vast destruction. Rail facilities were difficult to disguise and protect. German air attacks on the British rail system were particularly acute in the winter of 1940-1, with major damage to stations in London and Liverpool. German aerial reconnaissance and other target-allocation made much of identifying rail facilities for bombing. As a result, repair work, often by night, was crucial to the continual running of services, much of this work conducted while in danger of renewed attack.

In turn, the Anglo-American Combined Bomber Offensive on Germany included an Allied attempt to destroy German rail infrastructure, and with it the articulation of the German economy, as the integration of manufacturing on many sites was required, for example, to build tanks. With limited oil supplies and the resulting reliance on coal, as well as having fewer trucks than Britain and America, the German war economy concentrated on train links, as did that of German-allied and German-occupied Europe.

Despite the limited precision of bombing by high-flying aircraft dropping 'dumb' or free-fall bombs, Allied strategic bombing was crucial to the disruption of German communications and logistics, largely because it was eventually done on such a massive scale, and because the targets could not be attacked by any other means. Damage, including 45 per cent of the French rail network that was under German control in 1940-4, was extensive enough to preclude effective repairs, which indicated the potential for increasing returns to scale in the air offensive.

The deadly Anglo-American air attack on Dresden in 1945 was principally launched because it was a rail hub behind Germany's Eastern Front. The British Joint Intelligence Committee had established stopping German troop movements to the Silesian Front as a 'high priority'. The Soviet Union had also sought this assistance. The night before the attacks, Colonel Harold Cook, an American prisoner held in the Friedrichstadt marshalling yard in Dresden, described 'miles of freight cars loaded with supplies supporting and transporting German logistics towards the east.'

Rail systems of course have far less flexibility than road, switching routes is much harder. They are also harder to repair, the raw materials are less readily available and costlier to supply. Crucial points proved particular targets for attack. This was true of bridges, for example over the Seine in 1944, all below Paris being destroyed. It was also true of marshalling yards, for example the German one at Hamm near the Ruhr industrial belt in 1943.

There was also considerable strafing of individual trains, which were larger and more vulnerable targets than individual lorries, because obviously they moved in a predictable fashion. Aircraft carrying cannon proved particularly effective. On 8 August 1945, between the two atomic bomb attacks, American fighters machine-gunned railway stations and trains in Kyushu, notably Chikushi and Araki stations. One of the trains approaching Chikushi station had 'bodies piled on top of bodies in the carriages that were awash in blood'. There were no real Japanese air defences by the summer of 1945.

There were, as in the First World War and the interwar period, armoured trains as well as trains mounting powerful guns. China, Italy, Japan, Germany, Poland and, in particular, the Soviet Union used armoured trains to provide firepower. The Slovak National Uprising against the Germans in 1944 made use of rapidly adapted armoured trains. Armoured trains were vulnerable to air attack, though some carried anti-aircraft guns. Others used tank turrets or other guns. The Soviets deployed trains mounting powerful guns at Sevastopol, keeping them protected in tunnels from which they moved forward in 1942 to fire at the besieging Germans. The British deployed twelve armoured trains in 1940 when fearful of invasion and the last one was only withdrawn from service in November 1944.

Its vulnerabilities ensured that the rail system was also prone to partisan attack in occupied areas, as in Denmark and France. In many cases Resistance activity proved more effective than bombing, not least because the attackers could call on assistance from rail workers, as in France, as depicted in the film *The Train* (1964), which was very loosely based on successful efforts to stop the movement of seized art from Paris in August 1944. The Polish Resistance claimed to have damaged 6,930 locomotives and 19,058 wagons, to have blown up 38 railway bridges, and to have delayed repairs to 803 locomotives.

These vulnerabilities forced a heavy burden of defence on the Germans and their allies. It included adding troops and firepower to trains, the latter making them armed rather than armoured trains. The protection of the train system, however, was difficult. Moreover, particularly when needing to check for explosives, this protection greatly slowed up the speed of rail movements, and therefore the efficiency of their usage. However, the movement of oil from Ploesti in Romania was maintained despite air and Resistance attacks.

In invading the Soviet Union in 1941, confronting its vast space compared to the more limited extent of earlier campaign theatres, the Germans found that the railway system in Poland and the western Soviet Union collapsed the first winter of the war, with serious consequences for their forces on the Eastern Front. An unusually cold winter ensured that the poorly winterised German locomotives were hit hard, notably with their piping damaged. The lack of heated repair sheds added to the difficulties. In consequence, serviceability rates were only about 20-40 per cent for several weeks.

In contrast, the Soviets were more experienced in the use of their railways. These were significant for the rapid, epic, and highly successful move of factories eastward in late 1941 away from the range of German land and air attack. Rail provided the means to bring forward supplies and material once manufactured. So also with foreign supplies. The limitations of the supply route across Iran ensured the need to rely on Western supplies landed at Archangel and, further west, Murmansk, from which rail links to Vologda took supplies to near the front. The Germans and their Finnish ally failed to cut the vulnerable rail link from Murmansk, in part because of a limit to Finnish determination and German resources for the task.

American supplies were to be moved forward along the Trans-Siberian Railway, having been transported across the north Pacific. The key route to reinforce Alaska was a new road, the Alaska Highway, built in 1942. In the event, the road was of scant consequence as the vast bulk of supplies for Alaska was moved by sea. The speed of construction, with the use of poor switchbacks and pontoon bridges, would not have been possible for rail, and road restoration was more successful in 1943 in dealing with permafrost thawing than would have been possible for rail.

The Soviets also addressed the need for new rail links. For example, the Germans had planned a road bridge across the Kerch Strait east of Crimea to serve German strategic interests in the Caucasus. It was never completed because the Red Army advanced back into Ukraine in 1944. Instead, the bridge sections stockpiled at Kerch enabled the Soviets to complete it as a railway bridge, which reflected their particular logistical needs and capabilities. From October 1944 to February 1945, the bridge supported the Soviet advance by providing a transport route into Crimea, until it broke up under the pressure of ice.

More generally, railways were required to carry larger, heavier and different loads than in campaigns a half-century earlier, for example, large numbers of tanks. Despite being under air attack, the Germans continued to be able to do so, as in late 1944 when tanks were moved from the Eastern to the Western Front, in preparation for launching the offensive that was to be known as the Battle of the Bulge.

In Italy, the railways remained effective in 1943-5 in spite of the huge Allied air raids against the Brenner Pass and the marshalling points, notably Rome and Bologna, which never suffered decisive delays. Repairs were rapidly effective. As elsewhere, the capacity of the railways and the rolling stock required was of concern to the advancing Allies. in 1943, the year in which Sicily was invaded, the Americans took the trouble to record the railways as double or single track, steam or electric, as narrow gauge or standard gauge.

As in the previous war, existing passenger rolling stock moved large numbers of troops. The process of mobilisation and deployment at the beginning of the war was followed by the use of trains in successive campaigns to move troops toward the fronts. They also played a role in withdrawals.

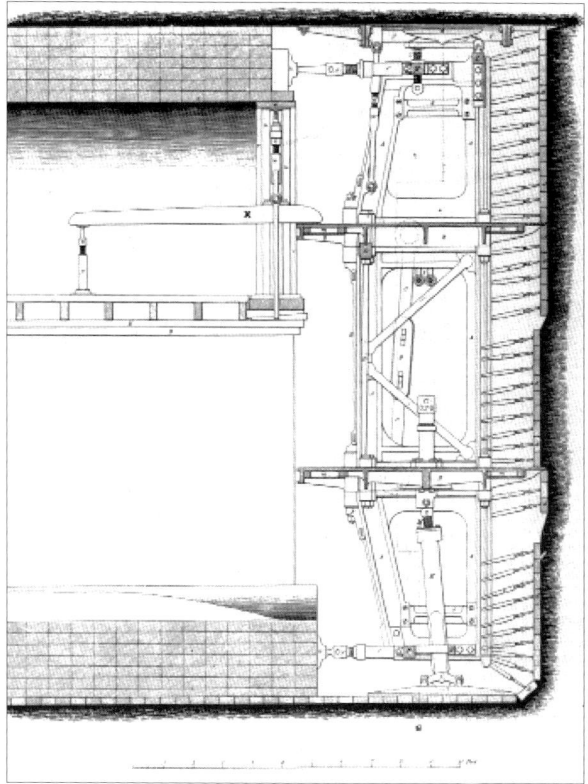

Right: Marc Brunel's tunneling shield was designed to drive a pedestrian tunnel through the clay and sand beneath the Thames, completed in 1843. The Thames Tunnel was converted to rail use in 1869 as part of the East London line.

Below: The working conditions inside a tunneling shield.

Above left: Herbert William Garratt served an apprenticeship with the North London Railway from 1879 to 1882 and later worked in Argentina, Lagos and Peru. His revolutionary design for articulated steam locomotives would be seen in Africa, South America, South East Asia and the Antipodes.

Above right: Financier, convict and blackmailer Charles Tyson Yerkes Jnr. played a role in developing mass transit not only in Chicago but also in London.

Above left: Japanese chief engineer Hasegawa Kinsuke oversaw the building of the Trunk Railway and is referred to as the father of Taiwanese railways – but his statue was removed in 1945 with the end of Japanese rule.

Above right: Édouard Percy Cranwill Girouard. Born in Montreal, the railway builder's reputation was so high that Kitchener personally requested his help in the daunting task of building the Sudan Military Railroad in 1896.

Military railroad operations in northern Virginia during the American Civil War, probably 1863 ...

... and some of the men who did the work.

Above and below: Elevated train at Greenwich Station, New York, *c.* 1885. The city, like any large conurbation by this time, was crowded, but unlike the problems faced by those going on a bear hunt, you can go over it and you can go under it. In October 1904 – despite the objections from the owners of the elevated railroad that was still running – the first New York City subway system opened to the general public at 5 cents per ride. The 9-mile line ran from City Hall to 145th Street and Broadway.

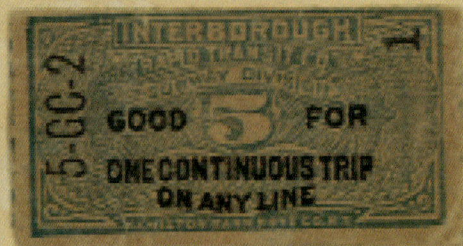

The train, as an enclosed but public space, has excited the imagination of crime writers from the outset. It has also been the location for several infamous real murders, as have stations.

From owning a single sailboat ferrying passengers across New York Harbor, Cornelius Vanderbilt went on to build the grandest personal fortune of the Gilded Age.

THE CURSE OF CALIFORNIA.

By 1901, when Edward H. Harriman acquired the Southern Pacific, the railroad had become known as 'the Octopus'. This 1882 cartoon from the *Wasp*, a San Francisco magazine, refers to its monopolistic grasp on farming, mining, and finance, and to the 1880 Mussel Slough Tragedy in which a dispute between homesteaders and the railroad resulted in seven deaths. The figures in the eyes of the creature are Leland Stanford (left) and Charles Crocker (right), two of the Southern Pacific's original controlling shareholders.

Right: Chicago, Burlington & Quincy EMD E5 No. 9911-A and the *Nebraska Zephyr* Budd-built streamliner crosses the Fox River at Oshkosh on 30 September 1993. The 1934 *Pioneer Zephyr* was the second internal combustion-powered streamliner built for mainline service in the US, and the first such train powered by a diesel engine. Shot welding, as developed and patented by the Budd Company, made the use of lightweight stainless steel in this way possible.

Below: A lot of work to be done, October 1935. Tanner Creek railroad viaduct complete, awaiting installation of the railroad tracks. Bonneville, Multnomah County, OR.

Left: Frank Julian Sprague, the father of electric traction. By 1890, more than a hundred electric railways using Sprague's equipment were being planned on several continents.

Below: A hybrid. Waiting at Wien Hauptbahnhof, Austria, 2018, this Class 187 locomotive is operated by RAILPOOL, a rail vehicle rental company, in whose livery it is seen. The Class 187 locomotives have a small diesel engine and can also run off the overhead wires.

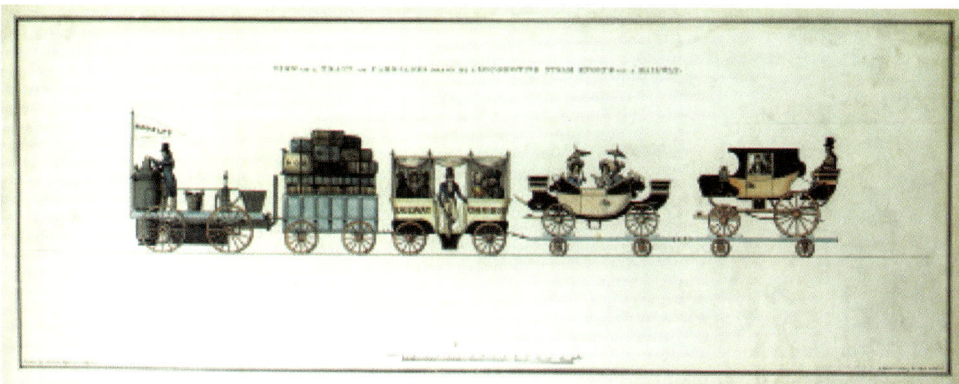

Let the train take the strain. This early lithograph from a painting by Charles Vignoles shows the locomotive *Novelty* pulling wagons that convey private carriages – the precursor of the Motorail era, *c.* 1830. It was pretty cheap in 1935 to 'Take Your Car by LNER'. (Artwork by Frank Newbold)

TAKE YOUR CAR
BY
L·N·E·R

WITH ONE FIRST OR
TWO THIRD CLASS TICKETS
THE RATES ARE

SINGLE JOURNEY 3d
RETURN JOURNEY:-
OUTWARD 3d
RETURN 1½d

PER MILE

Ask for particulars at L·N·E·R
Stations and Offices

LONDON & NORTH EASTERN RAILWAY

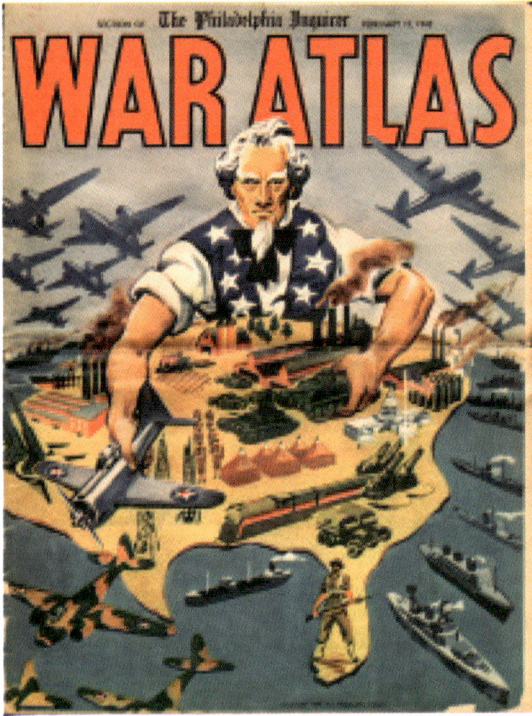

Uncle Sam doesn't forget the train as he tools up in the *Philadelphia Inquirer* War Atlas newspaper supplement, 13 February 1942.

Canadian National train 349 detours on Chicago & North Western's Adams line, passing under the venerable coaling tower at Clyman Junction for its trip west toward Superior, 13 April 1997.

Indian Railways Co-Co diesel-electric WDM2 No. 16264, based at Andal diesel shed, waits for departure time with a passenger train at Gorakhpur. 15 February 1994.

Co-Co diesel-electric double locomotive 2TE10L No. 1037, built at Lugansk (Voroshilovgrad) pictured at Kharkiv (Osnova) diesel depot, Ukraine, 11 June 1998. Between 1957 and 1961, a new, more powerful version of the TE3, the TEP 10, was developed for passenger duties. After 1961, work on the freight version of the new locomotive, the 2TE10L, was carried out at Lugansk.

Above: On the morning of 1 January 2001, in a temperature of around -40C, Datong works 1982-built QJ 3593 receives attention from the crew at Shuangyashan's servicing point. As the locomotive takes on water, the shed labourers break up the ice instantly forming around the servicing pits. Shuangyashan, 50 km east of Jiamusi, is a key railway hub for several deep coal mines in this extreme north-east tip of Heilongjiang Province, China.

Opposite top: Knottingley TMD was responsible for the day-to-day maintenance of locos working the heavy coal traffic between the Selby Coalfield and the power stations in the area east of Leeds. The depot is seen here crowded with locos on a Sunday in January 1991, with classes 08 and 56 visible. The Ferrybridge power station, which used vast amounts of coal, is in the background. Of the three original power houses, only one remains in use today – but now burns waste products and biomass.

Opposite bottom: 700mm gauge O&K 0-4-2 tank 4 (W/No.893 of 1901), by then the oldest working loco in Java, pauses between shunting duties at Merican mill's loading point on 12 August 2004, allowing traditional animal power to take priority. It was out of use by 2010, but steam continued in use at this Kediri region mill into the following year.

The southern portal of the Simplon tunnel near Iselle in Italy. From 1906 until 1982, this tunnel, between Brig, Switzerland and Domodossola in Italy, was the longest railway tunnel in the world. The two single-track tunnels were built nearly 15 years apart. The first to be opened was 19,803 m (64,970 ft) long; the second 19,824 m (65,039 ft). A treaty for its construction was signed in November 1895, which defined the border between the two countries as in the middle of the tunnel, allowing either country to block the tunnel in the event of war.

Since its construction, Tanggula Station, Tibet, has been the highest railway station in the world. Located 5,068 metres (16,627 ft) above sea level, this unstaffed station on the Qingzang railway opened on 1 July 2006. As of 2010, no passenger transport service was available since the region is uninhabited.

The Raurimu Spiral in the central North Island of New Zealand on the route between Auckland and Wellington. The terrain was simply too steep for a direct line. It looked like nine massive viaducts and a 20-kilometre detour were needed – until Public Works Department engineer Robert Holmes had a brainwave. Let the line spiral and cross over itself; no viaducts and only two short tunnels.

The 13.5-km (8.4-mile) long Marmaray Tunnel links Europe to Asia beneath the Bosporus Strait. Such a route was first proposed in 1860. The tunnel finally opened in 2013.

High-Speed Train 12ᵖ

1975 British Rail Inter-City Service HST

Above and left: Nearly gone but never to be forgotten, the British InterCity 125. BR Class 43 No. 43 137 (later Newton Abbot 150) in BR InterCity Swallow livery at Bristol Temple Meads, May 1991. Planned initially in the early 1970s as a stopgap to challenge the motorway network, the first HSTs running at 125 mph entered service on 4 October 1976. From 2019, HSTs in their original form were not permitted to operate passenger services on the National Rail network because of various access deficiencies, in particular, the need to manually open the doors.

Below left: Claude Monet depicts a train crossing a newly constructed iron bridge at Argenteuil (1874). It is intriguing that in his later paintings such incursions by the modern world are omitted. (Philadelphia Museum of Art)

Outside Europe, rail also played an important military role. For example, for the Italian war with Britain in Africa in 1940-3, Italy's Eritrean line was necessary in a colony almost without oil in order to supply the front line. In Somalia, the Juba front was supplied until February 1941 by rail as no other means were sufficient. In Libya, the small network between Tripoli, Zuara and Tagiura was used to move forward supplies, as was the Benghazi-Barce line, and the line from Tobruk to Marsa Matruh and El Daba that the British had built and the Germans and Italians seized. This use of rail saved oil and so reduced pressure on vehicles, an important plus for the Germans and Italians. Having conquered Ethiopia in 1936, the Italians had brought in locomotives with which they were able to cut travel times on the Djibouti-Addis Ababa line, and also planned new lines, from Addis Ababa to Massawa, and Gondar to Assab, in order to provide links between Ethiopia and the existing Italian colony of Eritrea, and also to Mogadishu to do the same for Italian Somaliland. None was built, the war speeding quashing plans that were of only limited viability; and since, none has been built.

For all the powers, the demands of war, both military and economic, were formidable and requests for locomotives and rolling stocks were frequently not met. For example, between May 1942 and September 1943, the government of India ordered 1,375 locomotives, but by the end of 1943 had only received 105. It proved necessary to turn more to coastal transport. India was not alone in having inadequate numbers of locomotives.

Rail logistics posed major requirements which were met by the combined use of peacetime skills and wartime capability, for example in doubling track, improving handling facilities, and providing relevant supplies. Thus, the Americans were able to deliver the locomotives and wagons necessary to increase dramatically the capacity of the rail system in Algeria, which they invaded in 1942. This increase was essential to support their very large force as it moved east to attack the Germans and Italians in Tunisia. The United States Military Railway Service ran operating and shop battalions, taking responsibility for the maintenance of rolling stock near the front line, as with the 765th Railway Shop Battalion when France was invaded in 1944. At the same time, the scale of the damage caused by Allied air attack caused major problems for the Allies as they advanced. So also did German destruction as their forces retreated. Partly as a consequence, but largely due to the necessary speed and scale and to the dispersed distribution pattern, Allied logistics in the advance across northern France depended heavily on trucks.

The necessary adaptability was not always demonstrated. The Burmese Railway proved resistant in 1941-2 to making the changes necessary to deal with the crisis of Japanese attack, changes advocated by Colonel Francis Biddulph, the Director of Military Transportation, who had run military railways during the First World War on the Western Front and in Italy. However, once the Japanese had conquered Burma, the British proved adept at militarising the transport system in north-east India, an area which had not hitherto had to make such preparations. In part, this was a matter of the interplay of imperial military traditions, and in the difficulties introducing what was seen in pre-war Britain as best practice. Biddulph had been Chief Instructor at Longmoor in Britain where running military railways was taught. His superior there, Lionel Manton, became India's first Director of Transportation. In contrast, Japan failed to make comparable improvements to the system they had taken over.

The interactions of diplomacy and blockade were significant to the movement of resources, and for neutrals as well as combatants. For example, the German-Soviet Pact of 1939 undermined the British plan to use blockade to weaken Germany.

There was a great expansion of German-Soviet rail traffic, although that had been limited by poor rail links and trains still had to stop to change gauges at the old border between Poland and the Soviet Union, a border within the Soviet Union after its conquest of eastern Poland in September 1939.

In the same month, neutral Switzerland closed its Alpine passes to the movement of German coal bound for Italy, which was desperately short of coal. While then officially neutral, Italy was allied to Germany. In turn, the Anglo-French total naval blockade begun in March 1940 prevented the shipping of German coal to Italy through the Low Countries, so that by 10 June, when Italy declared war on Britain and France, it had less than a month's supply. However, in the face of a rapidly successful German advance, the French armistice went into force on 25 June, and that day, the Swiss opened their passes and even helped with their own trains. They closed the passes again in February 1945, when Germany seemed to be facing total defeat. In the meantime, the Allies did not use aircraft to attack the trains in Switzerland. This would have been too conspicuous a breach of neutrality. In contrast, Soviet submarines attacked the freighters of neutral Sweden shipping its iron across the Baltic to Germany.

Avoiding Allied naval strength prompted the Axis powers to advance plans for new rail routes. These were also designed to lead to the articulation of new imperial spheres by replacing pre-existing territorial divisions and the associated gaps in rail provision. The German plans for Eastern Europe and the conquered parts of the Soviet Union included rail and road services.

In turn, the Japanese building of links between Thailand and Burma, the 415-km (258-mile) Burma Railway built in 1942-3, was an instance of this process, a fatal one for many of those used as forced labour, including British prisoners of war. Something like 90,000 Asian civilians died. The railway was designed to supply the Japanese forces in Burma and thus prepare for the invasion of north-east India, which, in the event, was launched in 1944. This route avoided the lengthy maritime one round Malaya, which would have absorbed considerable shipping resources and exposed them to Allied attack, against which it would have been necessary to deploy warships and aircraft. The Japanese reliance on unskilled forced labour was an aspect of the primitive nature of the execution of their plan, as was the need to use tracks and sleepers from dismantled railways in Malaya and the Dutch East Indies (now Indonesia).

The Japanese also formulated from 1939 a plan that proved to be the genesis of the bullet train. This was developed with the vision of building a vast economic zone connecting Japan proper, Korea, Manchuria, and conquered regions in northern China. The use of the existing rail lines connecting Tokyo and Fukuoka, at 1067 mm gauge, had by then reached close to their full capacity. The government expected growth in rail transport needs as their new economic zone developed. To do so, they wanted to add tracks. Those in Korea and Manchuria had already been at 1543 mm and it was thought that this size was best for the additional tracks. This route was planned for steam locomotion. A tunnel link between Kyushu and Korea was included in the plan. The land acquisition of the new rail route took place between Tokyo and Osaka and some of the tunnels were dug. The end of the war ended the idea of the economic zone; but the plan was revived for the later bullet train line, and the land and tunnels used.

A revival of past schemes was also seen with the Vichy interest in a trans-Saharan rail link, which was proposed as a way to retain control of French West Africa. Exploiting their maritime dominance, this had been attacked by British and Free-French forces from the summer of 1940. An unsuccessful attack was launched on Dakar that September, but the capture of Douala in August gave the Free French control of Cameroon and then

Congo-Brazzaville. Gabon followed in November. Away from the Atlantic, Chad and the Central African Republic had declared for Free France in August, and Vichy was therefore in danger of losing control of its colonies in the *sahel*.

In response, in March 1941, a line was authorised from Bouarfa in Algeria to Tassit, with the railway then splitting to go to Niamey, capital of Mali, and to Segou, both on the River Niger. This was a revival of a plan advanced by the French government in the 1920s, but not pursued due to the cost. Now, the railway was seen as necessary for national renewal. 3,500 kilometres were to be built, and power supplied by electrification and diesel, which was among the several over-optimistic aspects of the project. Forced labour camps were established, notably at Bouarfa, and Jews and other prisoners forced to work on the project in often deadly circumstances. Only a small portion, from Bouarfa to Oujda was built, and the implausible project, which lacked the necessary funds and powerful American locomotives, was anyway made redundant in November 1942 when Anglo-American forces conquered Algeria and Morocco. In the event, Niamey did not get a railway station until 2014 and then, as discussed at the start of chapter eleven, as part of an unrealised system. Some rail ambitions are never fulfilled.

Rail was also fundamental to the operation of the German concentration camp system – the problems affecting German trains in Eastern Europe in the winter of 1941-2 led to delay in the development and operation of the envisaged rate of mass slaughter. Jews were first deported by rail from Germany in late 1938 when those of Polish descent were expelled. Subsequently, the situation became far more deadly. Jews were moved long distances to slaughter, notably from Western Europe, and also from local ghettos, such as Cracow, Łódź and Warsaw, to extermination camps at Auschwitz, Chelmno and Treblinka respectively.

With the Transport Ministry playing an important organisational role, about 2.5 million Jews were taken to death camps by train in 1942-3 alone, and in conditions of cruelly imposed squalor. A comparison with the luxury of the private trains enjoyed by Hitler and the SS leader, Heinrich Himmler, as well as by Göring and Ribbentrop, is beyond irony. There has been debate as to whether the Allies should have bombed the railways taking Jews to the camps, and as to how effective that might have been. The great range of such operations and the consequences for aircraft vulnerability and bomb loads, the number of other targets – in accountancy terms, the opportunity cost – and the speed with which the Germans could repair the lines, are all germane factors. The only way to end the Holocaust was to overthrow the Nazi regime, which helped explain the salience of targeting the war economy.

Opened in October 1942, Auschwitz III, in contrast to the extermination camp Auschwitz II, was at first to supply forced labour for nearby industrial facilities run by the company I. G. Farben. Unlike the other extermination camps, Auschwitz was located in a key economic region, coal-rich Upper Silesia, a well-connected industrial zone. With the slave-labour force from Auschwitz, this zone acted as a nexus of co-operation between the SS and the Ministry for Armaments under Albert Speer. The I. G. Farben plant for the manufacture of synthetic rubber and oil was one of the largest German industrial projects, and the largest for these products. Synthetic rubber and oil were crucial to the German war economy, the latter especially so after the launching of Operation Barbarossa, the invasion of the Soviet Union in June 1941, brought about the end of the delivery of Soviet oil.

Trains were also used for deportation within the Soviet Union, as with Poles, Estonians, Lithuanians, Latvians, Chechens, Volga Germans and Crimean Tatars, with those deported moved to *gulags* (labour camps), especially in Siberia; and in America, Japanese-Americans were moved to camps. The extent to which the Second World War remains politically resonant is shown by the public memorialisation of such movements. Thus, the end of Soviet rule was followed by the display of wagons used for such deportations, as in the Latvian Museum of the Occupation.

In terms of the number of services, civilian rail was generally cut by the combatants, and the organisational burden of running rail rose greatly even without the disruptions and risk of enemy attack. This risk was much enhanced due to the increasing range of aircraft and the recognition that railways should be targets, with no differentiation for civilian use. Wartime increased freight load and therefore locomotive power. Scheduling was complicated by drivers operating in blackout, which increased the need for familiarisation with particular routes. Timetables were put under stress, and without any real regularity in demand. The special and specific nature of military requirements, as in the preparations in Britain for the invasion of Normandy in 1944, created even greater problems and pressure. Capacities, individual and collective, human and machine, were all put under stress.

Trains were used for the evacuation of civilians threatened by bombing. The evacuation of children and others from British cities at the start of the war saw 1.3 million people moved by train in a fortnight, an unprecedented movement. This was achieved by special trains. There was no comparable movement by road.

Road transport was hit hard with higher prices for fuel and limited availability. As a result, passenger usage of rail could rise, as it did in Britain. In part, this also reflected the extent to which wartime disruption to family life, and not only service leave, encouraged people to travel to see relations and others. With many trains taken up with wartime tasks, other services were fewer, more crowded, and often subject to cancellation. Trains were slower and usually dark in an attempt to prevent being spotting by hostile aircraft. Accidents increased, including falling off dark platforms. A lack of maintenance led to slower running of trains over more uneven track, and this resulted in more delays. Novels of wartime rail travel such as those of Edmund Crispin, were of dismal journeys, as in *The Moving Toyshop* (1946): 'I had a pretty bloody journey from London. Very slow train. Stopped at every telegraph pole – like a dog.' A more romantic context was provided by the British film *Brief Encounter* (1945) which was shot at Carnforth railway station, based on a 1936 play. In it, Laura Jesson goes on a weekly train journey to a town for shopping and an afternoon film, and falls in love.

The war saw government control of railways, as in the Inter-Company Freight Rolling Stock Control established in Britain. This control prepared the way for postwar nationalisation, notably in Britain, not least by reducing the financial strength of the companies. In that respect, wartime was a continuation of the Depression. In Britain, companies were only allowed to retain a portion of their profits, while useful sources of income, such as first-class travel (1941) and restaurant cars (1944), were abolished in order to increase capacity. Furthermore, routine maintenance decreased greatly, and there was no regular replacement of locomotives. Pre-war plans for improvement were abandoned, as was the practice of remaining fit for purpose. This had consequences in terms not only of wartime accidents but also a higher rate of accidents after the war than before it. So also with postwar breakdowns in locomotives. Obsolescence characterised rail systems, which were going to find the return of peacetime welcome but difficult.

8

POSTWAR FLUX

Amtrak Budd RDC No. 15 in the Chicago yard on 4 August 1975. (Tim kd5urs under Creative Commons 2.0)

The film *From Russia with Love* (1963) included a lengthy rail journey for James Bond by train from Istanbul, one that was indirectly based on the experience of Ian Fleming, the author of the 1957 novel. Having visited Istanbul for an Interpol conference in 1955, Fleming had travelled home by the Orient Express, although he disliked it as it lacked a restaurant car, and in his own copy of the novel he recorded, 'The Orient Express is a dull, dirty train.'

Set in 1947, Seishi Yokomizo's *Akuma ga Kitarite Fue o Fuku* (*The Devil's Flute Murders*, 1973) saw its protagonist take a 'semi-express bound [from Tokyo] for Kobe, feeling half-crushed to death... Even getting a train ticket was no mean feat ... found himself squeezed into this sardine-can of a train car looking like a crumpled handkerchief ... two hours late.'

Rail was generally exhausted in 1945, and certainly so in Britain. There, it had been employed with enormous energy, persistence, diligence and courage during the war, but it was clapped out, as Hugh Dalton, the Labour Chancellor of the Exchequer, noted in Parliament on 17 December 1946 when defending rail nationalisation.

Across the world, the future of rail had been made a more urgent issue in 1945 than it had been prior to the war, in part due to extensive wartime damage, but also to the need to respond to several years of inadequate investment and maintenance other than for immediate purposes linked to the war effort, and sometimes not even for those. Then there was the requirement in effect to 'demob' rail systems, but while enabling them to handle a range of acute and immediate issues including the movement of millions of victims and refugees, such as ethnic German expellees from Eastern Europe in 1945-6, as well as the supply of provision to people such as the Dutch population, who had become seriously malnourished during the last winter of German occupation. It was also necessary to make the systems fit for peacetime purposes, which, in Eastern Europe, China, North Korea and North Vietnam, included the ambitions of the Communist regimes that seized power.

There was much essential restoration of earlier networks and services as wartime damage was repaired. This task involved formidable effort against a background of major shortages of resources and coal and in the face of severe competition. However, the restoration was eased in many countries by labour availability, including, as in China, from prisoners of war. Across much of Europe and East Asia, this restoration involved repairing wartime damage that was far more extensive and serious than in the First World War because of more extensive, sustained and heavier bombing. All bar small parts of East Asia and North Africa and much of Greece and southern Italy had been damaged by conflict in the previous war. Much of the station infrastructure was badly damaged in Europe and East Asia, as were marshalling yards and bridges. Temporary replacements, which were often army-built wartime expedients, were also installed postwar, and had to be replaced by more permanent ones with better safety margins.

There was also the disruption attendant upon territorial changes, notably in the case of Poland's borders with Germany and the Soviet Union. In addition, there was postwar conflict, as with resistance to the imposition of Soviet control, particularly in Ukraine, the Baltic Republics and Poland, and these conflicts underlined the continued vulnerability of rail to sabotage and attack, as well as its military purposes. There were civil wars in China, Greece, and the Philippines between 1946 and 1954, as well as the birth of the Cold War and anti-imperial conflicts in that period, especially in Korea, Vietnam, Indonesia and Malaya. Conflict of a different sort was seen in labour disputes, as in France in 1953 when the Socialist and Communist trade unions used a dispute over terms and conditions both to compete with each other and to challenge the government.

Rail was a significant consideration in the Cold War, seen as important to the deployment of forces and vulnerable to disruption. *Casino Royale* (1953), Fleming's first James Bond story, centred on an attempt to end pro-Soviet subversion in the French rail industry. There was certainly an anxiety about a political dimension to industrial disputes in the rail industry, which in the period 1946-60 were serious in a number of states including Britain, France, and in French West Africa, particularly Senegal and Ivory Coast. Ousmane Sembène's novel *Les bouts de bois de Dieu* (1960; translated as *God's Bits of Wood*, 1962), used the railway strike in French West Africa in 1946-7 on the Dakar-Niger line to present the strikers as representing native unity and identity, although in practice wage scales were a central element of the strike, which did not accord with Sembène's Marxist and anticolonial narrative. Authoritarian states crushed strikers, notably in Ethiopia. In Communist states, there was also a determination to ensure only union activists who conformed to regime views held any power.

Politics involved priorities in provision and therefore expenditure. So narratives that do not include political factors are suspect. Thus, linked to restoration, there was an attempt postwar to improve services in accordance with both technological potential and politico-cultural priorities, notably with the use of diesel-powered locomotives and, separately, the expansion of electrification.

Diesel locomotives came into widespread use in America after the testing in 1937 of the EA/EB design, and even more after the testing of General Motors' FT freight design in 1939. The diesel is in effect an electric locomotive carrying its own power plant, whereas electrification and electric trains refer to the provision of electricity through overhead cables or a third rail. Diesels initially lacked the horsepower output of steam locomotives, which caused problems on gradients, but they were easier to maintain and refuel, had fewer labour needs and appeared modern and, as such, appropriate for states moving into such fields as nuclear power.

Regular use of diesel locomotives began in Britain in 1947. This was particularly useful because there were major pressures on coal supplies postwar, and much coal was of low quality. The Railway Modernisation Plan of 1955 in Britain noted: 'Many factors combine to indicate that the end of the steam era is at hand [including] the insistent demand for a reduction in air pollution by locomotives and for greater cleanliness in trains and railway stations.'

Across the world, the choice of electrification for particular lines was predicated not only on the availability and cost of energy sources, but also the prioritisation of specific services. Improvements after 1945 in India, for example, which gained independence in 1947, included network extension but also double-tracking and line electrification. Across the world, rail track became more reliable, with the use of welded in place of jointed track from the 1940s, and this became more or less universal by the 1960s.

The upgrading (electrification) of the existing Japanese lines (not the high-speed ones) continued well into the 1970s. The development of suburban railways by private companies started almost at the same time as the nationalisation of the trunk railways in 1906. Urbanisation led to their growth, especially in the 1950s and 1960s. The business opportunities for rail shifted from the industrial areas to the suburban ones. The unique business model of the Japanese suburban railways is that, typically, the holding company owns not only the railway companies but also the housing development company, the department store company, the supermarket chain company and often a baseball team and amusement parks. They raise income comprehensively in their business area, exploiting to the full the opportunity offered by the inflow of population. There is also the development of commercial facilities as an integral part of the terminus.

However, the spread of road use hit the viability of non-high-speed non-suburban lines, notably in remote areas, from the 1960s, as did the movement of people to the major cities. In addition, the decline in scale of the coal and steel industries hit some of the industrial lines. The public ownership of the Japanese National Railways prevented the rationalisation of the wasteful system. As a consequence, the privatisation and division of JNR in 1987 was highly significant.

The only two profitable lines among the non-high-speed lines were inherited by JR East, while the most profitable *Shinkansen* (new track) service used by the bullet train was inherited by JR Central. The other four regional JRs faced the heavy burden of maintenance with slim profit opportunities. In contrast, another offspring, JR Freight, enjoyed some recovery because it was liberated from the burden of the maintenance of the tracks, and thus had greater freedom to set competitive prices. The JRs are responsible for the operation and maintenance of *Shinkansen* routes, but the national entity for the construction of new routes is the Japan Railway Construction, Transport and Technology Agency (JRTT), which builds the tracks of the new routes for the bullet trains, owns the tracks it has built, and leases them out to the operating JRs. The funding sources of the JRTT's track constructions are the public works budget of the central government, the budgets of the local governments that benefit from the construction, and the leasing fees which have accrued through the operations of the trains.

There was postwar expansion in the patchy rail network of colonial empires, but it could be very limited. Plans to make mineral shipments easier were very typical of the resource-linked nature of imperial rail expansion and activity in the late 1940s and the 1950s. The discovery in 1959 of a major manganese deposit in Tambao in north-eastern Upper Volta (Burkina Faso), in French West Africa, led to plans for a rail extension from Ouagadougou, the capital, which the railway from Abjadan in Ivory Coast had reached in 1954. However, scant progress was made, such that there was reliance on lorries operating on poor roads that, far from being all-weather, encountered serious problems in the wet season. It was the same for countries that were not colonies, for example Brazil.

The British scheme of 1947-51 to develop large-scale groundnut (peanut) cultivation in Tanganyika was envisaged as a way to produce fats, a key food source, and employment, but it was totally misconceived and mismanaged. The scheme included initially the development of the harbour of Dar es Salaam and extensive use of the Central Line, for which more freight wagons were ordered, but subsequently, as interest shifted to production from the west and south of Tanganyika, a new deep-water port was planned at Mtwara and, to there, a new line, the 275-kilometre narrow gauge Southern Province Railway, partly opened in 1949, expanded in 1954-8 but closed in 1963. The Beneguela Railway in the Portuguese colony of Angola was more successful.

Further north, in 1960-5, there were plans to extend the Djibouti-Addis Ababa line from Adama to Dilla, but they were not pursued. In 1977-8, the Ogadan War with Somalia saw significant damage to the line. In 2008, service ended between Addis Ababa and Dire Dawa, and many of the rails were stolen.

Resource-linked rail expansion and activity was also to be true of post-colonial states, such as Cameroon and Mauritania. Due to decolonisation, rail projects could be suspended or called into doubt. Former imperial powers generally continued to provide a measure of support to their ex-colonies, but that was not always the case, as with France and Guinea from independence in 1958. Political independence, however, was not necessarily itself the key element of change. Indeed, whereas colonial governments frequently had an arm's-length relationship with non-state mineral producers, this was often not the case with independent states that were often open to partnerships. The latter could provide the liquidity necessary for investment.

Geopolitical considerations were far less to the fore for rail than had been the case. Instead, air dominated attention, and notably so for America, which replaced Britain as the leading source of liquidity and influence across much of the world. American geopolitical concerns and means were not centred on rail links and their construction. Instead, there was the desire for a global network of air bases, the links in between coming from air transport and, where necessary, by sea. Open skies agreements were the civilian equivalent for the Americans.

Rail was also in serious trouble in its heartlands. 'If we left the railways open to the full blast of the free unfettered competition of road transport the whole railway system within a few years would be totally bankrupt,' declared Hugh Dalton in the House of Commons in December 1946. Across much of the non-Communist world, the rapid increase in car ownership proved a serious problem for short- and long-range rail services. This was notably so in those prosperous countries where cars became ubiquitous, most particularly America, where losses on passenger services reached $723 million in 1957, but also Australia, Canada and New Zealand. Freight services meanwhile were hit by lorries in part because of their lack of flexibility compared to roads, not least as manufacturing became less focused on large factories fed by rail-borne coal. Road transport was helped by the availability of low-cost oil until 1973.

Rail freight had done well in America during the war. Road freight traffic fell as a percentage of total ton-miles during the war to only 5.6 in 1943, but this decline proved short term and by 1958 trucks carried 20 per cent of freight ton-miles, compared to 46 per cent for rail (75 per cent in 1929), 18 per cent for pipeline and 16 per cent for inland waterways. In 1955, President Dwight Eisenhower supported a plan for the federal funding of Interstate roads, pressing for a vast system of interconnected highways crisscrossing the country. Interstates, with their steadier and more predictable travel time offered opportunities to challenge the rail position in long-distance freight movement; hitherto, lorries were more significant only over short distances. The Federal-Aid Highway Act of 1956 was a key development, as the Act of 1944 had not included funding provisions. Road freight was increasingly important for higher-value goods, as well as making inroads in less valuable ones. Road competition was a crucial challenge to rail profitability, as it led to less of a margin to increase charges to reflect greater costs. This was not only the case in America.

The bankruptcy of major American rail companies, notably the Penn Central (the merger of the Pennsylvania Railroad and the New York Central) in 1970, led to the establishment that year of Amtrak (a government-funded body that took over intercity passenger services in 1971), and Conrail (the Consolidated Rail Corporation, a public body running from 1976, which was responsible for the lines of many bankrupt companies). Amtrak was a quasi-public, for-profit, corporation; but it depended on political support which led to inefficiencies, including running costly lines, notably in the South and West, although many services still were cut back. Thus, Las Vegas station was demolished in 1971, being replaced by a small waiting room in the hotel built on the site and, in 1997, that was closed with the end of the Amtrak service to the city.

Amtrak's far-flung network meant a constant need for federal subsidies, as well as a substantial repair backlog. Amtrak's separation from the private sector, both in financial and operational terms, made it harder to raise funds and to introduce efficiencies. In addition, the political tensions between state and federal governments and agencies did not help. Obsolescence was cumulative. Thus, in 2017, Amtrak's President, Charles Moorman, told the New Jersey State Legislature: '...the railroad is not, and frankly never has been, in a true state of good repair, meaning that many of the assets that make up the infrastructure are past the point at which they would normally be replaced.'

Technological changes provided rail with opportunities, notably in the shape of containers. They had been used already with railways in the nineteenth century, the Liverpool and Manchester Railway moving coal in rectangular timber boxes transferred by carts. In the early twentieth century, closed container boxes were in use; and, in 1921, the American Post Office contracted with the New York Central Railroad to move mail in containers. The Philadelphia Railroad began regular container services in 1928, opening a container terminal at Enola in 1932. The carriage of containers on flatcars became more common from the mid-1930s, and, in 1951, a Western European railway standard was developed. Container ships followed from the 1950s, and then double-stacked rail transport from 1977, with America the innovator and China a key copier. The world's first container ship's maiden voyage was in April 1956.

Containerisation required investment in new freight facilities but increased the speed and cut the cost of freight movements, greatly raising labour productivity on the railways, and changing the nature of marshalling yards. Interoperability with ships and lorries rapidly improved.

Linked to this, the deregulation provided by the Staggers Rail Act in 1980 helped make the freight system profitable, indeed highly profitable in the case of many lines, and thus attracting considerable investment. For example, Burlington Northern Santa

Fe (BNSF), owned by Berkshire Hathaway Inc., had revenues of over $5 billion in 2017. Conrail, meanwhile, had cut its network and was successfully privatised in 1987 by the Reagan government. In 2022, the leading railways in terms of annual freight wagons were, in order, BNSF and Union Pacific, both with over 8 million, then Norfolk Southern and CSX Transportation, both over six million, and then Canadian National, Canadian Pacific and Kansas City Southern. Both the Canadian railways bid to take over Kansas City Southern.

The 2015 Congressional hearing on the Staggers Act noted that since then 'the railroad industry has become more efficient, productive, and profitable.' The testimony from the American Chemistry Council, which opposed 'a reregulation of the rail industry', nevertheless drew attention to the consolidation made possible by the Staggers Act and the extent to which less competition meant higher charges. In turn, the rail industry representative emphasised the investment made possible by profit: 'We are preparing for tomorrow today all over the country, expanding internodal terminals, double-tracking hundreds of miles of track, installing millions of new rail ties, upgrading signal systems, and building new major rail yards.'

Although train derailments fell, from close to 800 annually in 2000-6 to fewer than 400 annually from 2015, there were still issues with accidents, for example the derailment in Ohio in February 2023 of a Norfolk Southern train carrying toxic chemicals and, in March 2023, in Minnesota of a train carrying ethanol, which is also flammable and toxic.

With America setting the norms of Western society, its combination of suburbanisation, low fuel, car parts and repair prices, and the very ready availability of them all, plus a failure to provide new rail passenger capacity, hit rail travel hard. There were low gas taxes and massive state support from the 1950s for roadbuilding with the interstate highway programme. These roads ensured that inexpensive bus services could provide competition for rail, not only locally but also long-distance. This interacting system of advantages from road availability then became influential in countries that followed the American example, such as New Zealand, where Auckland developed as a road-based city.

Advertising proved particularly important to the spread of the road model, and it was a sphere in which most rail systems, particularly nationalised ones, found it difficult to compete. In democracies, rail lacked the lobbying and popular appeal of road, and locomotive manufacturing that of car companies and factories. The latter attracted state support in a way that locomotive manufacturing did not. Air proved a key competition in large countries, such as America, Australia and Canada. Internal air services also provided competition in smaller countries, including Britain, France, Germany, Italy and New Zealand. As in Japan, these in part involved links between separate islands.

In this context, it was not surprising that in many states rail lines judged less important suffered from limited investment, which was a prelude to cuts in networks and services, as with the Beeching 'reshaping' in Britain, and major reductions in other countries, especially America. In Britain, a government-imposed ban on fare and freight increases led to a serious fall in net earnings in 1945-7, and share values, including of the profitable Southern Railway, fell on the anticipation of nationalisation by the Labour government, which occurred in 1948. Alongside a major increase in goods traffic as a whole, the proportion moved by road rose from 37 per cent in 1952 to 58.3 per cent in 1964. In turn, warehousing and distribution increasingly responded to supplies being carried by lorries. The rail network was moving from steam to diesel, although steam remained important, and not only on branch lines. In 1959, the locomotive *Sir Nigel Gresley*, built in 1937 and in the same series as *Mallard*, which achieved its higher speed when not pulling a full train of passengers, set a postwar steam speed record of 112 mph (180 km/h). It was to be withdrawn from service in 1966.

Diesel offered major operating conveniences, not least in working gradients, which challenged steam pressure, and also in saving labour. In place of the substantial workforce essential in order to get steam trains to operate – firelighters, lubricators, drivers and firemen – all that was needed with diesel was drivers. However, the strength of union opposition to change, as well as firmness over pay differentials and working practices, as in the 1955 seventeen-day national strike, helped undercut the investment made. So did the introduction of a number of diesel classes, which ensured the need for an expensive range of maintenance facilities.

Despite relatively strong freight and passenger usage in the 1950s, the operating deficit of British Rail increased from £16.5 million in 1956 to £104 million in 1962; although how much was lost would depend on which accounting convention is used, a point more generally the case when assessing rail financing. In the early 1960s, the Treasury pressed for clear financial targets and for economic charges by nationalised industries, in order to limit and hopefully drive down their debt and investment requirements, and the pressure thereby put on the rest of the economy through higher public expenditure, particularly at a time when economic growth was modest.

There were already cuts to the network in the 1950s; in Devon for example, the Princetown line in 1956 and the Teign Valley line in 1958. As so often, the process of closure was not immediate. Thus, the branch line to Moretonhampstead, opened in 1866, was closed to passenger service in 1959, but freight continued. The line closed only in 1964, and a last special passenger train ran in 1970, after which part of the track was lifted.

In the event, a major transformation was proposed. *The Reshaping of British Railways* (1963), a report better known after Dr Richard Beeching, the Chairman of the British Transport Commission and the first Chairman of the British Railways Board, which operated from 1963 to 2001, has remained controversial to the present day. Speaking for the government in the House of Lords, Viscount Hailsham, the Lord President of the Council, said that new investment alone was not the answer:

> A system which was built in the main about 1855 or before, and designed for purposes then, needs redesigning ... one-third of the system is not really being used adequately at all ... the people, whether they be consignors or freight or potential passengers, are voluntarily deserting the railways in droves and taking to the roads ... [for] the flexibility of road transport ... the danger is the force of inertia... What we have to do is to design a 20th-century rail system.

That theme, ensuring a 'modern system', was an established part of the rhetoric of rail, one that was frequently repeated and was important to British government in the period. In the early 1960s it lay behind the first attempt to join the European Economic Community, the forerunner to the European Union, and attempts at national economic planning. The Beeching Report should not be separated from this context.

The focus in the report was on a core network, one made possible and necessary by the move from steam to diesel, and one designed to provide speed, efficiency and profit. However, rural and small-town Britain changed as railways that had integrated it into an urban-centred network were removed. Branch lines were ruthlessly culled. As a result, largely rural areas, such as East Anglia, Lincolnshire, Mid-Wales, the Welsh Borders, north Cornwall and the Isle of Wight, were left with few or no services. In Devon, lines that closed included all those in West Devon, the Exe Valley Line, that from Exmouth via Budleigh, and those from Taunton to Barnstaple and Barnstaple to Ilfracombe. In Scotland, there were extensive closures, including in the Borders, South-West Scotland and North-East Scotland. The line north of Inverness was only reprieved through political lobbying.

Yet, that was not the sole issue with provision. In particular, on a longstanding pattern, and one that has continued to the present, the concentration on links that survived on routes into London, axial routes, was not matched by necessary attention to lateral ones, for example cross-country services. Thus, Trans-Pennine services are inadequate, as are those from, for example, Bristol to Weymouth, Great Yarmouth to Liverpool, and Birmingham to Cambridge. Similarly, double track lines became single track, as with most of the Salisbury to Exeter line in 1967.

There was also devastation-style rebuilding, as at Euston, and threats to redevelop other stations, such as Liverpool Street. As a result of Beeching and other changes, many stations were closed during this period. Railway works at major sites, such as Darlington and Swindon, closed. The last pick-up of mail by a moving train was made in 1971; thereafter, mail was only brought to rail stations by road, and aircraft and lorries were increasingly used to move post.

However, the dramatic cuts suggested as options in the 1982 report by Sir David Serpell, former Permanent Secretary at the Ministry of Transport, were rejected. One option, the headline one, would have reduced the system by 84 per cent, essentially to a few major routes, notably from London to Cardiff, Newcastle and Scotland via Manchester. The parliamentary discussion led

Lord Underhill, Labour's Opposition front bench spokesman on transport in the House of Lords, to claim that Britain seemed 'one of the few Western democracies which is behind in placing emphasis on the need for a strong rail system.' Lord Nugent of Guildford, a Conservative who had been Parliamentary Secretary to the Ministry of Transport, drew attention to the cost to the taxpayer and to archaic working practices. Born in 1907, he also commented on

> ... the sort of natural sympathy which most of us have for the railways themselves. I dare say that in my generation it dates back to our childhood wish to be an engine driver but, certainly, the sympathy is there and we do feel for the railways, especially if we could see a steam engine. That really does give us a thrill.

Instead of these cuts, the system, with passenger numbers reviving from the mid-1980s, stabilised at just over half the interwar mileage. This of course stripped out a lot of capacity, but also reduced the mileage that had to be maintained and the attendant costs. Whereas the number of a thousand million passenger-miles by rail had fallen from 24.2 in 1952 to 20.5 in 1976, it rose to 25.5 in 1990. This, moreover, was better than the figures for bus or coach: 50.3 in 1952, 32.9 in 1976, and 25.5 in 1990. Though these figures were totally dwarfed by those for car, taxi and motorcycle: 33.6 in 1952, 215.0 in 1976, and 352.9 in 1990. The construction of a motorway system began in 1958.

Alongside the reality of rail came the image or, rather, images, such as the romance of what was advertised as the most famous train in the world in Alfred Hitchcock's film *North by Northwest* (1959), with a journey for Cary Grant and Eva Marie Saint on the *20th Century Limited* express which ran from New York to Chicago from 1902 to 1967. It had been the most profitable train in interwar America as well as the most luxurious, and did not require elucidation, leading to remarks such as 'if the century was on time it was already at Grand Central' in Rex Stout's *Fer-De-Lance* (1934). The service did not survive the 1960s. Trains also continued to feature in music, as in the blues standard 'Night Train' released in 1952.

A very different form of railway journey as entertainment was provided by Walt Disney (1901-66), who was born in Marceline, Missouri, a town dependent on the railway. At Disneyland, his theme park in Anaheim, California, developed from the mid-1950s, the entire perimeter was encircled by the steam-powered 5/8 scale Sante Fe and Disneyland Railroad ride. There were also railways within the park, taking visitors into Nature's Wonderland, with a narrow gauge mine train operating through Rainbow Caverns in 1956. Another large-scale steam railway, the Carolwood Pacific, encircled Disney's home near Los Angeles. Railways were also prominent in other theme parks such as Legoland in Denmark.

Paradoxically, although luxury train services, not least night sleepers, were hit hard, the relative decline of rail travel did not end its hold on the popular imagination; although that attention focused on the now-discarded system of steam trains and, to a lesser extent, classic diesel types. Preservation groups and other enthusiasts re-opened a few lines and stations, notably in Britain and America, beginning with the Talyllyn Railway in Wales in 1951, and the Ffestiniog Railway, also originally a Welsh slate railway, in 1955. These reopened lines rarely link directly into a wider network.

Steam trains played a major role in films and television programmes, for example the British television series *Poirot* (1989-2013), in which the trains were spared the many problems and decline of Agatha Christie's lifetime (1890-1976), which included her being bitten by bed bugs on the Simplon-Orient Express. Rail was also written into plots, as in *Downton*

Abbey (2010-15), a television series in which Robert, Earl of Grantham loses his wife's money in the Grand Trunk Railway, a real Canadian company that due to poor management, including investment in expensive hotels, defaulted on loan payments in 1919 and was in effect nationalised in 1919-23. Very differently, and based on the London Underground, the satirical and, to those not in the know, baffling game 'Mornington Crescent' appeared on the BBC radio quiz-satire *I'm Sorry I Haven't a Clue* from 1978.

Model railways developed from the 1890s, but they became much less prominent with the rise of cars. Hamley's, the leading London toy shop, put a large working model railway system in a prominent place, but it was removed. Instead, in 2014, the store provided a fake Central Line tube map with a branch to the store's basement display of part of a real train cab. In New Zealand, the 'Forgotten World Line' on which scheduled passenger services stopped in 1983, can in part be used by means of converted golf carts, which was definitely not what the builders of the line in 1901-32 had in mind as they tunnelled hard.

In Communist states, meanwhile, although there were car industries, there was no increase in car use comparable to that in the West. Instead, there was a stress on freight rather than passengers, and on railway construction as a means to spread development, for example in the Soviet Union east of the Urals. This geographical pattern was a lasting theme in the Soviet period, during which long-range rail freight was practically an article of faith. Alongside the Communist commitment to electrification, there continued to be steam services, not least due to the cost of new locomotives. Indeed, with plentiful coal, Poland retained many regular steam services into the 1990s. Although China officially ended steam locomotion in 2002, it retained some services where gradients were a challenge.

Rail was seen as a way to integrate the Communist world, for freight, passengers, and the military; and services were established accordingly, for example from Moscow via Warsaw to East Berlin, and in 1972, the Leningrad Express to East Berlin. There was also a Moscow-Vienna service. In contrast, passenger transport across the Iron Curtain was less common, although it was comparatively easy for Westerners, as I discovered in 1978 and 1980. Until Russian troops withdrew in 1994, a special military train regularly operated between Moscow and East Berlin.

Whereas passenger numbers and freight were affected in the capitalist world by the emphasis on cars and aircraft, in the Communist world, rail remained far more significant. By the 1970s, French tourists overwhelmingly went to the Mediterranean by road. In contrast, East German workers went by the Leipzig-Varna express, via Prague and Bratislava, to the Bulgarian Black Sea resorts. Soviet workers going to Black Sea resorts such as Socchi went by train. As a result, the end of Communist rule in 1989-91 represented a major change for the global position of rail.

Elsewhere, however, uncompetitive lines could be kept in operation due to political support and government subsidy, which was a common process. In South Africa, the white-minority apartheid regime that ruled until 1994 drew heavily on support from farmers in the Transvaal and the Orange Free State, and as a result developed and maintained an uneconomical network that moved farm goods. These involved far lower revenues than the movement of coal and iron from mines to ports. Phrased differently, competition was politically defined and constrained, albeit not as clearly in Communist states. Cold War politics in the broadest sense, as well as the Cold War itself, had a profound effect on the fortunes of rail.

In Australia, fiscal pressures during the Second World War had continued the financial squeeze seen in the 1930s, but from the 1950s a determined effort was made to address the issue of variable gauges. There was also the opening of new lines, notably the completion of a standard gauge Sydney-Perth railway in 1969, and an Adelaide-Darwin one in 2004. The latter is the route of the celebrated Ghan train. The narrow gauge Central Australian Railway built between 1878 and 1929 had run between Port Augusta and Alice Springs, most laid without ballast, being replaced in 1980 by a standard gauge Tarcoola-Alice Springs line which avoided the floodplains that affected the original route. The line was extended to Darwin in 2001-4.

Freight is key to the Australian system, following the development of long-range bus services, as well as domestic air routes and, even more significantly, cut-price domestic air routes. The extent to which rail was not the answer for passengers was clear. On successive visits to Australia, although a rail enthusiast, I took aircraft for long journeys, and that is a typical response. In 1997-2004, there was the privatisation of much, but not all, of Australian railways, notably of Australian National Railways in 1997. This issue of ownership was part of the politics of rail that was so significant over the period and framed policy decisions. This is easy to see in recent decades but was also true of those immediately after the Second World War, a period in which many of the fundamentals of the present situation were created anew and much of the past of rail was rapidly discarded.

Due to a variety of factors, but principally a size that denied economies of scale and made closure an easier option, relatively small rail systems stopped operation in a number of countries, including Barbados (1937), Bermuda (1948), Cyprus (1951), Mauritius (1964), Trinidad (1968) and, after a decline in operations in the 1950s, Libya (1965). In Barbados, passenger traffic was discontinued as early as 1934, freight following in 1937. In Trinidad, the government railway (as opposed to plantation tracks) covered 173 km (107 miles) and in 1936 had 29 locomotives, but it was phased out from 1953. Three years later, the decision was made to close the system in Mauritius in the face of a deficit reflecting road competition. Passenger services stopped that year, freight following in 1964, in what was a typical sequence. Other islands that lost rail services included Jersey in 1936. In St Kitts, only a tourist line was to remain.

Bermuda's railway was typical of many small island systems. 21.7 miles long, it was formally completed in 1931, although sections had been open to traffic for several years. In most years, the railway made a small operating profit, but it was never able to handle depreciation or the replacement of its equipment, tracks and, in particular, bridges. As a result, the investors, who were out of pocket, threatened to shut the railway down in 1946, which led the government to purchase it. However, the necessary capital improvements led the government to abandon the railway in 1948 and turn instead to buses, the line becoming a walking route while the rolling stock was sold to (British) Guiana, now Guyana. The plan there for a line south to Brazil was never pursued, and after independence in 1966 the public rail system was closed, one line in 1972, the other in 1974; although industrial railways continued operation.

In Lebanon, closure, which was final in 1997, was more chaotic, with the civil war and foreign invasion causing major damage, not least explosions and the selling of part of the track for scrap metal. The steam-powered Beirut-Damascus line, finished in 1895, was closed in 1976.

Alongside new beginnings, there was a marked recession, notably the decline in the overall mileage of railways. That remains the case to the present, and that despite the huge rise in the world's population.

9

CHANGES OVER THE LAST
HALF CENTURY

The 300 km/h (190 mph) Frecciarossa and an E.444R at Milan Central Station in 2018. The E444R introduced in 1989 has a maximum speed of 200 km/h. (Christopher Down)

The photographs were impressive: Chinese high-speed train units being unloaded from ships in Indonesia for the Jakarta to Bandung high-speed rail project on the island of Java, Indonesia's most populous. Jakarta's population is over 13 million, and the population of the city and its five contiguous satellite cities is over 31 million, with the comparable figures for Bandung being over three and nine million. The two centres are 142 kilometres apart and the trains will operate at up to 350 kilometres an hour.

Over 80 kilometres will be elevated, while there are 13 tunnels. There will be a station near the airport in Halim. The Chinese were awarded the project in 2015, in part because they did not insist on Indonesian government funding; instead, the China Development Bank providing most of the loan finance, whereas the rival Japanese builders had demanded loan guarantees. The estimated cost was $7.5 billion, but the project will be well over budget, probably at $11.24 billion, and late. In August 2022, the Indonesian government had to inject funding in order to move completion forward. It is scheduled to be inaugurated by the President in August 2023 providing a key instance of the Belt and Road Initiative launched in 2013.

The delays were not only due to Covid but also as a result of funding disputes, environmental concerns, labour shortages and permit issues, the last owing a lot to popular opposition from communities along the route. Moreover, the original projection of over 60,000 passengers daily has already been cut to 31,000, while the standard ticket price, necessary to repay the Chinese loan of over $6.7 billion, makes the journey unaffordable to most Indonesians. In addition, the stations at the Bandung end are far distant from the city centre, which will necessitate costly connecting transport. The existing train trip is only three-fifths of the projected ticket price, and there are cars and mini-buses to provide completion. Both contribute to air pollution, but they offer a better price.

The problems affecting the project throw a sceptical light on China's global infrastructure ambitions. These are based on the replication of the Chinese model of consistent, strong and well-funded governmental support and a lack of opposition from civil society and political groups. This is generally not the case.

Separately, railway infrastructure may carry high potential for structural transformation and industrialisation, and the 'levelling up' pursued through British, Chinese, Japanese, Spanish and other new lines; but may also be superseded, as a nineteenth-century technology, the telegram, has been by mobile phones and computers. Whatever the case, project due diligence is a key issue for individual projects. Thus, in Africa, politics – or rather the lack of strong institutional government in many countries – not to mention corruption, has allowed China undue influence. China gets access to resources and in exchange promises to develop local infrastructure. In many instances, the African countries have ended up short-changed, with China delivering poor-quality infrastructure (built by Chinese contractors with Chinese workers), or not delivering at all.

The standard emphasis of course is on expansion, on new opportunities, new lines, new stations, new trains, persuasive images of the future. They can become a reality with plans coming to fruition, such as the British HST2; or, rather, not. This chapter and the next seek to show that the situation was, and is, far more complex, which helps direct attention as to how best to assess the future and to do so with appropriate scepticism.

While it is appropriate to devote space to expansion, it is also necessary to consider other trends and contexts. Many represent the continuation of earlier circumstances, but there are also new norms to assess. At the same time, the last half-century has seen the maintenance of many existing systems. This itself is a formidable and underrated task given rail financing, and the many and multiple strains affecting railway equipment, track and railbeds, strains arising from incessant use, as well as from climatic and geomorphological conditions. Maintenance is the key element for the far-flung rail systems in America, Russia and India, and with others of more modest range, such as Switzerland; and will become so with recently expanded systems, notably in China, which, because of its scale, will face a formidable maintenance burden. Accidents are frequently a product of failed maintenance.

Over the last half-century, there were significant improvements in networks and services in some areas. This was particularly the case in China, Japan, France, Germany, Italy and Spain. As so often, the process of change was scarcely value-free. Thus, the views of local communities, as well as traditional patterns of spatial organisation, were very much subordinated in the planning process for high-speed rail networks, and the concerns communities voiced about disruption had scant impact on the routing. This was not only in China, where the human costs of expansion are ignored.

The European system displayed considerable dynamism, in so far as individual countries as well as the continent as a whole was concerned. Attention was for a long time focussed on France. The first line of the prestigious TGV (*train à grande vitesse*), travelling at 270 km/h (168 mph), opened between Paris and Lyon in 1981 and bypassed Dijon, a longstanding rail hub that was thereby marginalised. The line was extended to Marseille in 2001, while separate lines followed, including to Strasbourg in 2016. The latter was politically significant because the European Parliament has regular meetings there and this was seen as a way to support France's case that the Parliament should continue to have that shared location.

As so often with the train, as distance was transformed by timetables, social divisions were seen afresh in new forms and also remoulded. Big, out-of-town stations on the new French lines were built to serve such cities as Avignon, Aix and Poitiers, encouraging wealthy Parisians to acquire second homes and driving up local house prices. Being out-of-town, the new stations were particularly convenient for those living in the surrounding countryside. This was reflected in the 'Parkway' title of some

British stations, planned or built, as in Bristol (opened in 1972), Tiverton (opened in 1986), Didcot (1985), Worcestershire (2020), Aylesbury Vale (2008), Haddenham and Thame (1987), Luton Airport (1999), Oxford (2015), Southampton Airport (renamed Southampton Parkway railway station in 1986), Whittlesford Parkway (renamed 2007), Buckshaw (2011), Horwich (1999), Liverpool South (2006), Bodmin Parkway (renamed 1983), Ebbw Vale (2008), Port Talbot (renamed 1984), Gloucestershire (1.4 miles east of Gloucester, not built), and Northampton (not built). Instead of the train being a central feature of urban life with the station in the city centre, it became, with the parkway stations, a key intermediary between the outer town and a wider world, and, as such, served the new social dynamics of commuters and second-home owners. The relative lack of comparable rail stations in America was notable, and in part a consequence of the different social background of rail passengers. There has not been an investment in America or Britain in new stations comparable to France, in part because there has not been an opening of new lines. Instead, Amtrak services, like British ones, use old lines and therefore old stations, or at least established station sites, even if there are new buildings, as in Wilmington, Delaware.

As always, political strategies played a role in the development of European high-speed lines, with politics understood both in the widest context, social or regional, and with reference to party politics. In Italy, where city centre to city centre travel is important, the high-speed rail line opened between Milan and Rome in 2007 was arguably intended to help national integration at a time when the demand for separatism from the Northern League was strong. As such, the politics of rail was part of an anti-populist stance, the central government using money accordingly. The line was also designed to move business from both air and road, and to a degree it succeeded in doing so.

The high-speed *Treno Alta Velocità* (TVA) network is intended in part to reduce the strain on existing rail capacity and improve choice for customers in service and pricing. The new lines are also planned to increase freight capacity by night, which is a EU goal. The main rail corridors are north-south, both west and east of the Apennine mountains, and east-west, from Turin via Milan and Venice to Trieste, and from Naples to Bari. Although Trieste was only added after the First World War, these corridors have been important from the early planning of Italian railways. Links to and between ports, such as Genoa, Trieste, Naples and Bari, have always been significant in the Italian rail system. As a reminder that the politics of rail continue, there have been renewed rail strikes in Italy since March 2023. A very different politics of rail was the bombing of a waiting room at Bologna Station in 1980, killing 85 people. Neo-Fascists were convicted, although exact responsibility for this terrorist attack remains contentious.

In Western Europe, there have been major changes in recent decades. In Germany, the unification of West and East provided the opportunity and need for new rail links, not least as earlier links to West Berlin could be supplemented. Thus, in 1991, construction began for a high-speed line from Erfurt in the former East Germany to Bamberg in former West Germany, only to be met by environmental criticism and pressure instead for upgrades to existing lines, and stopped by the new SPD-Green Coalition government in 1998. Subsequently, work on the line was resumed and it was opened in 2017.

However – and this in Europe's wealthiest large country – and one with a long rail history and a governmental system committed to rail, there were serious problems, not least with reliability. One in four trains was late in 2018, including many-long distance departures, a situation blamed in part on long-term underinvestment in favour of road, but also due to rising passenger numbers since the 1990s. Announced in 2022, a key remedy is a focus on high-performance corridors where infrastructure is to be improved to be able to take more freight and passengers. The previous year, plans were outlined to reopen 245 kilometres of disused lines. In March 2023, the German rail system was briefly shut as a result of a strike in pursuit of a 12 per cent pay increase. Six million customers were affected.

Whereas in Germany and Britain the focus was largely on existing lines, construction began in 1988 for the high-speed Spanish rail system, which, again, was part of a system and symbol of modernity, in a mutually supporting pattern. Spain drew strongly on the French example. The daily number of AVE (*Alta Velocidad Española*) passengers in millions rose from 4.878 in 2006 to 22.370 in 2019 (below Japan, France, Germany, China, Taiwan and Korea), before being hit by Covid. As is the norm, regional and local interests, lobbying and politics played a key role in deciding routes.

The interplay of national rail organisations and devolved government, which is a factor in Spain, has given a new dimension to a long-term relationship affecting networking. The related lobbying often leaves only a partial trace in the archives, yet the process echoes the situation in the nineteenth century. Lobbying was, and is, often linked with financial inducements in the forms of grants and borrowing facilities.

Separately, there was a major scandal in Spain in 2023 over ordering trains that were too big for some tunnels in the regions of Asturias and Cantabria, announced in 2020. This led to the resignation of the Transport Secretary and the head of Renfe, the state rail company, the order for 31 trains to be completed in 2024 being worth close to €260 million (£227 million). In response, the government made rail travel in the regions free until new rolling stock could be introduced, which is now predicted for 2026 at the earliest. The problem was a combination of current mismanagement and the legacy of the more independent system of the nineteenth century, which ensured that there were varying tunnel sizes. The trains were still in the design phase, not the manufacturing one, so that headline costs will be much lower than suggested when the scandal broke; but aside from the reputational damage of the scandal (akin to but rather more serious than that of 'the wrong' snow in 1991, or leaves on the line in 2010, or sunlight in 2016 in Britain), the design phase needs to be repeated. In contrast, when in 2014 SNCF in France ordered regional trains that were too wide for the network's platforms, responding to a similar failure to take note of older and different structures, the manufacturing phase had been completed and it was necessary to rebuild platforms at considerable cost. Such problems arise from centralisation and the consequently necessary standardisation.

The EU has repeatedly sought the creation of high-speed links, as in the improvement of services between Paris and Brussels and between France and Germany. The EU's Connecting Europe Facility was focused on this goal for rail, which is regarded as a benign alternative to air and road, not least as it avoids the extremely expensive as well as contentious issue of new airport construction.

A key element of the strategy is the wish to improve the Rhine-Alpine Core Network Corridor with its north-south rail freight services connecting North Sea ports to northern Italy, ensuring a freight corridor from Rotterdam to Genoa. One particular project, begun in 2014 and scheduled to cost €758 million (with the EU providing €311 million), was the upgrade of the line between Karlsruhe in Germany and Basle in Switzerland, in order to raise the number of tracks from two to four. This was designed to increase capacity and speed by enabling freight trains to use bypasses. The increased capacity is intended to link to the new Gotthard Base tunnel through the Alps, which is seen as a core facility.

The rate of return in relation to the huge costs of building such links, often over €40 million per kilometre, requires time perspectives well beyond the customary horizons of private finance, even before uncertainties over future revenues and risks are factored in. The financial dimension owes much to political contexts and loading, both within and between countries. An instance of the latter is greater Spanish than Portuguese interest in a high-speed line between Madrid and Lisbon. Announced in 2009 to be completed in 2013, cutting the journey from nine hours to 2¾, Portugal abandoned the plan in 2012. This was as part of the austerity programme of the conservative government of Pedro Passos Coelho (2011-15) and reflected conservative criticism of the cost voiced when in opposition from 2005 to 2011 to the previous government of the Socialist José Sócrates, who had championed the project. Spain criticised the abandonment, which was confirmed in 2012 when the decision was taken by the Portuguese government to improve freight routes from and to Portuguese ports instead, so as better to serve exports by sea and over land. In November 2022, Portugal released a new National Railway Plan envisaging new high-speed lines, including between Oporto and Lisbon, as well as to Madrid. The Lisbon-Oporto line is designed to continue to Vigo in Spain. The plan proposes to increase the rail percentage of passenger journeys from 4.6 to 20 by 2050 with freight rising from 13 to 40, to build a new bridge over the Tagus, and to link the ten largest cities by high-speed services. The viability of the scheme is unclear. Certainly, current rail journeys between Lisbon and Madrid are very slow and unpredictable. In February 2023, in order to tackle such circumstances, the European Commission announced a new emphasis on cross-border journeys, not direct funding for new lines but rather helping with coordination, regulations and promotion in order to break down barriers between rail operators and authorities in different countries. Coordination or its opposite has always been a significant aspect of operations, capacity and improvement. That is self-evident when considering the case of different countries, with France providing a level of protectionism that moved the Spanish government to formal complaint in 2020, and also of companies, competing or otherwise, within the same state.

The challenge is also seen within individual companies, whether state or privately owned, for in practice these are coalitions of competing divisions. In 2023, ten new services were announced as a pilot. The first was designed to connect Austria, Hungary and western Romania, with a rail service from Vienna to Budapest, and then one branch to Arad and another to Oradea. A new night service is to link Stockholm, Copenhagen and Berlin, as well as there being a day service between Hamburg and Gothenburg which might continue to Oslo. Other projected new services included Rome to Munich, Barcelona to Amsterdam, and Lisbon to Madrid. This is a far less expensive plan than that for new lines, and one that is more adaptable to political and financial capabilities.

In Britain, there were also attempts at modernisation, including new trains. The tilting Advanced Passenger Train did not prove a success. Tilting carriages, on which there were experiments from the 1950s, were designed to permit trains to go round curves on older and newer lines without reducing speed, notably on the West Coast main line. Prototypes were tested in the 1970s, but the first runs in service in 1981 did not go well. This led to a rapid withdrawal from service. A return of the tilting train to service in 1985-6 did not meet with favour, in large part due to the success of the high-speed diesel InterCity 125, and the trains were withdrawn from service; although the technology was to be used successfully for tilting trains in other countries. In contrast, on the East Coast Main Line from London to Edinburgh, fully electrified 225s, introduced in 1991, ensured journey times considerably shorter than they had been in the days of steam.

Opened in 1994, the Channel Tunnel has found it impossible to meet financial expectations. As a separate issue, post-Brexit border checks reduced peak capacity at London St Pancras by thirty per cent. However, the borrowing by Eurostar to meet the usage and revenue shortfall of the Eurostar service also reflected commercial and political choice: SNCF, the majority owner of Eurostar, was willing at the same time to spend about €600 million on a new high-speed operator in Spain, Ouigo España, which was founded in 2018 as a subsidiary of SNCF to develop services in Spain in competition with Renfe. So Eurostar had in large part to turn to commercial debt. Meanwhile, as an instance of the potential multiplier from new services, the high-speed line that linked St Pancras to the Channel Tunnel provided an opportunity greatly to increase rail services in Kent, with commuting times to London much reduced.

New trains and new routes can have geopolitical consequences. The road and rail Kerch Strait Bridge, opened in 2018 (originally a joint Ukraine-Russia initiative) provided a direct link between Russia and newly seized Crimea. It was attacked and damaged in 2022, probably by Ukraine, in response to the Russian invasion. This attack exemplified the vulnerability of the Russian logistical dependence on railways, although the bridge was fairly rapidly repaired.

The Channel Tunnel was not the sole rail tunnel built under a major shipping channel. A rail tunnel under the Bosporus was begun in 2004 and completed in 2008, rails added in 2009 and operations started in 2013. This is the deepest immersed tube tunnel in the world. The tunnel included a suburban service opened in 2019. The total Marmaray Project, 76.3 km (48 miles) long, included upgrading 63 km of suburban railway. The project was seen as important both in the local management of traffic and for the long-distance link between Ankara, the capital, and Istanbul, the largest city. Financing including soft loans from the Japan Bank for International Cooperation and the European Investment Bank.

Bridge-building or tunnelling is proposed by Russia for difficult waters in the Far East, as between Siberia and Sakhalin, and thence to Japan. The viability in engineering and financial terms of these ideas is unclear. The idea of a 11.7-kilometre tunnel under the Nevelskoy Strait between Siberia and Sakhalin was first proposed in the nineteenth century. Feasibility studies were undertaken in the late 1930s, at a time of huge tension with Japan, which then ruled southern Sakhalin to the south of the strait and had also occupied the north in 1905 and 1920-5. This geopolitical context was crucial to the plan, as a tunnel would have made possible the rapid reinforcement of Soviet forces in Sakhalin. The plan was postponed during the Second World War during which the Soviets concentrated resources on conflict with Germany and benefited from a 1941 non-aggression pact with Japan, only going to war with Japan in August 1945.

With all of Sakhalin under Soviet control from 1945, the scheme for a link between Siberia and Sakhalin was revived in 1950, again for military purposes, as Japan was now an American ally. A tunnel along with connecting rail lines on both sides was planned for completion in 1953 and full operation in 1955, the tunnel to be built by forced labour; but the project was abandoned in 1953. This abandonment indicated how little had been completed, but was also due to a lack of drive after Stalin's death in 1953, and to the post-Stalin amnesties reducing the labour force. A train ferry served as a substitute, but the plan for a link was revived in 2008-9, with talk of a bridge, an idea renewed in 2018. Nothing has happened about the plan for a bridge or tunnel link from Sakhalin to Hokkaido in Japan, or the even more implausible plan for a rail link over the Bering Strait, part of the 1890 idea of a 'Cosmopolitan Railway'. This plan was revived in 1904 and 2014.

Improved rail links between Russian Siberia and China are far more realistic. With China and Russia allies against America, there is a strong Chinese desire for Russian resources, a marked reversal of the situation in the late nineteenth century. There is, in a similar reversal, Russian concern about Chinese influence, even control. At the same time, concern has to be reframed to include regional interests, notably the economic benefits to be derived from improved links for freight shipments alongside pipelines.

Separately, the plan for a rail link between Japan and South Korea has been abandoned after little work was done. The Kyushu-Korea bridge project was longstanding, being advanced in the 1930s as well as during the Second World War. More recently, this link was supported on occasion by politicians close to the Unification Church, the Moonies. Based in South Korea, this church has many followers in Japan. The revival of the Kyushu-Korea tunnel plan was proposed by the Unificationists in the early 1980s but was never seriously considered, except for occasional lip service paid by Japanese and Korean politicians for the temporary political management of the bilateral relationship.

National prestige was generally at play in projects for bridges or tunnels across bodies of water; but with state encouragement, it more usually and clearly focused on the creation of long-distance rail systems, most notably in China. By 1951, 22,000 kilometres of track had been restored, and thereafter the emphasis was on new lines.

The ideological commitment to rail helps explain why the Chinese example is of limited applicability. A lack of realistic pricing or consideration of opportunity costs might be acceptable in a politically stable dictatorship benefiting from rapid and long-term economic growth and an unassailable ability to fix priorities and implement policies, but this does not describe most countries, including most dictatorships.

Lines were taken to far-flung parts of China, to Kashgar in 1999, a means of expanding the grip of the centre on distant Chinese Turkestan, and to Lhasa in Tibet in 2006, a formidable achievement across very difficult terrain. At 5,068 metres (16,627 feet) Tanggula railway station in Tibet is the world's highest, surpassing stations in Bolivia and Peru. The line included long tunnels and 675 bridges, and much is laid on permafrost. The carriages have enriched-oxygen and UV-protection systems. The line is frequently mentioned on television as a great Chinese achievement and was subsequently extended within Tibet. By the close of 2021, there were 150,000 kilometres of railway, 40,000 of which were high speed, the former the second largest in the world after America's 203,000, the latter the largest.

Developments continue. In 2022, a 825-kilometre line between Hotan and Ruoqiang was put into operation, which represented the final circling of the Taklimakan, China's largest desert, the shifting sands and sandstorms of which posed construction, maintenance and operational challenges. To try to reduce this, reed fences were installed as short-term windbreaks and sand-stabilising grids, as a preparation for the growth of the nearly 13 million trees that have been planted. Viaducts were built to allow sandstorms to pass beneath the tracks. Accounts of such lines were part of the heroic vision of rail beloved of the government.

As a result of the completion of this line, the length of Xinjiang's railways reached 8,977 kilometres, 3.2 times that of

2000. This was significant for a Chinese government seeking totally to suppress any possible separatist tendencies. In a 2022 border confrontation with India, rail speeded the ability to deploy troops, as had not been the case in the brief war with India in 1962. There was no matching Indian capability in 2022, and the line was important to sustain confrontation. In the Ukraine crisis of 2022-3, Russia used rail to move forward weapons and supplies, including reportedly the T-14, the latest main battle tank, thus reducing pressure on road. More generally in China and other authoritarian states, rail means that individual movements could and can be monitored in a determined surveillance state.

Across the world, there was over the last half century a marked reduction in rail use and services in some countries, while in others, rail proved uneconomic and heavily dependent on state aid; not that this necessarily stopped activity. The amount and source of investment were important and helped explain differences between countries. In America, in a very different context to India, which is a large system with insufficient investment, national passenger services did not attract support prior to the establishment of Amtrak. Government control is far patchier than in India. There was in America a continuing fall in railway mileage owned, from 217,552 in 1960 and 205,782 in 1970, to 183,055 in 1978. The fall was sharpest in areas of significant early activity, notably New England, so that, whereas the total owned mileage in America fell 26 per cent 1930-78, in Massachusetts it fell 57 per cent, to only 857 miles.

As a reminder of the importance of perceptions, provision now appeared over-capacity, and this was the case whether it was assessed in terms of usage, profitability, investment requirements, or the opportunity costs of capital. Massachusetts, moreover, was affected by a move from heavy industry to factories located near major roads.

There was a parallel in the decline of trolleybuses and other urban light systems. Thus, Cleveland's trolleybus system usage in 1996 was only just above 10 per cent of its 1946 peak. In part this was the result of urban decline in central Cleveland, but this was also more generally part of the decline of urban systems with competition from cars. There was a cultural and social move away from the public space of mass transit, one that was particularly pronounced in America. There was also a functional response to the remoulding of the cityscape as central city destinations declined and were replaced by suburb-to-suburb journeys: office-parks and new industrial capacity tended to be in suburban locations, and these were frequently linked to major roads, as were shopping malls. Such a linkage helped shoppers but also the just-in-time resupply of stores that was important to stock-management and cashflow and was linked to the location of distribution centres on the major roads and especially near important junctions.

Some rail travel to Southern cities was cut: Phoenix's passenger train service ended in 1996. In contrast, although stopped for a while by Hurricane Katrina in 2005, New Orleans, a far longer-established centre, is served by three Amtrak routes, the City of New Orleans from Chicago, the Crescent from New York, and the Sunset Limited from Los Angeles. Savannah is served by the New York-Miami Silver Service route.

Amtrak, which carried nearly 32 million passengers in 2017, was repeatedly attacked by Republicans, in part because of their opposition to Amtrak's major role on the East Coast and the resulting geographical-political tension. In April 2023, Amtrak unveiled proposals for the restoration of passenger services between New York and Scranton, mostly on existing track. In addition to construction and upgrading costs, the preliminary study predicted an annual operating cost of $19.1 million and revenue of $13.1 million, the difference requiring funding. Partly through a sense of regional advantage and disadvantage – and a process that presumably also goes on in other countries in which there is not such public discussion – Congress repeatedly delayed legislation to fund Amtrak other than over the short term. In 2014, there were 184 congressional districts in which no-one got on or off an Amtrak train, and 116 of them were represented by Republicans; the average number of rides in Republican districts was 41,000 compared to 261,000 in Democratic districts. The latter tend to be the most densely populated. Republicans argued that Amtrak was inefficient, wasteful, and overly prone to blame crashes, such as that outside Philadelphia in 2015, on infrastructure funding shortfalls rather than on the operating flaws that Republicans perceived. The Republicans opposed an annual subsidy of about $1 billion and drew attention to high wages and to 2012 figures that showed Amtrak accounted for just 0.14 per cent of passenger travel, compared to 87 per cent for road and 12 for aircraft.

Politics therefore played a significant role in the assumptions that framed the debate about financial support and they continue to do so. In America, as elsewhere, the return from Covid-level services has provided an opportunity to regroup and to reorganise transport priorities, but also reawakened political contention. The Amtrak Connects US plan announced in March 2021 was intended to create intercity corridors. How such plans would fare if Republicans returned to government is unclear. As a specific example, just before Donald Trump won the 2016 election, he threatened to rewrite NAFTA, hitting hard the share price of Kansas City Southern railroad, which was an important part of American-Mexican trade. However, this threat was not implemented, the share price rebounded, and the business boomed.

Meanwhile, Hillary Clinton's promise as Democratic candidate in her unsuccessful 2016 presidential campaign to create a 'world-leading' railway network was widely seen as fanciful. In America, new passenger links were classically between airports and city centres, as in Seattle and Atlanta. The 48-mile (77-km) Metropolitan Atlanta Rapid Transit Authority Rail network was opened in 1979 and had a ridership of 23 million by 2021. There is a colour-based route naming system, with the Yellow Line renamed Gold Line in 2010 in response to concerns from the local Asian community. However, the system failed to revitalise downtown Atlanta and did not match expectations of commuter usage. In part, this reflected the triumph of the car, but the network focus on low-density white areas rather than high-density black ones was also significant.

The wider economic potential of rail, however, remains important. In 2023, Siemens Mobility USA announced that it would build a rolling stock production factory in North Carolina to supplement its existing American factory in Sacramento. The location of the latter was related to the California High-Speed Rail Authority project for linking Los Angeles to San Francisco and the Brightline West Project for connecting Los Angeles to Las Vegas. There are hopes of completion by 2033 and 2027 respectively. However, problems with the LA to San Francisco line are instructive. Approved in 2008 with a predicted cost of $33 billion, $12-16 billion of which was to come from the federal government, the project was due to open in 2020. In the event, the federal government only allocated $3 billion and the project is now due to cost $105 billion. Completion is – problematic.

In the second case, Las Vegas had lost its rail passenger service in 1997 when Amtrak cancelled the Desert Wind service from Chicago to Los Angeles via Ogden, Salt Lake City, and Las Vegas. The same year, the Pioneer service from Denver to Seattle, another split off from the Chicago to San Francisco California Zephyr, was discontinued. Instead, an Amtrak Thruway motorcoach was introduced between Los Angeles and Las Vegas, such motorcoaches playing a major role in Amtrak services, increasingly so from 2014.

As with all projects, for Brightline West, show me the money. There is a high reliance for this project on tax-exempt private activity bonds issued by the states of California and Nevada XpressWest, a previous branding for the project, an instance of support for private ventures in the public interest. There were problems in making the bond sales attractive, and this led to their delay. This resulted in interest in switching money from the proposed High Desert Corridor freeway, which had been blocked on environmental grounds. The company also applied for funding under the federal Infrastructure Investment and Jobs Act of 2021. Success is uncertain.

Yet, alongside only limited provision and use of passenger service, deregulation in the 1980s and 1990s helped the railways profit as freight carriers. Moreover, there were fewer derailments, although in February 2023 one of a freight train on the Ohio-Pennsylvania border led to the spillage of dangerous chemicals and highlighted issues with maintenance and reliability. The question of reliability focused in particular on a rise in delays and, related to that, a cut in the service calls to collect freight. As a result, the efficient usage of freight carriages declined, with a heavy cost. Rail customers are often 'captive shippers', being only served by a single railway, so unable to negotiate for improved terms.

A major development from 2017 was the adoption of 'precision-scheduled railroading', which entailed freight services sticking to preset schedules rather than waiting for cargo to arrive. As a result, rolling stock spent less time in marshalling yards, and fewer trains meant fewer locomotives, which cut costs.

This was akin to lean manufacturing. Linked to this there was a smaller workforce, which greatly cut costs. Total employment for the seven largest North American freight railways fell from 159,000 in 2011 to 115,000 in 2021, a 28 per cent cut, during which time the amount of freight fell 11 per cent. In part, this was achieved by longer trains, some up to 3 miles. More revenue is gained from every ton of freight carried, which helps investors. Critics claim that new working practices contribute to derailments, and there has been a rise in complaints to rail regulators. There is certainly pressure on supervisors not to let trains stay in marshalling yards, while train inspection timeframes for features such as leaky bearings or improper loading have become much tighter.

The threat of an American freight train strike in late 2022 led to a wider realisation of the continuing economic significance of rail in the most car-obsessed country in the world. Food, energy, carmaker and retail groups urged Congress to intervene in the rail talks, noting that a freight shutdown could freeze almost a third of American cargo, pushing up inflation, hitting food and fuel supplies, and costing the economy an estimated $2 billion daily. About a quarter of American grain shipments are made by rail. Rail remains particularly important for bulk goods where the less than highly urgent real time constraint was compatible, for example in the movement of coal, iron ore and stone. As a consequence, there was something of a return to the original uses of rail, and this focus proved profitable for the four companies that together handled 90 per cent of American rail freight, notably Union Pacific, Norfolk Southern and Burlington Northern Santa Fe.

In 2022, with negotiation delayed by divisions between the unions over accepting a settlement, the pressure to ban strike action was successful, so that the strike was avoided. This led to debates over the need for more regulation, notably by the Surface

Transportation Board, particularly penalties for poor service, which the companies contested as likely to be a serious burden.

Meanwhile in America, as elsewhere, competition from air passenger services was supplemented by that from air freight, notably a major rise in overnight delivery services. These took a lot of high-value goods from rail and road. There was a hidden government subsidy in the running of the federally owned air traffic control system.

It is understandable that the emphasis in much discussion would be on growth including new lines, but the reality across most of the world was very different. This was a matter of economic, fiscal and political circumstances and developments, and their interaction with the pre-existing legacy, from terrain, which affected maintenance and running costs, to rolling stock. Terrain was a serious problem, as in Peru, or in Venezuela where the noted La Guaira-Caracas railway closed in 1951. In part this closure was due to storms, but a rival road link was also crucial. In Paraguay, where wood-powered steam locomotives were used until non-tourist passenger services ended in 1999, even the limited tourist steam train service was suspended in 2010. There is a limited rail link to Argentina, but the repurposing of the train station in the capital Asunción into a rail museum is an apt symbol of change.

The rail system did not change greatly in the last decades of the Soviet Union up to 1991, because the economic and political fundamentals remained constant, as did the regulatory and managerial structures and the related personnel. Soviet railways were crucial to an economy that did not rely heavily on road transport, despite the availability of oil. Road links were patchy, particularly good all-weather ones. The situation was produced by legacy factors from earlier Soviet history, as well as the ideology and practice of Soviet Communism. The particular Soviet route to modernisation was the electrification of 53,900 kilometres of the network. A State Electrification Committee had been established in 1920 and was important to the strategy of the Party, Lenin announcing in 1920 'Communism is Soviet power plus the electrification of the whole country.' The rail industry was a key element of this and clearly represented the central idea of state direction of the economy and of society as a whole. The power grid was seen as a way to unite and modernise the state, and the pace of electrification increased from 1926 with regional power plants aplenty and the annual output of billion kwh allegedly increasing from 1.9 in 1913 to 8.8 in 1931 and 48 by 1940, although Soviet figures are always problematic. From the late 1930s, the Soviet Union became the world leader in rail electrification, being surpassed in the 2010s by China. By 1990, over 60 per cent of Soviet freight was being hauled by electric trains. This provided greater efficiency than steam.

In turn, the fall of the Soviet Union was followed by an embrace of high-speed trains comparable to those in Western Europe. In 2001, a 200-km/h train entered service as the Nevsky Express on the St Petersburg-Moscow route, taking four and a half hours to cover the 635 kilometres instead of the six hours hitherto. In its place, from 2009, the Siemens-built Sapsam further cut the service time, with two and a half hours in the future envisaged once the infrastructure is updated. Other passenger-focused fast routes opened from Moscow to Ryazan, Tula and Vladimir. Streamlining has come in as has air-conditioning, wifi, and booking online, and there is a sense of being on an aircraft and not, as with Soviet rail, taking an endurance test. Russian Railways, the state-owned successor from 2003 to the Ministry of Railways, had cut its labour force greatly in the 2000s, but was badly affected by procurement corruption, which led in 2015-16 to major personnel changes linked to the appointment as new

Chief Executive of the First Deputy Minister of Transport. There are plans to extend the high-speed system in the 2020s including to Yekaterinburg and Rostov, but it is unclear that these plans will survive the crisis stemming from the Ukraine war, as Russian Railways receives financial support from the government. This is a more serious factor than the American sanctioning in December 2022 of the Chief Executive.

More generally, alongside change there are continuities. For example, the different advantages of trucks/lorries and rail remain unchanged, but the values involved can alter, as environmental lobbying indicates. Rail offers economies of scale that provide more efficient fuel use and cost-effectiveness, but trucks are generally faster and more flexible in their collection and delivery.

The technological development of railways has been relatively slow. Motive power has changed from steam to diesel and electricity, but these technologies have themselves developed slowly. Thus, the fuel consumption of diesel locomotives has not been widely addressed until very recently. High-speed trains, such as the French TGV, demonstrate some development, notably in-cab signalling and the measures taken to eliminate the effect of waves in the electrified catenary cables caused by the rapid movement of the train. Nevertheless, there has been no real transformation in operating costs.

Geography cannot always be conquered. The problems of frost-thaw and the resultant shifting of the soil poses problems for any use of high-speed trains across much of Canada. Terrain imposes costs, not least for tunnelling. Waterways can be bridged or tunnelled under, but these also represent major difficulties. Rail can change much, but not all.

10

WHAT NEXT?

Niamey airport station, Niger, opened in 2014 on the Niamey-Dosso line, now a sad testimony to the inability to bring plans to fruition that has so often characterised the history of rail. (Niger TZai)

The history of Niamey Railway Station, the first opened in Niger, and part of the AfricaRail project, can be as instructive as the repeated stress on new routes and services in much of the literature. The station was to be the terminus of a projected 563-kilometre line from Parakou in Benin (formerly Dahomey), which itself was the terminus of an existing 438-kilometre line from Cotonou on the Atlantic coast finished by the French colonial power in 1936.

As part of a €2 billion Blueline Project for a 3,000-kilometre rail loop including the line from Cotonou, there was a plan for a line to go on from Niamey, via Ouagadougou in Burkina Faso, to Abidjan in Ivory Coast, thus replacing the hinterland's reliance on lorries and cutting the costs of exports and imports. There was no emphasis on passenger traffic.

The opening ceremony exposed the gap between reality and ambition. The Presidents of Benin, Niger and Togo attended, but the inaugural train had only 500 metres of track to operate on, carrying the visiting dignitaries round and round. In 2016, a 145-kilometre line with seven other stations was opened from Niamey to Dosso in Niger. Yet, no trains have used the route since 2017, and there is no sign that this will change. The instability of the region is likely to discourage further investment.

As a reminder that entrepreneurial individuals still play a role in modern plans, the West African rail proposals highlighted a rivalry between Frank Timiş, a Romanian-Australian industrialist and head of Pan African Minerals who ran the major manganese mine at Tambao in north-eastern Burkina Faso close to Niger, and Vincent Bolloré, a Frenchman who played a major part in the opening ceremonies at Niamey. Bolloré was to hold 40 per cent of the project. African Minerals, which Timiş also controlled, went into administration in 2015 and was sold to a Chinese company. Tambao has very poor road links, which has led to interest in rail plans which, since 2010, have attracted Indian, Singaporean, Japanese and Brazilian concerns, including Mitsui Rail Capital.

From 1999, Bolloré had also been active in operating railways in Cameroon, with mineral exports a key element. In Niger, his company built the line between Niamey and Dosso, but it was affected by litigation with rival companies: Petrolin Group, headed by Samuel Dossou-Aworet, an oil industry figure from Benin, and Geftarail, a French company, both claiming rights to build between Niger and Benin. As a result, construction by Bolloré stopped six kilometres south of Dosso, leaving a scene that is as worthy of record as those more impressive tributes to technology that tend to be reproduced in books on rail. Subsequent neglect has left much of the track damaged, while in Niamey heat has similarly made the line unusable. The punctured hopes at Dosso, now a town of unfinished buildings, do not bode well for plans for a 248-kilometre line from Maradi, Niger's second city, to Kano in Nigeria, a plan designed to provide a link to the Atlantic via the Nigerian rail system. Nor, indeed, does the significant level of instability in northern Nigeria, which includes protection payments to local powerbrokers for economic activity.

A greater use of rail, nevertheless, is being encouraged by a range of factors that vary in impact in particular countries. First, potential demand rises due to the increase in world population and global economic activity. The population was about one billion in 1800 and three in 1960, reached eight in 2023 and is predicted to grow to about 9.8 billion in 2050. There are particularly high growth rates in South Asia and sub-Saharan Africa, and even though rates are lower, there has been growth to high figures elsewhere, notably in China and the United States.

This situation creates a demographic conundrum. A decreasing percentage of the global population may travel by rail, but even if the percentage falls, possibly sharply, the aggregate number of those so doing may still rise. This creates issues of provision, funding and equity, with competing demands for more and less expenditure on rail. If that is the case for passengers, it will also be so for freight.

At the same time, the context will vary greatly as national populations follow very different paths. This will include political, social, environmental, and financial factors. These can be clearly seen in the case of the rail versus road battle. For European middle-class commentators, that has been, and generally remains, a debate over public rail versus private car, but there is the very different perspective provided by buses, which provide public and/ or private transport, generally for the less affluent. When rail is in private or public-private ownership, the accompanying debate is on profits. Public ownership, however, does not necessarily mean free from profit for vested interests, or rentiers, including those who in effect corruptly own aspects of the state.

To complicate the picture still further, fertility rates are falling in many countries and it is possible that the world population may peak in 2050. The rich world currently has about three people of working age for everyone over 65. By 2050 there could be less than two. That implies higher taxes and lower returns for savers, which means investors in rail. Just how many workers will be commuting into New York or Shanghai in the middle of the century?

A rail-centred narrative would focus on China, the source of much expansion both there and elsewhere. In 2013-19, Chinese companies signed $61.6 billion worth of rail construction contracts with 34 countries. 47 per cent in Asia and 34 per cent in Africa, Malaysia and Nigeria being the largest parties in each category. From the 2010s, trade from China overland by rail to Western Europe developed. Services via Kazakhstan, Russia, Belarus and Poland, or via the old Trans-Siberian axis of Russia, Belarus and Poland, were part of a developing network of links, such as from Chongqing, Wuhan and Xian to Duisburg, and from Yiwu to Hamburg; they were interrupted during the Covid pandemic of 2020-2, but then resumed. The market is very important. By 2022, 20 per cent of the EU's imports came from China, compared with 12 per cent from America. Nevertheless, plans for new services and routes have not always come to fruition.

Chinese financing has a difficult imprint. Debt burdens have already hit hard, notably in Sri Lanka, Pakistan and Laos. Granting resources, including control over ports, as collateral for debts increases the problem. Corruption has also been an issue, with the Chinese-backed East Coast Rail Link in Malaysia linked in 2015 to claims that the Prime Minister, Najib Razak, embezzled money in a plot linked to inflated costs. His successor only agreed to maintain the project when the cost was cut substantially. Moreover, stronger Chinese capital controls create increasing commitments to match the cost implications of inflation. As a result, the exportability of the Chinese rail model is problematic, and in countries such as Angola, where it revamped the rail system, China's infrastructure-resource, economic-financial model has proved difficult to sustain as the true costs to both sides have become apparent.

Chinese activity, nevertheless, is still far-reaching and includes rail links to ports. China financed parts of a (largely) freight route from Budapest via Belgrade to the Greek port of Piraeus, a route, however, that was delayed in construction and will leave Hungary and Serbia with a very substantial debt to China. South of Belgrade, it is the EU that is providing the upgrade to the line. The upgrade from Budapest to Belgrade will cut the time taken from eight to three and a half hours, but most of the work has gone to Chinese companies and subcontractors, as well as to Lörinc Mészáros, a friend of Viktor Orbán, Prime Minister of Hungary.

Strategic issues proved particularly significant for Chinese rail plans, but not only for them. Concern about Chinese and Russian plans gave rise to rival attempts to develop rail links, notably the Rail Baltica project for a high-speed standard-gauge link from Berlin, via

Warsaw and Vilnius, to Riga and Tallinn. This route was intended to bypass the Russian Baltic enclave of Kaliningrad, a former Cold War rail hub. Agreed in 2017, the reason for the project was bluntly spelt out that year by Maris Kucinskis, the Latvian Prime Minister: 'We have to continue to strengthen our defence capability.' A link to Finland through a connecting undersea rail tunnel was also envisaged but is in a different league in terms of mileage costs.

The Rail Baltica project in part represents a corrective to that under the Cold War when east-west links focused on Russia predominated, as they had done when these countries were part of the Russian Empire. The completion of Rail Baltica, however, has been postponed from 2026 to 2030. Estonia, Latvia and Lithuania quarrelled over management. This has led the EU to threaten to block its funding, which is crucial for a scheme that is due to cost €6 billion ($6.5 billion).

The Soviet influence meanwhile continues. Ukraine's railway is on the 1.52 metre gauge, rather than the 1.435 metre one used in Poland and most of Europe. In 2022, Denys Shmyhal, Ukraine's Prime Minister, declared that the railways there would be rebuilt to the European gauge, which would help through transport. Lviv in western Ukraine might then become a major hub, with rail links to south-west Poland, Ostrava in the Czech Republic, and Košice in Slovakia. This enhanced capability would counter the Russian ability to blockade Ukraine's Black Sea ports, notably Odessa. In 2022, a blockade had exposed the inadequacies of the current rail system of Ukraine and the inability of its westward links to replace all of its maritime trade. As a result, an export terminal was developed at Izmail, a river port on the Danube, with redevelopment also at nearby Kiliia. This put pressure on the rail link from Odessa which was vulnerable at its bridge crossing over the Dniester estuary at Zatoka. Damage from missile attacks forced business back onto an overloaded road from Odessa.

The Ukraine war of 2022-3 saw rail links as of continuing strategic importance. Rail hubs, such as Kupiansk and Melitopol, remained significant for operational goals. Yet, at the same time, most supplies were moved by road. In Kiev, the rail tunnels were used to provide shelter against Russian missile attacks.

War is not at the forefront of rail planning in most states. Instead, in many countries, often related to international financial aid or at least investment, but also separate from it, governments make bold plans for railway improvements, keen to develop their state's infrastructure as a politically attractive means to economic development. In particular, on a longstanding basis, such infrastructure is seen as necessary for the movement to ports of bulky raw materials for export. Such rail movements are supported not so much because they are environmentally appropriate, although that argument is advanced, but because they help overcome the limitations of large-scale road movements. The use of containers facilitates this process, and there have been developments in containers, lorries and rolling stock in order to permit easier and faster loading and unloading.

At the same time, and conforming to a different form and content of strategy, environmentalism encourages investment in rail as a contrast to road. This is notably so with rapid transit systems in America and Europe, some of which followed previous rail links, as in Boston and Tyneside.

Aside from being designed to reduce pressure on crowded roads, electric passenger trains are seen as significant in reducing carbon emissions, with the European Environment Agency estimating in 2021 that, although some generation of power used fossil fuels, nevertheless trains averaged a fifth of the greenhouse-gas emissions per passenger-kilometre of aircraft and less than half that of buses. This factor has greatly encouraged EU support for the expansion of rail. However, there are still significant costs. Thus, a study published in 2023 by the Technische Universität Dresden for the Bavarian railway agency reported that it would be technically possible to replace the diesel trains in the hilly Bayerischen Wald with battery traction, but that this would require significant infrastructure investment. Also in 2023, a study undertaken by the University of Queensland suggested that batteries or a combination of batteries and hydrogen fuel cells could feasibly replace diesel traction for for heavy freight trains, while Poland's national rail authority certified for operation a hydrogen locomotive on which work had begun in 2019. This is designed to lead to a prototype electric and hydrogen bi-mode passenger train for completion by the end of 2026. Separately in 2023, the leaders of six private German rail freight operators published an open letter to the federal Transport Minister pressing the government to revise pessimistic forecasts for the sector's future growth.

Interest in rail in a number of areas, for example California, where there are plans for a high-speed rail system, is an aspect of environmentalism. The situation in California, however, offers a caveat about the problems faced by such plans. Thus, in the Bay Area, Facebook hoped from 2017 to revitalize an 18-mile rail route from Union City on the east side of San Francisco over the abandoned Dumbarton Rail Bridge, opened in 1910 but requiring revitalisation, and up the San Francisco Peninsula. This was intended to make commuting easier and to cut emissions. These linked goals were regarded as particularly significant as local housing costs ensured that many could not live near their place of work, which led to long commutes, congested roads and pollution. In the event, being a key part of the world's most prosperous economy could not ensure success. As an instructive instance of the more general need to consider a range of factors as playing a part in success and failure, other than solely resources, there was the regulatory environment. Across the nine counties of the Bay Area, there were 27 transit agencies, and their views, issues, and planning cycles did not coincide. This affected plans for operation of the new system by 2028. There were also specific factors that complicated demand prediction, in particular the Covid pandemic of 2020-2 and the decline of office work. Facebook abandoned its project in 2021. In practice, the administrative impasse was the key issue.

Environmental goals are also important to the development of new locomotives and rolling stock. In France, following a programme launched in 2015, SNCF prepared for TGV M, or Avelia Horizon trains, the TGV of the future, to enter service in 2024. The train is predicted to cut CO_2 emissions by 37 per cent and is made of 97 per cent recyclable components while also carrying 20 per cent more passengers thanks to being a double-decker, a high-speed practice also seen elsewhere, as in Spain, but not in Britain or America. The maximum speed is designed to be 320 kilometres per hour and the lengthened nose offers an increase in aerodynamic quality. SNCF's order of 115 TGV M trains is worth €3.3 billion, and manufacture by Alstom keeps the business in France. The international role of major companies, such as Alstom, is another aspect of the competitive power politics of rail, as governments such as France can play a major role in supporting such contracts. Indeed, in 2023, the incumbent company, SNCF Voyageurs, beat a rival bid from Transdev, a private group that is well-established in the Île de France, to win the Hauts-de-France region's first competitively tendered contract for the operation of passenger train services. Yet there were problems. In 2023, French demonstrations against proposed government legislation on the retirement age led to the severe disruption of train services, with strikes in that traditionally radical sector seen as a way to maintain pressure on the government.

New technology is a possible factor in any new developments, although the consequences are unclear, as with 'Maglev' (magnetic levitation) systems. These use electromagnetics to move the train up off the track, thus ensuring a lack of friction, and to move the train ahead. Although patented in America extraordinarily enough in 1905, such trains have seen only limited development. They are operational, notably in China, Japan, and South Korea, but none are particularly long. More generally, the application of software has made it easier to ensure that timetables are workable and robust, while also saving labour. By the twenty-first century, the image of rail travel conveyed by visual advertising remained important to sales, but practical information was more accessible by internet. Software is key to automated working across the rail system, from signalling to driving. The spread of digital rail technology offers both savings in the form of labour costs and also more efficiency. Safety factors are a key element. Thus, remote monitoring and control of critical equipment requires the seamless operation of advanced control with a high level of precision. The sophistication of monitoring has increased greatly to include the use of satellite-based radar data and a relevant algorithm to derive soil moisture value, thus offering guidance on earthen structures such as slopes along lines.

Less positively, many areas of major population growth see few realistic plans for new provision, while plans elsewhere have been pushed back or postponed. This was notably so in Brazil, Latin America's most populous country, where there were longstanding plans for new high-speed lines between Rio de Janeiro and São Paulo, relatively close, as well as more fanciful ideas of a route on to Manaus on the Amazon, one in which riverboats provided most of the coverage. One such plan for a line between Rio and São Paulo was launched in 1989 but rapidly dropped due to the cost and the lack of public and private funding. All plans for a Brazilian high-speed train system were put aside. They were revived from 2000, with plans for lines between those cities, as well as Brasilia and Goiãnia, Belo Horizonte and Curitiba, and Ribeirão Preto and Uberlãndria. None, however, has been started. In part, politics played a role, but it was no simple case of the Right being opposed to rail. Instead, the right-wing government of Jair Bolsonaro, the President from 2019 until 2022, was interested in private investment in rail as a means to improve the economy. He backed Ferrogrão, a 1,000-kilometre railway into Amazonia, as part of his controversial plan to develop the latter, including making it less expensive to move soybeans and grains to the coast. This plan had scant concern for the environment or indigenous people and reflected Bolsonaro's strong links to agribusiness.

The National Logistics Plan in 2022 reported that 67.7 per cent of cargo in Brazil travelled by road, compared to 21.5 per cent by rail and 9.5 per cent by waterways, and it was planned that by 2035 the percentage by rail would be increased to 40. The Brazilian freight load was overwhelmingly iron ore (73 per cent) and agricultural products (14 per cent). A theme in the new plans was that of natural unification, as with the title of schemes, for example the Midwest Integration Railroad. In 2021-2, Bolsonaro sought to encourage more private sector investment in rail, and bids for nearly 22,250 km of railway construction were received.

There was less boldness in other Latin American countries, though still some expansion with the first metro service in Ecuador's capital, Quito, opened in 2023. The Huancayo Metro in Peru was all too typical, the plan announced in 2012 for a 7-kilometre stretch of an old *Ferrocarril Central Andino* line to become a metropolitan railway, with a second 42-kilometre stretch to the city of Jauja. The scheme was abandoned in 2013. A different challenge to the Lima to Huancayo rail line in 1992-2003 arose from the very active Shining Path terrorist movement, while in 2023, there was disruption to rail services during large-scale demonstrations against the government. In some states, such as Paraguay and Venezuela, there was contraction.

In the latter, despite oil wealth, mismanagement helped stop work on the 468-kilometre Tinaco-Anaco high-speed railway for which there was a Chinese $7.5 billion contract. This was a project to connect the east and west of the country and help in the development of the plains south of the coastal mountains. President Chávez said at the ground-breaking: 'It is the great railway of the northern plains axis.' There was to be technology transfer and four factories to produce sleepers, rails and rolling stock. Agreed in 2009 as part of the 2006 National Socialist Plan for Railway Development for 15 new lines comprising 8,500 miles by 2030, only 31 per cent of the line was built by 2011 when work was halted for the first time, and by 2013 the state rail authority owed $400 million to the Chinese consortium, and work stopped. In 2015, the Chinese managers left while facilities in a railway factory in Zaraza were looted and vandalised by an armed group of local residents. Aside from financing, there were serious labour and environmental problems and by 2021 only 40 kilometres were in operation. There was no stable electricity supply. So also with other aspects of the 2006 plan.

In Africa, there was a marked sense of unfulfilled hopes. In Nigeria, Africa's most populous country, and one with a very high rate of population growth, there has been expansion in services with trains running from Abuja, the new capital, to Kaduna, in the north from 2016. However, in 2022, there were bombs on the track and the kidnapping of passengers for ransom. In Nigeria, there is separatism in the South-East and acute lawlessness across much of the north.

These issues of stability and vulnerabilities greatly affected the plan advanced from 2008 for a 4,000-kilometre railway to link the Atlantic port of Dakar with the Red Sea's Port Sudan, thus providing a transcontinental railway from Senegal to Sudan via Mali, Niger and Chad, and one that avoids the sea routes round the Cape of Good Hope or via the Mediterranean and the Suez Canal. There were already railways from Dakar to Koulikoro, Mali (1,287 km), opened in 1924 and a product of French imperialism; and another (of a different gauge) from Nyala, Sudan, near the border with Chad, to Port Sudan. The plan made even more implausible by bitter civil war in Sudan in 2023 as well as the linked deterioration in relations between Sudan and Chad.

This new plan was linked to the idea of West African regional rail integration, notably building a line from Bamako, the capital of Mali, to its border with Ivory Coast, as part of a new system also involving Burkino Faso, Benin, Nigeria and Ghana. Progress, however, has been very limited. The breakdown of stability in the region, notably in Mali and Niger from the early 2010s, made the plan unworkable. Moreover, the existing Senegal-Mali line is in a poor state, and notably so for passenger traffic, with serious problems of investment and management affecting the rolling stock and track, such that speeds are low.

Mineral extraction is a key reason for rail links, as in the 704-kilometre line in Mauritania from the iron workings at Zouérat to the export port of Nouadhibou, which was built in 1960-3 and nationalised in 1974. Due to Mauritania's annexation of the south-western part of Southern Sahara in 1976, after Spanish forces withdrew from what had been the Spanish Sahara, the line running close to the frontier was attacked by Polisaro forces, which hit Mauritania's economy. After withdrawal from Spanish Sahara by Mauritanian forces in 1979, use of the line was resumed. The trains are very long and move about 16.6 million tons of iron a year. This line carries a few passengers but underlines the extent to which the most profitable and predictable use of rail is for freight. There are similar plans elsewhere, as for a 1,100-kilometre Botswana- Zimbabwe-Mozambique route to take coal from Serule to a port at Techobanine Point, Mozambique, and thus make it available to Asian markets. A memorandum of understanding was signed but has not been brought to fruition. Such economic benefits make it possible to envisage confronting the problems posed by the cost of constructing and maintaining rail over large distances.

The largest country in Central Africa, Congo, or the Democratic Republic of Congo, had in 2022 5,033 kilometres of railways, but the lines were in four districts, not an interconnected network, operating on three gauges and run by separate companies. Most of the lines were in the east, linking to neighbouring countries, Angola and Zambia. Part of the earlier system cannot be used. Corruption was a major problem under the Mobutu regime from 1965 to 1997, and warfare in the 1990s contributed to disruption. Road traffic is responsible for 97 per cent of Congolese freight movement. In response, there have been bold plans for renovation and new development, including elevated monorail high-speed trains in five corridors of 10,800 kilometres, more specifically 485 in the first phase. The monorail lines are seen as less disruptive to existing infrastructure and also better suited to cross the numerous rivers of the country and to deal with flooding. The route from the capital, Kinshasa, to the port of Matadi is the main initial goal. Other proposals over the last two decades have included lines from Congo to Uganda and to the Kenyan port of Lamu.

South Africa has a poor rail system, with corruption and violence problems. Mismanagement of rail freight by Transnet, a state-owned enterprise, is linked to inadequate expenditure on maintenance, especially on the locomotives, but bountiful spending on wages and contracts. As a result, there is increased reliance on lorries, notably to move coal, iron and chrome and, therefore, less revenue coming into Transnet. One possibility is for South Africa to follow Mozambique, Tanzania and Zambia in developing private-public partnerships. Thus, in Mozambique, Vale, a major Brazilian mining firm, invested in 2010 in the Northern Development Corridor and built a line, completed in 2017, to move coal from its mines to a coal export terminal. Indian public-sector rail-based consortia have leased the Beira railway. However, that solution requires a stable operating context, which is absent in South Africa.

China is the leading investor in African rail, with personnel as well as funds. Chinese expertise, investment and technology in financing and building railways have played a role. Investments include a standard gauge railway in Kenya from Mombasa to Nairobi (in place of the inadequate colonial narrow-gauge line), which the World Bank refused to finance and which, since becoming operational in 2018, has made a heavy and politically damaging loss. This ensured that the planned extension to Uganda, let alone new connections to Rwanda, South Sudan and Ethiopia, did not materialise. Instead, there has been a revamping of the British colonial rail link. The Lamu Port, South Sudan and Ethiopia Transport Corridor was presented as a way to open up northern Kenya and was designed to be part of a rail land bridge to Douala in Cameroon, thus linking the Indian and Atlantic Oceans. In January 2023, Uganda cancelled a $2.3 billion contract with China Harbour Engineering Company to build a 170-mile railway from Kampala to the Kenyan border town of Malaba, instead turning to a Turkish company. There has also been an electric line between Djibouti, a port that is a centre of Chinese investment and a major naval base, and Ethiopia; a projected service in Nigeria between congested Lagos and Ibadan; and a Chinese role in the Senegal-Niger service.

Chinese assistance can apparently involve bribery. Thus, South Africa's Transnet allegedly bought overpriced locomotives from China and then had a dispute that led to the Chinese refusing to supply spare parts. The terms that Kenya agreed were prohibitive. In 2013, China and Tanzania agreed to build a port at Bagamoyo able to handle 20 million containers a year that was to be connected to the Tazara Railway, with China's Export-Import Bank providing most of the finance. The port was in the home district of President Jakaya Kikwete, but his successor, John Magufuli, cancelled the construction contracts saying the Chinese demands were excessive. In turn, in 2021, the negotiations were resumed by the new president who had links with Kikwete.

The problems of Africa are highly pertinent not only to that continent, but also to whether the Chinese model of rail construction and operation can be exported anywhere, and thus with reference to the general global situation. The evidence so far is that this is unsatisfactory for African states and people. Debt sustainability is a key issue.

Areas of inadequate rail provision in Africa include the rapidly expanding cities in sub-Saharan Africa, such as Kinshasa in Congo. In 2023, Africa Finance Corporation and Trans Connexion Congo announced plans for a 325-kilometre refurbished and expanded rail network in Kinshasa, MetroKin. The first phase is a 25-kilometre connection from the central station to the airport. This will not be enough to address the mobility needs of a population that has risen from 0.2 million in the 1960s to over ten million in 2010, and over 16 million in 2018. The infrastructure has failed to cope, not only with the annual population growth rate of 3.5 per cent but also with basic issues of maintenance, leading to obsolescence. The plan included modern trains and modest fares. The proposal documents note advantages but also weaknesses and threats including financial dependence on foreign partners, poor means of guaranteeing investment costs, skill shortages, road competition, lawlessness, and landslides due to torrential rain.

The situation in Africa, where the urban population, understood as settlements of 10,000 or more, is forecast to rise from 50 per cent in 2015 to over 70 per cent by 2050, is complicated by the tendency, also seen elsewhere, as in Japan, Britain or France, to focus on major cities and notably capitals, such as Kinshasa, rather than the towns and cities where much of the population live.

Thus, in 2015, about 60 per cent of Africa's urban population lived in cities with a population of less than one million. Mass transit systems designed for megalopolises are not appropriate for these cities, and this serves as a reminder of the range of urban environments that have to be addressed, and the mistake of a one-size-fits-all solution, whether or not focused on trains.

In contrast to much of Africa, in the Middle East, more affluent and more stable Dubai, Doha, Riyadh and Tel Aviv saw the development of metro systems, while Tunis has had one since 1985 and it has subsequently greatly expanded. However, the very much delayed suburban rail system for the city only began operation in 2023. A metro system was also planned for Baghdad. Such a scheme was advanced in the 1970s, only to be stopped by the Iran-Iraq War of 1980-8 and Iraq's subsequent international isolation. In 2008, Baghdad's municipality invited bids for a bolder scheme, with 40 stations (instead of the 14-15 since envisaged). In 2011, a preliminary agreement to build the metro, which was expected to take five years to complete, was signed. In 2013, an agreement had been signed for the design studies, but there has been delay since. Iraq, able to draw on oil wealth, signed a $2.5 billion letter of intent with Alstom in 2020 to accelerate the implementation of the Baghdad Elevated Train, a 22-kilometre elevated railway, French technology providing a way to address Baghdad's polluted congestion, including a link to the airport.

The situation in Iraq is more generally indicative of the difficulties of moving from proposals to implementation, and particularly of fixing deliverable time horizons. The plans of recent decades have included urban rail projects for the city of Basra as well as a Baghdad-Basra high-speed line that was agreed in 2011, both again with Alstom. This scheme for transport at speeds of up to 155 mph was not executed, but there were improvements to the service on what was called the Southern Rail Line, and in 2020 a delivery of Chinese diesel trains capable of 100 mph. The failure of the 2011 agreement did not prevent fresh plans and promises. The 2023 Iraqi budget included a railway from the Gulf port of Faw to northern Iraq, to provide a route on to Turkish ports, and thus a link from the Persian Gulf to both the Black Sea and the Mediterranean. This offered both Iraq and Turkey a means to bypass the Suez Canal, and also to avoid the civil war in Syria across which the existing route ran but had been blocked by that conflict. This plan also competed with the revival in 2022 of rail links between Turkey and Iran.

In part due to different political, governmental, economic and fiscal contexts, India, a rapidly growing economy, is failing to match developments in China. The treatment of rail was long an aspect of the corporatism of Indian politics and also of a more general failure in publicly regulated rail systems (whether or not state owned), to allow for a return on capital sufficient to attract more investment. There are plans for high-speed lines, notably between Mumbai and Ahmedabad, Hyderabad and Nagpur, Nagpur and Varanasi, Patna and Guwahati, Chennai and Mysuru, and Delhi to Ahmedabad and Amritsar, but completion goals have been overly optimistic. In 2019, the government announced that it would invest substantial sums by 2030 to improve the rail system, with the National High Speed Rail Corporation

Limited established to that end in 2016 to connect the Diamond Quadrilateral, the major cities of Delhi, Mumbai, Chennai and Kolkata. The first was to be the Mumbai-Ahmedabad line, but it is behind schedule.

The Indian rail system has proven highly vulnerable to accidents, which in part is due to poor maintenance but also to a difficulty in preventing trespassing on the line by individuals, vehicles and animals. I have noted at Chennai's main railway station not only that security precautions were not working for humans, but also that a cow was wandering on a platform. There have also been serious incidents of disaffection with the government leading to the disruption of rail services and damage to rolling stock. In 2022, railway stations and coaches in the major provinces of Bihar, Uttar Pradesh and Bengal were vandalised in protests over a new military recruitment plan designed to lower the average age of service and cut pension costs. There were also hundreds of train cancellations. The railways suffered a loss of 259.44 crores aside from passenger refunds.

Under-investment is a major issue for the future of Indian railways, in part arising because ticket prices were held down for political reasons. The high rate of population growth in India, to reach 1.43 billion by 2023, passing China, and predicted to reach 1.6 billion in the next three decades, makes its situation of particular significance for the global development of rail systems. Nevertheless, despite some important activity, the Indian influence on projects elsewhere has been much less than that of China.

More generally, much of the freight need in India is met by road transport and notably so given the difficulties of matching freight requirements to rail provision. It is easier to improve or cope with roads than install new rail links. So also in Sri Lanka, where, in 2001, in terms of ton-kilometres carried, only two per cent were by rail, compared to 97 per cent by motor vehicles and one per cent by water transport.

Motor vehicles dominate in poor or conflict-wracked states, such as Palestine, Lebanon, Libya, Sudan, Syria and Yemen, that cannot match Saudi Arabia, Israel, Iraq, Morocco, or the United Arab Emirates in their plans for rail. Population growth can be a factor in addressing the need to increase rail capacity, as with financially weak Egypt. In 2018, after a long period of no real changes to Egyptian rail, plans were advanced to build three high-speed lines, with a total length of about 2,000 kilometres (1,200 miles). The first, 660 kilometres long, designed for completion in 2027, the 'Suez Canal on Rails', was to link Mersa Matrouh on the Mediterranean west of Alexandria to Ain Sukhna on the Gulf of Suez, leading into the Red Sea. The second (1,100 km) was to go from the new capital, 6th of October, up the Nile to the Sudanese border, and the third (225 km) to link the mid-Nile to the Red Sea port of Safaga. The German Siemens company as well as Deutsche Bahn are key participants, as is a Chinese-Egyptian consortium. The entire network, which in part made sense of the new capital, and which would give Egypt the sixth-largest network in the world, had a projected cost of $23 billion and is therefore dependent on the international financial support received by Egypt. The network was designed to be fully electrified and to cut pollution.

Many projects across the world are not financially sound nor environmentally prudent, as in Mexico when President López Obrador has supported the Tren Maya Scheme in the Yucatán peninsula that, in linking tourist sites, would benefit the hotels of supporters. Construction began in 2020, but the estimated cost has risen from 150 billion pesos (2018) to 321 billion ($18.5 billion) in 2020. How this cost would be met has been the cause of great controversy, as have the environmental consequences and the implications for indigenous people. More generally, political uncertainties in Mexico as elsewhere discourage foreign investment, a long-term problem for rail with its capital and income requirements.

Global fiscal and monetary tightening from 2022 suggested a worsening situation for the future of rail. In particular, pressure on investment availability is a product of a more general strain on liquidity, while the marked rise in interest rates meant that return on capital became more problematic, greatly affecting investment options. Inflation eroded the value of international financial backing, requiring a greater volume of support at the same time that its availability diminished. More generally, the current financing environment for railway development is poor, with rail unattractive to private capital in part as a result of the very long time required to gain any decent return, and also due to the flawed direction of many new infrastructure projects, the slow pace or lack of technological development, and the running costs and poor management of railways.

Poor management may owe something to the natural monopoly that most rail enjoys, whether the ownership is public or private. In two sectors, there is really no competition: heavy freight and mass transit. In land haulage of low unit value heavy products, such as coal, ore, aggregates, and grain, there is no competitive transport mode. Before arriving in many supermarkets, bottled water has been moved by rail at some stage, as it is heavy and cheap. The same applies to commuter transport. Consequently, there is little incentive to improve efficiency, cost and service. Rail management is also generally closed-minded, with each railway typically increasing procurement costs by imposing their own unique specifications on equipment purchased, rather than buying standard locomotives and rolling stocks. As a result, costs rise and reliability can fall. In the modern world of just-in-time reliable deliveries, rail finds it difficult to compete with road. It has an in-built inflexibility that means it needs to hold more buffer stock. With low unit value goods, the purchase and financing cost of the stock holding is low. For other dry products, containerised long-distance traffic, akin to maritime transport, is effective by rail, but only for very long distances. Otherwise, containers are inefficient because of the need for, and cost of, double handling – the splitting of a full container load into parts for final delivery to customers. There have been attempts at forms of inter-model transport, such as making rail truck bodies that can form trains for the longer part of the journey from supplier to customer. However, the rail network can be very inflexible in its interpretation of regulators and safety requirements, and the traders can face problems in taking the load that a normal road trailer can, because they were heavier and had restricted dimensions in order to clear tunnels and other 'obstacles'. These are issues for both manufacturing and retailing.

The state, and its borrowing possibilities, have provided the principal exception to investment constraints. Indeed, state borrowing capacity combined with Quantitative Easing can be directly linked to the expansion of Japanese, Spanish, Italian, French and German rail capacity. This is not necessarily related, as in China, to the degree of economic growth; although the fiscal underpinning of some Chinese lines can be questioned.

In the current fiscal crisis, however, governments are increasingly subject to the pressures of opportunity costs and interest rates. The current recession has also hit government tax revenues. The most dynamically active railway builder, China, has seen growth rates fall and domestic pressures rise, and this is likely to limit fresh state investment in rail, at least in the short term; and there is no room in the Chinese system for foreign investment. For China, there is also the question of whether there are more marginal benefits in future construction, as those lines which are most likely to be of great value have already been built. At the same time, the emphasis placed in China on new rail schemes is such that it is likely to continue its investment.

In Britain, fiscal crisis has played a role in the downscaling of plans. Driving new lines through densely populated areas is costly. Tunnelling in particular is very expensive. In France with its lower population density, the original TGV line cost £15 million per mile at 2022 prices, but HST2 could cost just under £400 million a mile. And that at a time when long-distance rail journeys represent only 0.17 per cent of journeys. The business case presented by the government for HST2 saw a steady deterioration in outcomes such that in 2022 it suggested a benefit-cost ratio of 0.92 – it would cost more to build than the advantages it can bestow. The underlying claims, for example that the line would create half a million jobs, were groundless, although the case offered by capacity pressures on the London to Scotland lines remains pertinent, not least as improving existing lines is both costly and highly disruptive. By constructing in effect a new line for long-range passenger services separate to the existing one that would be for local and freight services, speed and capacity would increase, and it might be possible to move freight from the roads.

By March 2023, the estimated cost of what was then the largest infrastructure project in Europe, had risen from £32.7 billion, when it was approved in 2012, to £72 billion, and the opening of the line to Birmingham had been pushed back from 2026 to between 2029 and 2033, with the second part of the line to Manchester and a truncated eastern leg from 2033 to 2035-41. In 2022-3, inflation hit hard as the cost of timber, steel, aggregates, fuel, energy and labour all rose. This led to an increase in anticipated costs, possibly to £100 billion, and suggestions of fresh delays, with the line possibly reaching Euston only in 2041. Postponements push up the long-term cost. This example is of particular significance given Britain's role as the original trendsetter and powerhouse behind rail.

In May 2023, services run by TransPennine Express were brought under government control as the Operator of Last Resort when its contract expired, as a response to a very high rate of cancellations in part due to industrial action: that February, nearly a quarter of its trains were cancelled. At a more modest level, in April 2023, plans to reintroduce a passenger service (closed in 1961) on the freight-only Isle of Grain branch on the Hoo Peninsula were postponed, Medway Council citing 'high inflation, significantly increased construction costs and pressures on public spending'.

More impressive, not least because far less resources are at stake, are recent developments in Scotland, where the emphasis has not been on exorbitant blue-skies conventional new construction. Instead, with the Scottish government arguing that regional-inclusive growth is held back by poor infrastructure links, the major change post-Beeching has been the (re-) opening in 2015 of the 35-mile Borders Railway, closed in 1969, that connects Edinburgh to Galashiels and Melrose. Moreover, from the opening of Transport Scotland in 2006, there has been a focus, imperfect but present, on integrated services reflected in subsidiary commuting developments. Another line reopened was the Stirling-Alloa-Kincardine line in 2008. The Edinburgh tram, light-rail system faced numerous problems but has been completed. Railways in Scotland were renationalised in 2022 as Scottish Rail Holdings Ltd and the Crossborder Sleeper service was nationalised in 2023.

Politically stormy debate surrounds not only new plans but also existing provision. From within the rail industry, there can be strong pressure challenging the maintenance of current capacity, notably underused rural lines, for example in France. This pressure is driven by regulation and the demand for uniformity, for safety requirements demand significant investment if many of these lines are to remain open. The social investment of support for uneconomic lines is generally a frozen-case scenario of sustaining past commitments, not a progressive one of deciding that such lines should be maintained or even constructed to face present and future concerns. Thus, in France, lines in rural and upland areas, such as the Massif Central, used by relatively few, are sustained, rather than constructing similarly uneconomic but new schemes in urban areas where public transport pressures are acute. Legacy issues include inadequate investment and, as in America, there is generally a greater, often much greater, willingness to invest public funds in new and existing road links than in rail.

The Greek railway system has many trains travelling on single tracks. That was a contributing factor to the head-on collision in 2023 near Larissa. Signalling and automatic control systems are inadequate or non-existent in many areas of Greece, and if there also appears to have been human error in the Larissa accident, the extent, nature and reliability of backup systems is also, as with other countries and accidents, pertinent. In recent decades, Greek governments have tended to invest more in road than rail. In part, this reflects the political and social significance of motorists, but it is also a product of the importance of road freight. Greece sold its rail operator to the Italian state company in 2017 as part of the country's bailout; but hundreds of millions of Euros were to have been invested in rail infrastructure for necessary improvements. This has not yet been the outcome.

Nevertheless, plans for rail expansion and increase in services are frequently advanced. Some are aspects of long-developing systems such as those in Japan for lines from Kanazawa to Osaka, Tokyo to Nagoya via an inland route, and the Hokkaido extension to Sapporo, the last scheduled to open in 2031. The initial high-speed *Shinkansen* Tokyo-Osaka service, opened in 1964 with its exclusive track on the 1453 mm gauge (compared to the existing lines with their 1067 mm gauge), was successful partly because the acquisition of land started before the end of the Second World War: the line was originally planned for military purposes. The initial success was emulated by newer routes, which owe much to regional development ideas and levelling up, but with diminishing success due to issues of political intervention in routing and problems with financing. Nevertheless, despite the limits in financing and the questionable economic viability of the newer routes, they have been managed quite well.

There has been the development in Japan of trains with a narrower loading gauge allowing services to go on narrow gauge lines, although at lower speeds, an experimental *Shinkansen* (high-speed) train which can switch between standard and narrow gauges. Similarly in Spain, alongside upgraded services there are also improved lines; for example, in 2022, there was an upgrading of the route to Extremadura which may eventually go on to Lisbon.

Recent examples include the new Israeli government's further development of existing new light rail lines in 2022, notably in Jerusalem, so as to improve services there and with Tel Aviv. There are plans for 13 trains an hour each way between the two cities by 2040 as part of the Israel Railways 2040 Strategic Plan. There is also a plan for a major expansion of Tel Aviv's light rail system. As so often, politics plays an integral role, a factor accentuated by the coalition nature of Israel's governments and the very frequent changes of ministry. Thus, alongside support for light rail, there has been opposition, and the same for standard rail routes to

Kiryat Shmona and Eilat. The latter is designed to provide a route from the interior and, indirectly the Mediterranean, to the Red Sea, and thus to offer an alternative to the Suez Canal. Rejected in 2013 as not economically worthwhile, this plan was revised in 2022 with the new government and, in particular, the return as Minister of Transportation of Miri Reger, an ally of Benjamin Netanyahu, replacing Merav Michaeli of Labour who had held the post in 2021-2. Labour was more attuned to the urban constituencies attracted by urban light railways.

At a very different scale, Australia has advanced a whole series of plans for high-speed trains, notably from Sydney to Melbourne (which is close compared to Adelaide and Perth), since the 1980s; but each has been turned down. These included the XPT and Very Fast Train project, in the 1990s CountryLink and Speedrail, and in 2022 the failure of Fast Rail, announced in 2018, which involved plans for high-speed lines from Sydney to Newcastle, Wollongong, Canberra, and Orange/Parkes. This would have led to much tunnelling in pursuit of a 'truly polycentric city region' according to the New South Wales Greater Cities Commission in 2022.

The New South Wales government pulled out because of the rising costs and the difficulty of securing land, and instead pressed for the Federal Government to take over the cost, a shift from the position of the previous government. HST2 had been cited as a model and Andrew McNaughton, the Strategic Advisor on the latter, was the Fast Rail Panel Chair. Instead, in 2023, the New South Wales government announced plans to quadruple the tracks at the more frequent services, rather than increasing speed by means of new high-speed lines. In April 2023, the Turkish Transport Minister announced a 1 hour 29 minutes 'super high-speed' railway between Istanbul and Ankara compared with the 4 hours 5 minutes over the 533-kilometre high-speed route built in 2008-14 as part of a planned major expansion of high-speed Turkish services.

There are many other instances of nation-based plans, not least where rail links with other countries are limited or non-existent. Thus, also serving as a reminder that not all foreign investment in Africa is Chinese, Britain is funding a new rail hub in central Nairobi. This project links British geostrategic interests with the Kenyan wish to revitalise the centre of Nairobi in the face of suburban development. The current central station is to be preserved within a larger modernised replacement.

Expansion plans are also frequently international. Some sit within existing international political and/or rail networks. The European Green Speed project launched in 2019 plans the creation of a rail network linking 430 cities, with trains travelling at least 100 mph by 2040 and streamlined cross-border ticketing. This plan focused on a merger of the operators Thalys and Eurostar, both majority-owned by SNCF, so as to connect Britain, France, Belgium, the Netherlands and Germany.

Somewhat different, the establishment of strategic rail links in Asia can have non-Chinese manifestations, as with developments in South-West Asia. The railway between Turkey and Iran was a welcome release from isolation for Iran during the 1980-8 war with Iraq, but it was suspended in 2015 due to opposition in Kurdistan. It has been revived as a wider scheme, with the first train from Pakistan arriving in Turkey via Iran in January 2022, a 5,981-kilometre (3,666-mile) route that took 12 days and 21 hours. This is an aspect of the geopolitics of Asian rail links. In the case of Turkey, Iran and Pakistan, the geopolitics was not that of anti-Communism, but, instead, an Islamic alignment aimed at providing unity against both the West and Russia. Moreover, the three powers had shared interests in opposing separatism, respectively by Kurds (Turkey and Iran) and Baluchis (Iran and Pakistan).

As a reminder of the significance of rail alignments, this newly revived railway is different to the interwar Trans-Iranian Railway, which ran north to south and was extended in 1961 to Gorgan near the Soviet frontier east of the Caspian Sea. In contrast, in the context of the period prior to 1947, the newly revived east-west railway would have linked British India to the British zone of influence in Iraq, and, for this reason, some interwar British commentators had wanted the interwar Trans-Iranian Railway to be east-west.

As a further instance of the geopolitics of rail, in 2014 a new line linked Gorgan in Iran to Etrek in Turkmenistan. This connected Iran to Turkmenistan and then Kazakhstan. The scheme was related to the International North-South Transport Corridor agreed in 2002 and designed to move goods, by sea and rail, from India, via Iran and Russia, to Europe. Initiated by India, Russia and Iran, the Corridor produced its first India-European train shipment in 2021. So also was the building of new rail links in Iran and Azerbaijan, with the Rasht-Astara section completed in 2016. This activity shows the continuity of imperial interests and geopolitical concerns in railways in particular areas. Iran has pursued good relations with Muslim Azerbaijan in opposition to Christian Armenia. In contrast, in December 2021, thanks to EU pressure, the presidents of Armenia and Azerbaijan offered verbal agreement to reopen a railway. Earlier that year, Azerbaijan began reconstruction of the 100-kilometre Soviet-era railway to reconnect Nakhichevan to the core of Azerbaijan, thus cementing the result of victory over Armenia the previous year. Alongside the catch-all vocabulary of far-flung trans-continental and inter-continental corridors, there are also more specific alignments and limited networks at issue. These can build on the more far-flung ideas, not least to enhance the rhetoric or encourage constituencies of support, particularly securing foreign support; but that approach does not necessarily explain the logic of the specific project.

While rail continues to seem an answer to links between regions, and notably major urban communities, it is also still regarded as an important means of transport for those within them. This has become more significant with rising population numbers and the growth across the world of super cities of great size, for population growth has overwhelmingly meant urbanization and the rate of the latter is even greater than that of the former. Commuting is a key element but not the sole rail requirement for transport within the megalopolis.

As far as their external links are concerned, in place of, or in addition to, earlier linkage with ports, has come that with airports. The rail linkage to major airports is excellent in some cases, as with Amsterdam, Copenhagen, Frankfurt, Lisbon, Oporto, Paris, Stockholm, Toulouse and Zurich airports. The process continues. In 2023, a contract for a metro extension to Bucharest airport was awarded.

In comparison, the situation is less happy in Britain, Iceland, Australia and, even more, America. In the US, some airports were linked up to rail access, notably Atlanta, Chicago, Newark, Orlando, Philadelphia, and Seattle. Others were not, for example La Guardia, or only after major delays, such as Dulles, the main Washington airport. Indeed, rapid light-rail systems within airports between terminals, as at John F. Kennedy Airport, New York, were often put in more rapidly than those between airports and nearby cities. In America, they were long delayed by the emphasis being on passengers arriving by car, such that large car parks were more important for the planners than access to any railroad. Out-of-town railway stations again tend to have very large carparks. This is an aspect of what can be a disjuncture between local (private) travel and distant (mass) travel, although the relationship varies by country.

Driverless technology can play a role in airport rail links, as for London's City Airport, and more generally, for both passengers and freight. Thus, by the end of 2020, 97 kilometres of the Delhi metro network was driverless, while in 2023 the bids for a contract for a new metro line for Naples included the supply of driverless trains. The introduction of such technology around the world, however, is in part subject to the power of unions which tend, as in Britain, to be resistant to change. Nevertheless, across the world, there is much rail automation, not least in the transport of freight and the loading and unloading of cargo.

There needs to be an urgent and public discussion of costs and benefits, one that is specific to particular circumstances. This specificity is both long-term and short. Comparisons with the construction achievements of the late nineteenth century are unhelpful, as labour then was plentiful and machinery more expensive and often hard to find. More particularly, there is the change in the cost of capital that has been so prominent over recent decades, and that indeed throws light on the earlier history of rail. These changes affect private financial markets, state provision, and the interaction of the two, an interaction that has been, and is, crucial to new developments.

The period since 1970 saw major issues in funding, with no consistency as a result. This was true both of general economic difficulties, as well as those more specifically of financing. The oil-linked crises in 1973 and 1979 were followed by widespread economic problems in the early 1980s, early 1990s and late 2000s. In addition, there were particular financial crises in many countries, including, in the 1980s, much of Latin America, and in the late 1990s, Russia and many Asian states. These all put pressure on government funding and on tax revenue.

In contrast, the crisis of the late 2000s was countered by a general quantitative easing that continued until the early 2020s. Accompanied by low interest rates, this ensured a low cost for new projects and for the running of existing lines. That was seen for example in both Europe and Japan, and is a key way to consider recent expansion and, conversely, the nature of current plans in the shadow of the Covid pandemic and the financial problems of 2022-3. For example, plans for the development of railway sites that are understandably disliked intensely, such as that of Network Rail to build a skyscraper that would overshadow the splendid concourse of London's Liverpool Street Station, built in 1874, reflect the need to derive profit from sites in order to compensate for serious operating losses.

It may be that the present moment should be seen as a 'correction', a situation that has often been the case, as with the earlier periods of overconfidence, for example in 1873, 1893, 1929 and, for different reasons, 1914 and 1939. If so, it is clear that the long timespan of many contemporary projects, not only in construction but also with reference to the anticipated period of repayment, and thus financing, are unrealistic. That presents a valuable way to present rail history, that of the multiple interactions of hope and experience, expectation and reality.

And so also with the prospect of war. The prospect of war has increased greatly from the early 2020s. This entails the possibility of a devastation of infrastructure far greater than that in either world war. In addition, even if large-scale conflict is avoided, there is likely to be far more expenditure on military provision by several of the states mentioned in this chapter, including China, Japan, Iran, Israel, Saudi Arabia, Britain, France, Germany and the US. It is highly unlikely that this situation will not affect plans and implementation. To imagine otherwise would be foolish. Trains were cancelled in Japan in April 2023 in response to North Korean missile tests. Moreover, the spreading conflicts in sub-Saharan Africa in the 2020s, notably in the *sahel*, made ideas of long-range African train links seem pipe dreams.

Thus, the story is being shaped anew by international imperatives, financial pressures and technological developments, and that approach undercuts a progressivism and inevitability of development that, instead, may become an anachronism. In particular, as indicated throughout this book, the high cost of creating, maintaining and running railways has helped make them more problematic, in terms of individual lines, and of plans for new or enhanced systems as a whole. This cost includes a permanent way that is more complex than that of a road, a system that is more vulnerable than a road one, and large and therefore generally expensive labour forces. The last is notably so in Western countries where labour forces are much harder to control than in authoritarian states.

Environmental demands, not least for 'clean fuel', also pose difficulties, in terms of practicality and cost both of switchover and in operations. In April 2023, biofuels used to cut carbon emissions in England clogged up some diesel train engines' fuel filters in south-west England, with algae growing in fuel tanks leading to the withdrawal of some trains. As a result, there was a switch in these trains from biodiesel to standard diesel.

The idea of a technological magic bullet that will restore and/ or ensure the profitability of rail comes up against the realities not only of technological possibilities for its competitors, but also of longstanding issues and costs that amount to a systemic vulnerability in the present and one that shows no signs of diminishing. The geography of rail remains a key factor, and one that poses a central contrast between areas where rail is significant and those where it is occasional or even absent, and not least if population growth is thrown into the equation. There are obviously changes, not least Chinese, as opposed to European, capital and geopolitical standing across much of the world. Although as a reminder that Chinese achievements must be put in context, the Chinese rail system in 2015 moved 13 per cent of the country's freight volume. Far more went by road, while waterborne transport, notably coastal shipping, was also very important.

A global history of rail should be about Africa as well as Europe, the US and China, or Paraguay, where the system essentially largely ceased operation over the last quarter-century, as well as Paris. The reasons for this contrast cannot be finessed by technology or hope.

PICTURE ACKNOWLEDGEMENTS

Page 13: *The World's Last Steam Locomotives in Industry*, Gordon Edgar.

Page 14, top: HP Baumeler under creative commons 2.0. Bottom: Hiroki Ogawa under creative commons 3.0.

Page 15, top: Duane Wilkins under creative commons 2.0. Bottom: MEOGLOBAL, Muhammed Enes Okullu under creative commons 2.0.

Page 16, top and middle: *InterCity HST 125*, Hugh Llewelyn. Bottom: Courtesy of the Philadelphia Museum of Art.

All of the books cited above are available from Amberley, featuring some of the best railway photography in print.

Anglo Scottish Sleepers, David Meara. 978-1445672328

Death Ride from Fenchurch Street and Other Victorian Railway Murders, Arthur and Mary Sellwood. 978-1848684959

Diesel Locomotives Around the World, Peter J. Green. 978-1398108523

Electrifying the Underground: The Technology that Created London's Tube, Graeme Cleves. 978-1445622033

German Traction, Andrew Cole. 978-1445666945

Heavy Freight Locomotives, George Woods. 978-1398101999

InterCity HST 125, Hugh Llewelyn. 978-1445634180

Iron Empires: Robber Barons, Railroads, and the Making of Modern America, Michael Hilzik. 978-0358567127

Railroads of Wisconsin, Mike Danneman. 978-1398103177

The World's Last Steam Locomotives in Industry, Gordon Edgar. 978-1398108103

INDEX